# Gender and the Radical and Extreme Right

*Gender and the Radical and Extreme Right* takes up an important and often-overlooked intersection across scholarship on the radical right, gender, and education. These subfields have mostly operated independent of one another, and the scholars and practitioners who attend to educational interventions on the far right rarely address gender directly, while the growing body of scholarship on gender and the far right typically overlooks the issue of educational implications.

This edited volume steps into this space, bringing together seven chapters and an afterword to help readers rethink the educational implications of research on gender and the radical right. As a starting point for future dialogue and research across previously disparate subfields, this volume highlights education as one space where such an integration may be seen as a fruitful avenue for further exploration.

This book was originally published as a special issue of *Gender and Education*.

**Cynthia Miller-Idriss** is Professor of Education and Sociology at American University, Washington, D.C., USA. She also directs the International Training and Education Program and runs the bi-annual Global Education Forum. Her research is focused on far right youth subcultures and on the organization and production of knowledge about the world within U.S. universities. She is the author of *The Extreme Gone Mainstream: Commercialization and Far Right Youth Culture in Germany* (2018) and *Seeing the World: How Universities Make Knowledge in a Global Era* (with Mitchell Stevens and Seteney Shami, 2018).

**Hilary Pilkington** is Professor of Sociology at the University of Manchester, UK. She has a long-standing research interest in youth and youth cultural practices, post-socialist societies and qualitative, especially ethnographic, research methods. Her most recent books include *Loud and Proud: Passion and Politics in the English Defence League* (2016) and *Understanding Youth Participation across Europe: From survey to ethnography* (2017). She has been coordinator of several large, collaborative research projects, including the FP7 MYPLACE project and the H2020-EU funded project DARE (Dialogue About Radicalisation and Equality).

# Gender and the Radical and Extreme Right

## Mechanisms of Transmission and the Role of Educational Interventions

*Edited by*
**Cynthia Miller-Idriss and Hilary Pilkington**

Routledge
Taylor & Francis Group

LONDON AND NEW YORK

First published 2019
by Routledge
2 Park Square, Milton Park, Abingdon, Oxon, OX14 4RN, UK

and by Routledge
52 Vanderbilt Avenue, New York, NY 10017, USA

First issued in paperback 2020

*Routledge is an imprint of the Taylor & Francis Group, an informa business*

*British Library Cataloguing in Publication Data*
A catalogue record for this book is available from the British Library

ISBN 13: 978-0-367-58451-1 (pbk)
ISBN 13: 978-1-138-33568-4 (hbk)

Typeset in Myriad Pro
by RefineCatch Limited, Bungay, Suffolk

**Publisher's Note**
The publisher accepts responsibility for any inconsistencies that may have
arisen during the conversion of this book from journal articles to book chapters,
namely the possible inclusion of journal terminology.

**Disclaimer**
Every effort has been made to contact copyright holders for their permission to
reprint material in this book. The publishers would be grateful to hear from any
copyright holder who is not here acknowledged and will undertake to rectify
any errors or omissions in future editions of this book.

# Contents

# Citation Information

The chapters in this book were originally published in *Gender and Education*, volume 29, issue 2 (March 2017). When citing this material, please use the original page numbering for each article, as follows:

For any permission-related enquiries please visit:
http://www.tandfonline.com/page/help/permissions

# Notes on Contributors

**Kathleen Blee** is a Distinguished Professor of Sociology at the University of Pittsburgh, USA, specializing in social movements, race, and violence. She has published extensively on women in radical right movements, including her books *Inside Organized Racism: Women in the Hate Movement* (2002), *Women of the Klan: Racism and Gender in the 1920s* (1991), and *Women of the Right: Comparisons and Interplay Across Borders* (co-edited with Sandra Deutsch, 2012).

**Alexandra Koronaiou** teaches Sociology of Work and Leisure as well as Sociology of Media at Panteion University, Greece, she also teaches 'Introduction to Adult Education' at the Hellenic Open University, Greece. Since 2011 she has been the team leader of various EU projects at Panteion University. Her research interests include extreme-right radicalization, youth radicalization, sociology of work and free time, education, sociology of youth, and gender issues.

**Marcel Lubbers** is Professor of (Political) Sociology at Radboud University, the Netherlands. He has published internationally on understanding radical right voting and euroscepticism. He has also researched nationalism and cultural consumption. His current work includes a focus on immigrant integration – his most recent project is on Migrants' Welfare State Attitudes.

**Jennifer Meyer** completed her PhD in History of Political Thought and History (bi-national doctorate) at the École Normale Supérieure de Lyon, France, and the University of Erfurt, Germany, in 2014. Her research focuses on the history of feminist movements, the intersections of gender and race, and the history of anti-Semitism. She co-edited the trilingual volume *Intersectionality und Kritik* (with Vera Kallenberg and Johanna M. Mueller, 2013).

**Cynthia Miller-Idriss** is Professor of Education and Sociology at American University, USA. She also directs the International Training and Education Program and runs the bi-annual Global Education Forum. Her research is focused on far right youth subcultures and on the organization and production of knowledge about the world within U.S. universities.

**Hilary Pilkington** is Professor of Sociology at the University of Manchester, UK. She has a long-standing research interest in youth and youth cultural practices, post-socialist societies and qualitative, especially ethnographic, research methods. She has been coordinator of several large, collaborative research projects, including the FP7 MYPLACE project and the H2020-EU funded project DARE (Dialogue About Radicalisation and Equality).

**Alexandros Sakellariou** is currently teaching Sociology at the Hellenic Open University, Greece, and is a Postdoctoral Researcher at Panteion University of Athens, Greece. He received his PhD in Sociology from the Department of Sociology of Panteion University. Since 2011 he has worked as a Researcher at Panteion University on EU Projects. His scientific interests include sociology of religion, sociology of youth, youth activism and civic participation, and right-wing extremism.

**George J. Severs** is a PhD student at Selwyn College at Cambridge University, UK, where he is researching a history of HIV/AIDS activism in the UK c.1982–2000. Previously, he studied for an MPhil in Modern British History at Pembroke College, Cambridge with a thesis exploring the Church of England's responses to the HIV/AIDS epidemic. In 2016 he graduated with a First Class Honours degree in History from Royal Holloway, University of London, UK.

**Niels Spierings** is Assistant Professor in Sociology at Radboud University, the Netherlands. His research interests include political behavior; gender and sexuality; populism; social media; Islam; migration; democratic politics; and quantitative, qualitative and feminist research methods. On these topics he has published journal articles and monographs. In 2015 he co-edited a special issue on gender and the populist radical right in *Patterns of Prejudice* with Andrej Zaslove.

**Anita Stasulane** is Professor of History of Religions and Director of the Institute of Humanities and Social Sciences at Daugavpils University, Latvia. She graduated from the University of Latvia (1985) and Pontifical Gregorian University, Rome, Italy (1998). She has been working on mainly the new religious movements and youth cultures; currently she is conducting research on religious fundamentalism.

**Andrej Zaslove** is Assistant Professor in the Department of Political Science at the Institute for Management Research at Radboud University, the Netherlands. His research focuses on populism (with a current emphasis on measuring populism, foreign policy and populism, and gender and populism). In 2015 he co-edited a special issue on gender and the populist radical right in *Patterns of Prejudice* with Niels Spierings.

# In search of the missing link: gender, education and the radical right

Cynthia Miller-Idriss and Hilary Pilkington

## Introduction

There is to date no systematic examination of how scholarship on gender and education intersects with studies of the radical right. While there is considerable practical and scholarly work attending to educational interventions and initiatives related to radical and far right movements, little of this work directly addresses gender or gender differences in far right engagement. Similarly, the significant body of scholarship addressing gender and the far right has not typically engaged the issue of educational implications directly – whether through discussions about how radical and extreme right groups try to educate their own constituents and broader public or by identifying strategies for educational interventions, which more directly address gender as a factor in extremist or radical right engagement. This special issue steps into this space. It brings together seven articles and an afterword that we believe assist in rethinking gender and the radical right through the exploration of how and why participation in far right and radical right movements remains gendered, and what links they might have with education. In particular, we hope this special issue provides a starting point for future dialogue and research across, and integration of, previously disparate subfields, with education as one space where such an integration may be seen as a fruitful avenue for further exploration.

## Situating the radical right on the spectrum

Given that our primary objective was to spark discussion of the intersection of three categories – gender, education and the radical right – we maximized the scope for contributions by deploying each of those categories broadly. In mapping this spectrum of scholarly interest and engagement, we used the term 'radical right,' on the one hand, as a shorthand for a range of ideological positions associated with classic political movements and parties of the far right, through the new family of 'populist radical right' (Mudde 2007, 25) parties that have enjoyed significant electoral success and public visibility in recent years. We also focused on looser single-issue (anti-Jihadi, anti-Islamist) movements, subcultural groups or scenes. This broad approach recognizes that there is variation both across disciplines and across countries in how the adjectives 'radical,' 'extreme' or 'far' are used in relation to the right of the political spectrum. There is also ideological contestation:

for example, while the term 'hate group' is often used to refer to groups within and beyond the radical right spectrum, far right-wing groups may position others as the 'haters' (Shafer 2002, 84).

On the other hand, to avoid using conceptual terminology loosely, we start from the position of recognizing that the radical right has certain distinguishing characteristics. We use Rydgren's (forthcoming) definition of the radical right as a subset of right-wing extremism, which is hostile to democratic governance or constitutions but not necessarily actively opposed to democracy per se (also see Mudde 2000, 2005; Miller-Idriss forthcoming-a). When radical right movements and activities fall within legal bounds, they typically are subject to the protections of free speech and are generally regarded as a contested, but legitimate, part of the democratic spectrum. However, such groups and movements also merit broader societal attention, monitoring, and educational inter-vention when they are associated with xenophobic, anti-democratic, authoritarian, anti-immigrant, anti-Semitic, anti-government, fascist, homophobic, ethno-nationalist, Islamo-phobic or racist values, beliefs, actions and goals (Rydgren, forthcoming). This is particu-larly the case when such attitudes and actions lead to violence. In a 2016 *Washington Post* interview (Itkowitz 2016) about her research on Donald Trump's campaign rhetoric, for example, legal scholar Susan Benesch argued that Trump's tone and messages increase the risk of inter-group violence. Invoking his supporters' potential use of the Second Amendment against Hillary Clinton was a barely veiled call to arms against a presidential candidate, while his repeated statement that President Obama and Hillary Clinton were founders of the Islamic State is what Benesch calls a 'hallmark of dangerous speech to describe an in-group member as the enemy.' Such language can inflame angry supporters to create unrest or commit violent acts (Itkowitz 2016). Rhetoric espoused by some popu-list and radical right movements has been clearly linked in recent years to hate crimes and violence against migrants and religious, ethnic, and racial minorities. Hate crimes in the UK increased 41 per cent post-Brexit (Weaver 2016), for example, while the number of hate groups in the US increased by 14 per cent from 2014 to 2015; the number of anti-Muslim groups alone in the US has increased by 42 per cent during that period. These figures are part of longer-term trends – the overall number of hate groups in the US has doubled since 1999[1] while anti-Muslim or anti-Islam sentiment in the general popu-lation of the UK is rising[2] – but are also clearly affected by populist and far right rhetoric. Elsewhere, direct violence against immigrants has also risen. In Germany, for example, there were 740 right-wing extremist attacks on refugee homes from January to mid-October, in 2016. This represents a four-fold increase over 2014, dozens of which involved arson, and 10 cases involved explosives.[3]

In adopting the term 'radical right' as a shorthand, we start from two important pre-mises. First, we are confronting a broad spectrum of opinion and activism; however, most radical right movement activists are not directly engaged in violence. Second, radical right and populist ideas are increasingly found not at the pathological margins but among increasingly broad swathes of society. This, we suggest, makes the study of the intersection of the radical right with both gender and education of particular impor-tance. In relation to gender, as these ideas and their political vehicles extend their reach into the population, we should anticipate that the constituency of their support is also likely to expand, so that being a woman, or being LGBT may diminish as a 'protective' factor – that is, a factor that would make individuals less likely to support or engage in radical right movements. In relation to education, if the terrain of engagement is ideas, not violence, then the opportunity for educational intervention seems particularly significant.

## Gender and the radical right

There is a substantive research literature attending to the gendered dimensions of right-wing radicalism, generally creating a consensus amongst scholars that gender acts as a protective factor (in the case of women) and a risk factor (in the case of men). Summarizing the field, Kitschelt (2007, 1199) suggests that one of only two incontrovertible facts about the 'radical right' is that such parties attract more men than women while Mudde (2014, 10) contends that women are significantly underrepresented across the extreme right spectrum. However, it has been argued recently that right-wing women are not so much absent as 'overlooked' by scholarship in the field (Blee and Deutsch 2012, 1). This argument for revisiting what we know about gender and the radical right is strengthened by empirical trends that lead us to suppose that the relationship between the two is under-going change. There is evidence, for example, that the gender gap in support for the growing array of populist radical right parties and movements across Europe is narrowing (Spierings and Zaslove 2015, 139–140) while the incorporation of gender equality and gay rights platforms (often as part of broader anti-Islam or anti-multiculturalist ideologies) extends the potential appeal of the radical right to women and LGBT communities (Akker-man and Hagelund 2007, 199). Moreover, we are likely to see a rise not only in electoral support for the radical right among women but also increasing activism in such move-ments. As their ideas are increasingly 'mainstreamed,' any associated stigmatization typi-cally discouraging women's participation in the radical right decreases and we are already witnessing women's increasing visibility in these movements, including in leadership positions.

To date, however, these changes are not fully reflected in the literature. Close-up studies of the far right and populist radical right movements suggest that women rep-resent only a small minority of activists and primarily hold traditional supportive roles (Ezekiel 2002, 54; Kimmel 2007, 207; Blee and Linden 2012, 107). While there are both psychological and social reasons why gender propensities may be apparent (Rippl and Seipel 1999; Ferber and Kimmel 2008), most work has focused on single-country case studies and explained women's relative absence through references to exclusively mascu-linist or homosocial spaces where women and sexual minorities feel uncomfortable (Ezekiel 2002, 57; Kimmel 2007, 207; Pilkington, Omel'chenko, and Garifzianova 2010, 158; Blee and Linden 2012, 103–105). In this special issue, we seek to capture emergent changes in this picture through contributions which address the question of the extension of support for far right and radical right parties and movements to new female and LGBT constituencies (Pilkington 2017; Spierings, Zaslove, and Lubbers, 2017), and which chal-lenge, or paint in more nuanced colors, the purely masculine worlds of these movements.

## Education and the radical right

The term education refers not only to formal schooling but also education across the life course, in formal and non-formal settings, such as popular culture. We therefore refer not only to educational interventions intended to combat physical and symbolic violence associated with the radical and far right, but also the educational implications of radical right discourse for the broader public and the role that institutions (such as the media) play in amplifying the rhetoric and ideas of the radical right in shaping how people think and act. The radical right, in other words, also have educational goals (Meyer, this issue). On the intervention side, educational work includes both school- and university-based interventions – such as anti-racist curricula in the UK or 'teaching tolerance' and 'courageous conversations' programs in the US – as well as formal and informal programs designed for out-of-school youth and adults in settings such as soccer retreats, summer camps, after-school clubs, youth clubs, theater troupes, or other kinds of activities organized by non-profit organizations, local and state agencies or community groups. Although there has been substantial work related to educational interventions and extremism (Prevent), there have been strikingly few syntheses tracing trends across what are ultimately distinct subfields: anti-racist education, countering violent extremism (CVE) work, work on prevention, research on inter-group relations and prejudice, research on gangs and youth violence and research on de-radicalization.

Assessing the state of the research on education and the radical right is further complicated by the fact that much of the work in this area is not specific to far or radical right populations per se, but rather targets related areas such prejudice reduction or the promotion of tolerance (e.g. Beelmann and Heinemann 2014). This is particularly the case for formal, school-based initiatives, which tend to focus on broad areas deemed critical for civic engagement and democratic participation, such as teaching tolerance of diverse viewpoints through required courses like citizenship education in the UK or government and civics classes in the US rather than on interventions specific to a radical right population. When such initiatives take place in formal school settings with high populations of young people who are engaged in, or at risk for, radical right participation, they fall within the purview of interventions for the radical right. But in many other settings, the same initiatives are not thought of as work engaging the far right but as educational initiatives for the general population. This makes tracking the impact of such programs for particular groups somewhat challenging. A related example is in official, formal school, university and stadium policies, which seek to ban particular ideological symbols or clothing through the enforcement of dress codes. Such policies often have a target population in mind (e.g. the extreme right-wing), but frame the policies more broadly, and are not typically understood as educational interventions for the radical or far right per se.

Informal interventions are more likely to specifically target far-, radical- and extreme right-wing youth and adults for their programing. EXIT-Germany, for example, does educational work with drop-outs from the far right scene, and has reached out to far right populations in unconventional ways; for example, in 2011, the group's 'Trojan T-shirt' project gave away free souvenir t-shirts designed with far right iconography and messaging that – once washed – revealed a message and telephone number to help people exit right-wing extremism.[4] Elsewhere in Germany, the federal government has promoted volunteer firefighting brigades as a site for civic engagement for youth at risk for extremist engagement.[5] Such interventions – which fall well outside the boundaries of traditional schooling – are educational initiatives specifically designed for young people or adults who are at-risk for extremist engagement or are already involved in radical and extreme groups.

Part of the challenge with developing effective interventions to engage right-wing radical young people is that well-intended initiatives can backfire, sometimes fueling the very attitudes and behavior that educators seek to change (Johansson 2013). Tom Cockburn's work with far right young people in the North of England showed, for example, that anti-racist education programs failed because they were premised upon a naïve assumption that contact among diverse groups would create greater tolerance. However, because far right young people felt ostracized and blamed, the programs drove them further away rather than building trust and empathy (2007). The young men Cockburn studied felt 'nobody was interested in listening to them, or realistically engaging in their ideas, or challenging their beliefs in a way that showed respect' (554). Cockburn argues that such approaches led to the suppression of racism at school, moving beyond the school corridors into public space. As an alternative, he advocates for interventions that allow for more personal reflection, a strengthening of all identities, and building trust and empathy rather than (simply) challenging and confronting discrimination and prejudice (558).

It is also clear that top-down interventions cannot address the specific needs of young people and adults who are at-risk for extremist engagement in every local setting. On the one hand, this is because local cultural variations shape the appeal of radical groups in different ways; while young people in one place may be motivated by the anti-migrant rhetoric of radical right movements, in other places, the appeal may be more substantially grounded in anti-government or Euro-skeptic sentiment or economic arguments about the labor market. There are even opposing variations on the same themes: some far right groups draw movement support by arguing against same-sex marriage in favor of 'traditional' or 'Christian' values, while other groups argue that protections for same-sex relationships must be safeguarded against the potential imposition of Sharia law from Muslim immigrants. Far right positions on gendered issues are not as clear as previous scholars have assumed (Pilkington, this issue). Interventions seeking to limit the engagement of young people in violent radical right actions cannot therefore create universal curricula but need to understand the concerns, fears and motivations of particular youth populations. This is also true on the implementation side; centrally organized policy and curricular initiatives are subject to varied interpretation and differences in implementation which make it hard to compare their effectiveness. For example, Carrington and Bonnett (1997) show that there are significant geographical and regional differences in how particular states or provinces within a nation interpret and implement anti-racist or multicultural educational initiatives.

## Interventions specifically addressing gender-based issues

There is little known about educational intervention work that specifically targets gender-based issues in studies of far right movements, despite consistent findings about the role that issues such as traditional masculinities play in the appeal of the radical and extreme right. One persistent challenge is that most educational interventions target youth populations, in part because of consistent evidence about the persistence of political attitudes formed during adolescence and early adulthood (Siedler 2011, 175), but also because of a lengthy history of youth support for far right parties and engagement in far right youth subcultures (Mudde 2014). Young people are more likely to support far right-wing parties when compared with adults (Arzheimer 2009; Mieriņa and Koroļeva, 2015) and to engage in extreme and radical far right subcultures (Mudde 2014, 5), which are predominantly responsible for far right youth violence. While not all far right young people engage in violence, they are more likely than adults to engage in far right violence and are the disproportionate perpetrators of far right-wing attacks on immigrants, migrants and ethnic or racial minorities. While it therefore makes sense that interventions are heavily slanted toward work with youth populations, the fluid nature of young people's attachments to subcultures and identities adds another challenge to any associated educational interventions. Miller-Idriss' (forthcoming-b) research with German young people, for example, calls for more research focusing not only on clearly bounded 'far right youth,' but rather on youth who are 'in and around the far right scene,' thereby acknowledging the ways that young people experiment through participation with various subcultural groups, shifting from the core to the periphery of particular groups over time. This fluid nature of subcultural scenes has implications, she argues, both for the ways in which scholars understand the porous nature of young people's identities and their complex and contradictory nature. However, there are educational implications as well, as she notes, particularly when such identities are embedded in scenes where violence is valorized: 'Acknowledging that young people in the far right have flexible engagements in far right scenes does not therefore imply that those engagements are any less consequential or worthy of intervention' (Miller-Idriss, forthcoming-a).

It is not just subcultures in general that generate flexible engagements; younger generations are also increasingly experiencing more fluidity around gender identities as well (Pascoe 2007; Pascoe and Bridges 2015). Educators therefore need to be aware of the shifting dynamics and realities around gender and sexuality as well as changing social norms around traditional notions of masculinity, and potential backlashes from conservative social movements, including the far right, to such developments. While there has been some work within research on gender, education and extremism suggesting the need to combat the 'reproduction of dominant masculinities in schools and the collusion in male violence as "normal,"' (Davies 2008, 613) there is less attention focused upon how far right groups are navigating changing legal policies and social norms related to gender and sexuality. Davies (2008) argues that both formal educational work in schools and non-formal educational work in out-of-school settings such as youth groups and sports clubs needs to help promote a 'range of differing ideals of manhood and femalehood' and challenge authoritarianism, encourage female political engagement, educate both sexes towards emotional literacy, productive economic activity, democratic engagement and equal rights and participation in public life (616). We need significantly more scholarship tracing whether and how such interventions and educational work are effective, as we discuss in further detail below.

## The missing link: introducing the contributions through the lens of education

For the reasons we have noted, the educational implications of how gender and the radical right are rethought in contributions to this special issue may seem at times implicit rather than explicit. We now move towards a summary of each of the articles with a focus on identifying some of the potential educational implications of each author's claims and findings.

Two of the articles in this special issue draw directly on formal educational settings or curricula. *Jennifer Meyer's* historical analysis of early twentieth-century *völkisch* feminism in Germany demonstrates a clear need to reconsider history curricula around how women's engagement in the Third Reich has been narrated. Meyer focuses on the *völkisch* movement's writer Sophie Rogge-Börner, who developed a theory that rejected patriarchy because of its 'Jewish' character and argued that gender equality was intrinsic to a true 'Nordic-Germanic' nature. Meyer closely analyzes Rogge-Börner's writings on gender and education within and beyond formal schooling, including her arguments about how best to educate a racially superior Nordic-Germanic race through both girls' and boys' schooling, co-education and girls' access to equal higher education and professional opportunities. The Rogge-Börner writings are particularly important for this special issue because they are one of the few cases where radical and extreme right-wing ideologues have directly addressed the relationship between gender relations and nationalist movements. In terms of educational strategy, Meyer's article highlights a key case where formal schooling is targeted as a tool for both racial separation and gender equality within a white nationalist framework.

*Cynthia Miller-Idriss'* article on masculinity and the body in far right youth culture in Germany draws on interviews with vocational school students and image analyses of symbols and commercial clothing brands to identify the ways in which youth subcultures reflect aspects of Connell's hegemonic masculinity. First, commercial iconography actively promotes idealized notions of male body image and traditional notions about masculinity as representing strength, power, heroism, loyalty, integrity, belonging and togetherness. Second, symbols and iconography market rebellion to young people and position the far right as a place to express aggression, violence and resistance to mainstream and adult authority. Miller-Idriss' analysis suggests that educational interventions which fail to acknowledge the role that masculinities play in the appeal of far right ideologies and subcultures are unlikely to succeed. While educational interventions aimed at preventing extremist engagement or de-radicalizing young people already on a path toward violence have often focused on rational argumentation – for example, providing accurate information about immigrants' employment or civic engagement – Miller-Idriss argues that the appeal of far right and extremist movements is often more emotional in nature. It would seem that far right youth culture is closely connected to male fantasies about a romantic, pure and untroubled national past, and young men's potential to restore a lost civilization or era. Such fantasies provide a landscape for navigating uncertain labor markets and transitions into adulthood, yet have been largely ignored by policymakers and educators seeking to prevent violence or extremist engagement. Educators need to confront the emotional appeal of extremist groups for young men, particularly if they are to create alternative spaces for them to express the twin desires for male comradeship and rebellion against the mainstream.

While formal schooling has historically played an important role in how the public understands radical right movements and parties, education also happens outside of formal settings. One mechanism through which the public is educated about radical right movements is through the linguistic choices that scholars and the media make in analyses of the far right. This has been evidenced most recently in debates about journalists' ready adoption of white supremacist groups' self-definition as 'alt-right,' for example, which critics argue has the effect of softening or legitimizing racist or radical right ideologies and platforms. *George Severs'* article extends this tradition with an analysis of a historical case from the UK. *Severs'* analysis of three episodes through which the British National Party (BNP) established clear anti-gay activism during the 1980s and 1990s highlights the critical importance of using conceptual terms that accurately reflect social attitudes and phenomena. Severs carefully differentiates what scholars have typically described as *homophobic* policies and attitudes on the part of the BNP from what he argues should more accurately be labeled *homohysteria*. While the former term refers to attitudes toward homosexuals grounded in fear and abjection, Severs shows that BNP policies and engagements were not only attitudinal, but also served as active opposition to homosexuality. Severs draws on three historical examples to illustrate the nature and extent of the BNP's homohysteria in general and the centrality of the party's opposition to gay men in particular. Severs' work highlights the ways in which particular linguistic choices can shape the public's – or scholars' – perceptions of nationalist political platforms, revealing one of many ways in which publics are educated about the radical right.

The potential for public discourse to shape voter behavior and civic understanding is also a key finding in *Anita Stasulane's* work on Latvia. Stasulane analyzes the role of women in the radical right Latvian National Front (LNF) – a case which is intriguing both because there is little English-language work on Latvian radical right movements and because of the unique role that women play in LNF leadership and party politics. The LNF blends esotericism with political goals and glorifies the feminine in its esoteric emphases. Women are highlighted as spiritually superior to men, tasked with leadership and positioned as pioneers who safeguard the nation. The prominent position given to women is correlated with higher female participation in the LNF compared to other radical right movements: approximately half of LNF members are estimated to be female. The LNF case illustrates how particular ideological frames can work to actively recruit women – and as Stasulane suggests, there are implications for how radical right groups will, and are trying to mobilize, female voters with anti-migrant and Islamophobic rhetoric that is specifically tied to women's rights, sexuality or assaults on women – such as the case of the 2016 New Year's Eve attacks in Cologne. While there has been significant attention to the role of masculinity in attracting men to far right groups, we have paid less attention to the potential for (re)framings of femininity, women's role in the nation, or discussions of women's rights to be used for recruitment or radicalization by far right political parties and movements. This could be important for interventions which may have overlooked the appeal of discourses which position women as strong leaders in national politics, or imply that their rights will be threatened through migration or expanded understandings of multiculturalism and diversity.

Like George Severs' work, *Niels Spierings, Andrej Zaslove*, and *Marcel Lubbers* also address the issue of attitudes toward sexuality by utilizing a quantitative analysis of voter data from 29 elections across 10 European countries to explain whether and how support for gay and lesbian rights is related to anti-migration attitudes. The term 'sexually modern nativism' refers to populist platforms which have shifted away from promoting 'traditional' family values and practices and instead proclaim that Western democratic traditions and values include a wider range of sexualities and tolerance toward the LGBTQ community. This platform is then positioned in contrast to a perceived Islamic threat as increased migration is said to weaken gay and lesbian rights, tolerance for sexual difference and secular modernity. Among other educational implications of Spierings et. al.'s work, their findings about the context-dependent nature of voting behaviors (with clear effects evident in some countries but not in others) show that national context matters; while comparative data is important for understanding trends and variations across national and cultural contexts, specific voter or activist behaviors may not correspond to similar ideological claims across contexts.

*Hilary Pilkington's* ethnographic study of the English Defence League (EDL) challenges a number of prevailing assumptions in research on gender, sexuality and the extreme right. Pilkington argues that while support for, and activism in, the extreme right remains numerically dominated by men, it is no longer a closed or ideologically inhospitable environment for women or LGBT activists. In the EDL, while women remain a minority, they mostly join on their own initiative, play an active role, and share in the camaraderie of activism. The study shows a degree of instrumentality in the movement's adoption of gender equality and LGBT rights platforms to 'expose' what is envisaged as an oppressive and intolerant Islamist ideology. However, the analysis reveals a contradictory picture. It exposes the limits to progressive views on gender and sexuality within the movement whilst also providing observational evidence that declarations of greater openness to women and LGBT supporters constitute more than lip-service to the top-down imposition of a strategically beneficial ideology. In practice, attitudes and behaviors among activists are diverse, ambivalent and conflicted; as such they arguably constitute a more radical variant of mainstream population attitudes rather than a highly ideologised, pathological fringe. These findings have important implications for educational interventions. While EDL supporters might be targeted through anti-racist interventions aimed at preventing extremist violence, activists view themselves as distant from, and indeed opposed to, the traditional far right. No simple, linear relationship can be assumed, therefore, between movement activists and ideological positions, including around issues of gender and sexuality. Educational interventions that fail to recognize these differentiations simply reinforce activists' suspicions that educational institutions are complicit in the wider agenda of government and liberal 'do-gooders' who label all those who 'tell it like it is' as violent, racist thugs. In this context, formal educational settings such as school or college often appear as sites of exclusion, expulsion or persecution, while the EDL is experienced by young members as the place they learned *not* to be racist (Pilkington 2016, 99).

Finally, *Sakellariou and Koronaiou's* article on the Golden Dawn's ideological platform in Greece – and discourses about women within it – points to the ways in which radical right political discourse can have an educative effect on their own constituents and the broader populace. Like other European far right parties, the Golden Dawn positions women as reproductive engines of the nation, focusing in particular on mothering boys who will be future Greek soldiers. But in contrast to similar parties, which have maintained traditional fascist and far right ideologies about women yet simultaneously elected women into leadership roles (such as France's Marine Le Pen), Sakellariou and Koronaiou show that the Golden Dawn calls for women to embrace their primary role as wives and mothers, only entering the workforce or more public roles in areas aligned with women's purportedly natural, feminine roles as nurturers in the private sphere. Through these efforts, the Golden Dawn aims to change women's behavior in ways that align with the protection and reproduction of the nation and its (white) populace, while far right cultural values are physically embodied through biological and natural roles.

It is this latter point that makes the Golden Dawn case such a compelling contribution to this issue, because Sakellariou and Koronaiou identify the ways in which radical right discourses can work to shape the ideas and beliefs of the broader public. Discussions of education and the radical right are not only about interventions to prevent far right violence. We must also examine the ways in which radical right groups aim to educate their own membership and shift broader public discourse about their key ideological beliefs in relation to women's rights and public roles in the labor market. To the extent that such positions take hold within the broader populace, it seems important to incorporate how a national(ist) habitus might take shape in any intervention aimed at disrupting radical and extreme right movements.

Finally, *Kathleen Blee's* insightful *Afterword* re-asserts the role of gender and of education to the historical and contemporary strategies and agendas of the radical right. Blee shows how the contributions to this issue help tease out the gendered processes through which people accept radical right ideologies and identify key educational implications of the gendered aspects of radical right politics and movements. As she points out, this issue goes to press just as these issues have been thrown into particular relief by the election of a new US president on a wave of support from 'white supremacists, xenophobes and anti-feminists' and 'aided by torrents of fake news items meant to undermine Trump's female opponent.' The gendered and educational implications of this historical moment will be investigated for years to come, but it is clear, as Blee points out, that this is a particularly critical time to attend more carefully to the relationship between gender, education and the radical right.

## Implications and future directions: gender, education and the radical right

'If education alone cannot counter extremism, what it can do is not make things worse,' Lynn Davies (2008, 620) writes. Davies' point is that pedagogical approaches which aim to 'teach' people the 'right' attitudes and beliefs may not only be ineffective but can also backfire, leading individuals to retreat even further into narrow worldviews. Beyond 'not making things worse,' though, what do we know about what works in educational programs with radical right populations? What do the articles in this special issue teach us, collectively, about education, gender, and the radical right?

First, the scholarship makes clear that educational initiatives aimed at reaching far right and radical right populations need to start from a standpoint of empathy for the uncertainty and precarity of young people's lives, the contexts in which they live, as well as the appeal of the clarity which clear dualisms (good/evil, enemy/friend, etc.) provide to some far right communities (Davies 2008, 620–621; also see Davies 2009). Engagement with far and radical right movements is not only driven by rational decisions but also by affective responses (Miller-Idriss 2017). Interventions which seek to shut down individual concerns – including expressions of fear and hatred – without acknowledging the affective registers of young lives are unlikely to succeed. As many articles in this issue suggest, this includes grappling with traditional notions of masculinity, femininity, fatherhood and motherhood. Davies suggests that school-based interventions, for example, focus on breaking down 'otherness' and addressing issues of free speech while acknowledging and addressing misconceptions (2008, 621–623).

Second, educators need to develop initiatives that can account for the fluid and contradictory aspects of identity within far right movements, particularly for young people. Individuals do not always express personal beliefs that align with party platforms (Pilkington, this issue). Adolescence and early adulthood are key phases of identity formation, and educational work with this population must account for potential differences between what people do in public and what they say in private, as well as the contradictions individuals must necessarily negotiate. Gender identities are also complex; women activists who themselves mock, and transgress, traditional notions of femininity may fail to challenge (or even recognize) a largely unreconstructed masculinity that governs everyday interactions and communications (Pilkington, this issue).

Finally, these contributions clearly suggest that national context matters and further comparative research across countries and regions is necessary. There is no universal intervention; regional differences in the appeal of various populist and radical right platforms and rhetoric abound (Spierings, Zaslove, and Lubbers, 2017). Radical right groups' educational platforms and programs related to gender need further investigation, whether through the study of radical right groups' formal curricular objectives for girls' and boys' schooling, as Meyer (this issue) analyzes, or through the role of radical right-wing populist discourse intended to mold a national(ist) habitus about gender roles, as Sakellariou and Koronaiou (this issue) detail.

We would also call for more research on the intersection of formal and informal schooling. There is some evidence suggesting that pedagogical interventions around right-wing extremism, anti-semitism and xenophobia are most effective when formal and non-formal educational partners work collaboratively in more intensive engagements with smaller numbers of schools and communities (Johansson 2013). While non-formal partners can develop intervention strategies that are more specific to the at-risk group, Johansson points out that school-based educators, who spend more time with young people overall, often have important contextual and family background information about young people which may increase the success of interventions. But there is little data available that helps trace how such collaborations work in general or whether and how gender might play a role in their relative impact.

The choices that journalists, scholars and educators make about what kinds of language to use to describe particular groups of people can have a major impact on social attitudes in general and on the appeal of the radical right specifically. As the outcomes of the referendum on EU membership in the UK (June 2016) and the American presidential elections (November 2016) demonstrate, anti-immigration, anti-Muslim and racist rhetoric can quickly move from the periphery to the center of political debate. These events reveal, moreover, that simple strategies of condemnation or the silencing of distasteful views are often counterproductive; to those who already feel unheard, they confirm the disdain they experience, not only from politicians but also from the wider 'liberal' elite. If as scholars and educators we want to retain some authority in shaping public opinion, therefore, we need to recognize and respond to growing popular and critical scrutiny of our right to do so. In this special issue, we take a step in that direction as we attempt to rethink, more complexly, some of our assumptions about the relationship between the radical right, its gender constituency and the implications for education in its broadest and most strategic sense.

## Notes

1. See the Southern Poverty Law Center's hate map for more information. Accessed November 4 2016. https://www.splcenter.org/hate-map.
2. A meta-analysis of the findings of 64 opinion polls (2007–2010) on attitudes toward Muslims suggests that Islamophobia is higher than it was in 2001–2006 (Field 2012, 158). According to Field (Field 2012, 158), depending on the specific question asked, between one fifth and three quarters of the UK population hold anti-Muslim or anti-Islam attitudes.
3. Statistics on Germany come from the Bundeskriminalamt and were reported by Die Zeit (2016).
4. See 'Trojan T-shirt targets German right-wing rock fans,' *BBC News*, Accessed October 25 2016. http://www.bbc.com/news/world-europe-14465150.
5. See 'Mit der freiwilligen Feuerwehr gegen Extremismus,' *Deutsche Welle*, July 13. Accessed November 4 2016. http://www.dw.com/de/mit-der-freiwilligen-feuerwehr-gegen-extremismus/a-19398283.

## Disclosure statement

No potential conflict of interest was reported by the authors.

## Funding

The authors are grateful to Alessandra Hodulik for research assistance and to the participants in a series of Economic and Social Research Council (ESRC) funded seminars on Right Wing Extremism in Contemporary Europe (2013–2015, Award no. ES/L000857/1) in which gender was a central theme and in which some of the ideas explored here first came to light.

## References

Akkerman, T., and A. Hagelund. 2007. "'Women and Children First!' Anti-Immigration Parties and Gender in Norway and the Netherlands." *Patterns of Prejudice* 41 (2): 197–214.

Arzheimer, K. 2009. "Contextual Factors and the Extreme Right Vote in Western Europe, 1980–2002." *American Journal of Political Science* 53 (2): 259–275.

Beelmann, Andreas, and Kim Sarah Heinemann. 2014. "Preventing Prejudice and Improving Intergroup Attitudes: A Meta-analysis of Child and Adolescent Training Programs." *Journal of Applied Developmental Psychology* 35 (1): 10–24.

Blee, K., and S. Deutsch. 2012. "Introduction." In *Women of the Right: Comparisons and Interplay Across Borders*, edited by K. Blee and S. McGee Deutsch, 1–17. University Park, PA: Penn State University Press.

Blee, K., and A. Linden. 2012. "Women in Extreme Right Parties and Movements." In *Women of the Right: Comparisons and Interplay Across Borders*, edited by K. Blee and S. McGee Deutsch, 98–116. University Park, PA: Penn State University Press.

Carrington, B., and A. Bonnett. 1997. 'The Other Canadian 'Mosaic'- 'race' Equity Education in Ontario and British Columbia." *Comparative Education* 33 (3): 411–431.

Cockburn, T. 2007. "'Performing' Racism: Engaging Young Supporters of the Far Right in England." *British Journal of Sociology of Education* 28 (5): 547–560.

Davies, Lynn. 2008. "Gender, Education, Extremism and Security." *Compare: A Journal of Comparative and International Education* 38 (5): 611–625.

Davies, Lynn. 2009. "Educating against Extremism: Towards a Critical Politicisation of Young people." *International Review of Education* 55 (2/3): 183–203.

Die Zeit. 2016. "BKA zählt fast 800 Angriffe auf Flüchtlingsunterkünfte." October 19 2016. http://www.zeit.de/gesellschaft/2016-10/asylunterkuenfte-angriffe-800-straftaten-fluechtlingsheime.

Ezekiel, R. 2002. "An Ethnographer Looks at Neo-Nazi and Klan Groups: The Racist Mind Revisited." *American Behavioral Scientist* 46: 51–71.

Ferber, A. L., and M. S. Kimmel. 2008. "The Gendered Face of Terrorism." *Sociology Compass* 2 (3): 870–887.

Field, C. D. 2012. "Revisiting Islamophobia in Contemporary Britain, 2007–10." In *Islamophobia in the West: Measuring and Explaining Individual Attitudes*, edited by M. Helbling, 147–161. London: Routledge.

Itkowitz, C. 2016. "This Professor Devotes her Life to Countering Dangerous Speech. She Can't Ignore Donald Trump's." *The Washington Post*. October 24 2016.

Johansson, Susanne. 2013. "Innovative Methods and Models of Collaboration in the Field of Pedagogical Prevention of Xenophobia, Anti-semitism and Right-wing Extremism: Chances and Perspectives for a Better Cooperation between Formal and Non-formal Education in Germany." *Social Theory, Empirics, Policy and Practice* 7: 119–132.

Kimmel, M. 2007. Racism as Adolescent Male Rite of Passage: Ex-Nazis in Scandinavia. *Journal of Contemporary Ethnography* 36(2): 202–218.

Kitschelt, H. 2007. Growth and Persistence of the Radical Right in Postindustrial Democracies: Advances and Challenges in Comparative Research. *West European Politics* 30 (5): 1176–1206.

Mieriņa, I., and I. Koroļeva. 2015. "Support for Far Right Ideology and Anti-Migrant Attitudes Among Youth in Europe: A Comparative Analysis." *The Sociological Review* 63 (S2): 183–205.

Miller-Idriss, C. forthcoming-a. "Youth and the Radical Right." In *Oxford Handbook of the Radical Right*, edited by Jens Rydgren. Oxford: Oxford University Press.

Miller-Idriss, C. forthcoming-b. *The Extreme Gone Mainstream Commercialization and Far Right Youth Culture in Germany*. Princeton: Princeton University Press.

Miller-Idriss. 2017. "Soldier, Sailor, Rebel, Rulebreaker: Masculinity and the Body in the German Far Right." *Gender and Education*. doi:10.1080/09540253.2016.1274381.

Mudde, C. 2000. *The Ideology of the Extreme Right*. Manchester: Manchester University Press.

Mudde, C. 2005. "Racist Extremism in Central and Eastern Europe." *East European Politics and Societies* 19: 161–184.

Mudde, C. 2007. *Populist Radical Right Parties in Europe*. Cambridge: Cambridge University Press.

Mudde, C. 2014. "Introduction: Youth and the Extreme Right: Explanations, Issues, and Solutions." In *Youth and the Extreme Right*, edited by C. Mudde, 1–18. New York: IDebate Press.

Pascoe, C. J. 2007. *Dude, You're a Fag: Masculinity and Sexuality in High School*. Berkeley, CA: University of California Press.

Pascoe, C. J., and T. Bridges. 2015. *Exploring Masculinities: Identity, Inequality, Continuity and Change.* Oxford: Oxford University Press.

Pilkington, H. 2016. *Loud and Proud: Passion and Politics in the English Defence League.* Manchester: Manchester University Press.

Pilkington, Hilary. 2017. "'EDL Angels Stand Beside their Men … not Behind Them': The Politics of Gender and Sexuality in an Anti-Islam(ist) Movement." *Gender and Education.* doi:10.1080/09540253.2016.1237622.

Pilkington, H., E. Omel'chenko, and A. Garifzianova. 2010. *Russia's Skinheads: Exploring and Rethinking Subcultural Lives.* London: Routledge.

Rippl, S., and C. Seipel. 1999. "Gender Differences in Right-Wing Extremism: Intergroup Validity of a Second-Order Construct." *Social Psychology Quarterly* 62: 381–393.

Rydgren, Jens. Forthcoming. *The Oxford Handbook of the Radical Right.* Oxford: Oxford University Press.

Shafer, Joseph A. 2002. "Spinning the Web of Hate: Web-Based Hate Propagation by Extremist Organizations." *Journal of Criminal Justice and Popular Culture* 9 (2): 69–88.

Siedler, T. 2011. "Parental Unemployment and Young People's Extreme Right-wing Party Affinity: Evidence from Panel Data." *Journal of the Royal Statistical Society. Series A (Statistics in Society* 174 (3): 737–758.

Spierings, Niels, Andrej Zaslove, and Marcel Luabbers. 2017. "Sexual-modern nativist voters: do they Exist and do they Vote for the Radical Right?" *Gender and Education.* doi:10.1080/09540253.2016.1274383.

Spierings, N., and A. Zaslove. 2015. "Gendering the Vote for Populist Radical-right Parties." *Patterns of Prejudice* 49 (1–2): 135–162.

Weaver, Matthew. 2016. "Hate Crimes Soared After EU Referendum, Home Office Figures Confirm." *The Guardian*, October 13 2016. https://www.theguardian.com/politics/2016/oct/13/hate-crimes-eu-referendum-home-office-figures-confirm, accessed November 4, 2016.

# Towards equality for women and men of one race: Sophie Rogge-Börner's racial-feminist philosophy of education

Jennifer Meyer

**ABSTRACT**

Since 1933 marked the end of autonomous and democratic women's associations, historiography tends to neglect the study of feminist voices under National-Socialism. This paper looks at one of *völkisch* feminist movement's leaders, writer and journalist Sophie Rogge-Börner (1878–1955), whose claims for gender equality were rooted in anti-Semitism and scientific racism. In its first section, the paper will present the core aspects of her racial-feminist discourse. The second section will discuss Sophie Rogge-Börner's philosophy of education in detail to compare her conceptions to the official national-socialist ideology. By doing so, this paper will address the issue of women's engagement, agency, and autonomy in the radical right.

> Women and men of *one* race are blessed with the same intellectual capacities (…). This is why both sexes have the right to the same education of the mind. (Sophie Rogge-Börner, 1933c, 174).

## Introduction

From the immediate aftermath of the Second World War to the *Historikerinnenstreit* in the early 1980s, feminist interpretations of the Nazi past tended to portray all women as victims of the sexist and racist politics of the Third Reich, and to describe the National-Socialist ideology as the most extreme form of patriarchy.[1] This was consistent with a perception of radical right movements as male-dominated and deeply misogynistic, which has been challenged by recent historiography (Evans 1986; Grossmann 1991). In the past decades, these ideal-typical representations have been abandoned in favour of more nuanced and complex descriptions of the variety of women's experiences under the Third Reich, shaped in particular by their 'racial' and social origin, as well as their support for and participation in radical right movements (Heinsohn, Vogel and Weckel 1997; Gehmacher 1998, 2001; Kandel 2004; Allal 2006). Nowadays, the main question is not whether, but to what extent, for what reasons, and at what levels women were involved in the radical right. As a result, it is to be asked whether the presence of women in radical right movements challenges their defence of traditional gender roles, heterosexuality, and patriarchal values.

Driven by these questions, this article takes a look at the German-*völkisch* women's movement, which emerged in the 1920s as a reaction to the democratic and (partially) internationalist impetus of the 'old' women's movement, and to the strong anti-feminism within the radical right. Historiography generally distinguishes two modes of argumentation within first-wave feminism: difference (or relational) feminists praise genuinely feminine qualities and seek the recognition of women's specific contributions to society; equality (or individualist) feminists advocate for women's full emancipation as a universal human right. In both cases, however, gender appears to be the main category of feminist analysis and politics. This paper proposes to challenge this gender-centred perspective in adopting an intersectional approach (Kallenberg, Mueller and Meyer, 2013) to examine the interlocking of the categories of race, class, and gender in the writings of *völkisch* journalist and writer Sophie Rogge-Börner. Although she did not manage to persuade the majority of *völkisch* women to accept her radical conception of gender equality, and faced a violent anti-feminist backlash from all streams of the radical right, she can be considered one of the *völkisch* women's movement leaders (Crips 1990; Ziege 1997; Streubel 2006; Breuer 2008; Meyer 2013). As the first child of Prussian officer Eduard Börner (1852–1921) and Pauline Scharpenberg (1855–1921), she was born on 24 July 1878 in Warendorf in Westphalia but lived in various garrison towns, following the regular transfers of her father. At almost thirty-two years old, she married military doctor Max Rogge (1871–1946) in April 1910 with whom she had a son, Ralf, a year later.[2] Like for many German women, the war and Germany's defeat woke her interest in politics (Heinsohn 2000, 2007). She joined the *Deutschnationale Volkspartei* (German-National People's Party) in 1919, which supported the restoration of the monarchy, and she campaigned for Germany's 'racial' renewal. Disappointed by the party's conservatism and anti-feminism, she played an active role in the openly racist and anti-Semitic *Deutschvölkische Freiheitspartei* (German-Völkisch Freedom Party) and the *Nationalsozialistische Freiheitsbewegung* (National-Socialist Freedom Movement) but avoided an affiliation with the *Nationalsozialistische Deutsche Arbeiterpartei* (National-Socialist German Workers' Party, or NSDAP).[3] Encouraging the alliance between all parties and groups of the radical right, she gathered local national-socialist and völkisch supporters under the name *Völkisch-sozialer Block* (Völkisch-Social Bloc) for the 1924 parliamentary election. After a brief career as a teacher before the First World War, she focused on writing and published many fictional novels and short stories, poems, and political essays. Furthermore, she worked as a journalist and was the chief editor of *Die Deutsche Kämpferin. Stimmen zur Gestaltung der wahrhaftigen Volksgemeinschaft*, literally: *The German (female) fighter. Voices for the shaping of a true community of the people*, from 1933 to 1937. On an average, the magazine reached a circulation of 2500 exemplars per month. In comparison, *Die Frau*, the bimonthly organ of the *Bund Deutscher Frauenvereine* (Federation of German Women's Associations) did not exceed a circulation of 8000 exemplars.

As a very prolific journalist and writer, Sophie Rogge-Börner gained a certain popularity in the 1920s but she never succeed in convincing the *völkisch* movement to convert to feminism, nor *völkisch* feminists to equality feminism. As both a radical advocate of full gender equality and a virulent anti-Semitic, she also failed at assembling non-*völkisch* women under the banner of her racial-feminist project. Her ongoing conflict with the national-socialist regime regarding its women's policy marginalised her even more in the political arena. After 1945, she did not regain her former popularity even if she tried to reconnect with völkisch ideologues and especially with feminists. Published in 1951, her last book *Planet im Absturz?* may give the impression that she focused solely on her feminist project. However, an in-depth analysis and an insight into her private correspondence with former colleague and friend Lenore Kühn reveal quickly that she was forced to reformulate her racial views to avoid censorship but did not abandon them. In her eyes, the only crimes one could condemn Hitler and the Third Reich for were their sexism and the death of German soldiers and civilians. She was very careful to not fully deny the Holocaust but never named its main victims, the Jews, and stated outright that the expulsion of Germans from the Eastern European countries decided during the Potsdam Conference was in no way less inhuman or less cruel (Rogge-Börner 1951, 13). This equivalence echoed to the development of the 'victim theory' – or 'victim myth' – that founded Austria's national identity after 1945 but also granted a sort of moral amnesty to a large part of the German population. The designation of Adolf Hitler and the national-socialist elites as the real and sole perpetrators led to a victimisation of individuals that tended to present the Germans as the victims of Hitler's power of manipulation and of his insatiable militarism and imperialism, the victims of the Allied Forces, and the victims of the expulsions after the war, and to restrict the collective examination of the various forms of complicity that took place. Two letters addressed to Lenore Kühn in 1951 and 1952 reveal that Sophie Rogge-Börner was still in contact with her long-time friend and colleague Bernhard Kummer, a fellow representative of Nordicism, but was unable to propagate feminist ideas within neo-völkisch and right-wing circles. She was also rather disappointed by the pacifist, internationalist, and democratic stance of the majority of the newly founded feminist associations, such as the *Deutscher Frauenring* (German women's circle, 1949), and refused to cooperate with them. However, she also had a few occasional successes, for example, when a few activists from Berlin invited her in 1952 to read one of her new plays. Three years later, in February 1955, Sophie Rogge-Börner died and was buried in Düsseldorf where she had lived since October 1948. Although Sophie Rogge-Börner remained a controversial and marginalised figure within the radical right, from 1933 onwards, her ideas experienced a new conceptual development and a surge of interest in pagan Unitarian circles through the work of philosopher and Ludwig F. Clauss's scholar Sigrid Hunke (1913–1999), a scholar of Ludwig F. Clauss (Junginger 2004).

In its first section, this article will expose the three key aspects of Sophie Rogge-Börner's racial-feminism: (1) the construction of the myth of the Nordic-Germanic race's original and total gender equality, (2) the narrative of 'racial degeneration', allegedly provoked by the introduction of 'Jewish' patriarchy, and (3) the presentation of the re-establishment of gender equality as the solution of the 'race question'. In its second section, this article will focus on the link between education and the radical right in taking a closer look at Sophie Rogge-Börner's claims for gender-equal and gender-neutral education.

## The racial-feminist thought as the symbiosis of racial anti-Semitism and equality feminism

### The myth of the Nordic-Germanic race's original and total gender equality

Like the majority of twentieth-century racial theorists, Sophie Rogge-Börner referred to popular and widely manipulated texts such as Tacitus' *Germania*, Johann J. Bachofen's

*Mother Right*, and stories of the Norse mythology compiled in the *Edda* and the sagas, which allegedly proved the racial superiority of the Germans (Laffont 2006; Davies 2007, 2009; Baden 2009). However, her feminist interpretation of these knowledge sources remained profoundly controversial within the radical right, as well as within the various strands of the feminist movement. Claiming that the specific power relation between men and women was the primary criterion to not only delimit the frontiers between the various races, but also to determine their ranking in the global racial hierarchy, she asserted that peoples of the so-called 'Nordic-Germanic race' in ancient times were characterised by gender equality when they remained racially pure; conversely, patriarchy and the most brutal oppression of women reigned within the inferior 'Jewish race'. Sophie Rogge-Börner's focus on the social organisation, rather than on biological elements, in her definition of the Nordic-Germanic 'race' finds an explanation in her adhesion to Nordicism's minority 'racial psychologist' stream. Literally the 'science of the race's soul' (*Rassenseelenkunde*), racial psychology was developed by Ludwig F. Clauss as a reaction to Hans F. K. Günther's 'raciology' (*Rassenkunde*). It postulated that cultural and psychological aspects were of higher importance than purely biological elements to define a 'race' (Wiedemann 2009).

According to Sophie Rogge-Börner, Nordic-Germanic gender equality would have resulted from minimal sexual differentiation. Primary sex characteristics (external genitalia, internal reproductive anatomy, and gonads) were the only distinction between male and female humans of Nordic-Germanic 'race' based on physiological characteristics that she did not challenge since they were necessary to human reproduction. However, she considered that they had no social relevance and therefore did not generate an imbalance of power distribution between men and women, nor sexism. She also affirmed that secondary sex characteristics, like stature or strength, did not exist within the Nordic-Germanic 'race' at the beginning of humanity, but were rather a long-term result of the introduction of so-called 'Jewish' patriarchy. Likewise, during this 'pure' period of time, sex-specific differences in brain structure were inexistent, so that intellectual capacities and psychology could differ between individuals but were not caused by their gender. The similarity between genders, or rather the absence of a sex-specific differentiation, was the key to gender equality.

Although she adopted an essentialist conception of the category of 'race', Sophie Rogge-Börner rejected the feminist arguments based on a differentialist definition of gender, which emphasised specifically feminine qualities and aimed at extending the so-called female sphere rather than achieving full equality in all domains. Affirming that the whole Nordic-Germanic social organisation was built on the principle of 'not taking gender difference into consideration' (Rogge-Börner 1935, 7–24), as well on a strongly defined elitism between an 'elite' and a broader 'mass', she stated that Nordic-Germanic women had the same right as men to work, to contribute to the political and legislative process, to administer justice, to perform religious functions, and to participate in armed battles against enemies.

Although Sophie Rogge-Börner referred to both Ludwig F. Clauss and Hans F. K. Günther in her early works, certainly to gain respectability and legitimacy as a scholar of scientific racism, she stridently criticised their strong anti-feminism, particularly Hans F. K. Günther's engagement in the *Männerbund* (Men's League) along with Nazi ideologue Alfred Rosenberg and their assertion that patriarchy was of Nordic essence and, as a result, the sole authentic and appropriate social system for peoples of Nordic origin, that is, in the first instance, the Germans. Led by Rosenberg, the *Männerbund* radicalised and racialised the convergence of stereotypes of Jews and women that had emerged in fin-de-siècle Europe and, with as its corollary the entanglement of anti-Semitism and anti-feminism, became central to the discourse of race and gender within the radical right (Braun 1992, 1994). But Rogge-Börner also opposed the supporters of Herman Wirth's racist and anti-modernist reinterpretation of Johann Bachofen's work about the origins of matriarchy that he propagated in his book *Der Aufgang der Menschheit* (The ascent of Mankind) in 1928 and his translation into German of the Ura Linda Chronicle in 1933 (Davies 2007). While fully subscribing to the essentialist, racist, and especially anti-Semitic principles that laid the foundations for their beliefs, Sophie Rogge-Börner could not adhere to Günther's and Rosenberg's idea of a Nordic patriarchy that explicitly aimed at sending women back into the domestic sphere, but she could not support the idealisation of ancient matriarchy spread by Herman Wirth either because it also tended towards a limitation of women's potential in the end in sacralising motherhood. As a result, her open disapproval of recognised ideologues and her forceful defence of a 'Nordic-Germanic' gender equality led to her further marginalisation within the radical right.

### The narrative of 'racial degeneration' provoked by the introduction of 'Jewish' patriarchy

Since gender equality was the criterion characterising the Nordic-Germanic race and measuring its superiority, the deeply asymmetrical power relation between men and women at the beginning of the twentieth century was, for Sophie Rogge-Börner, proof of an extreme 'racial' degeneration. Influenced by racial pessimist authors like Arthur de Gobineau and Alfred Rosenberg who stated that 'racial' mixing always caused the degeneration of the superior 'race' (and never the improvement of the inferior 'race'), Sophie Rogge-Börner affirmed that encounters between the Nordic-Germanic and the Jewish 'races' led to the disappearance of the gender-equal golden age. This biological and cultural mixing could not have contributed, by any means, to reducing, even less ending, women's oppression in patriarchal 'races'. This founded the call for a radical anti-Semitic, racist, and feminist agenda rooted in the 'de-Jewification' of society and the exclusion of Jewish women from the liberation's project. Building on Johann J. Bachofen's thesis of a simultaneity between the apollonian patriarchal phase and the development of the Christian religion, which was considered influenced by the 'Jewish spirit' within *völkisch* and neo-pagan circles, Sophie Rogge-Börner argued that cultural and biological encounters provoked by migrations, the Roman conquest, and especially the Christianisation of the Germanic (and Nordic) peoples led to the progressive introduc-tion of 'Jewish' patriarchy. This evolution not only caused a radical transformation of Nordic-Germanic laws and traditions, which led to the development of an unnatural gen-dered division of labour imprisoning women in the domestic sphere. It also created 'arti-ficial differences' between genders to justify male dominance and female oppression afterwards. It may appear surprising that Sophie Rogge-Börner drew on socialist pedago-gue and philosopher Mathilde Vaerting's work, and especially on the two volumes of her *Neubegründung der Psychologie von Mann und Weib* (A New Basis for the Psychology of

Man and Woman) published in 1921 and 1923, to support the revolutionary idea that the unequal power relation between men and women did not derive from pre-existent, innate, and immutable differences, but from the socially and historically constructed gender hierarchy, which reinforced and legitimated its own existence in making gender differences appear natural (Wobbe 1994, 1998). In fact, Mathilde Vaerting was contributing to the controversies caused by the revival of Bachofen at the beginning of the twentieth century and her interpretation of the jurist's work about matriarchy was widely discussed within feminist circles, on both sides of the political spectrum.

However, there were central differences between the two feminists. First, Sophie Rogge-Börner re-essentialised Mathilde Vaerting's thesis in postulating the racial origin of the three possible constellations of power relations between genders: patriarchy, matriarchy, and gender equality. Secondly, and as a result, her criticism of the imbalance of power between men and women did not lead to a criticism of other types of social inequalities since her ideology was rooted in the racial theories of her time. By contrast, Mathilde Vaerting used her comparison of sexism to racism and to anti-Semitism to offer both a broader analysis of the mechanisms of power that shape modern society and a potential path of emancipation. Not only was she heavily criticised by the majority of *völkisch* supporters whose anti-feminism and anti-Semitism expressed a specific cultural identity developed in Imperial Germany (Volkov 2000a, 2000b), but many völkisch feminists such as Mathilde Ludendorff and Bertha Eckstein-Diener (who often published under the pseudonym Sir Galahad) also rejected her thesis because she refused to take the new racial theories into consideration and/or because she considered patriarchy as well as gender itself as a historically and socially constructed phenomenon that could be overturned. With her support for Mathilde Vaerting, Sophie Rogge-Börner was, once again, relatively isolated within right-wing (feminist) circles.

### The solution to the 'gender question' (Geschlechterfrage) is the solution to the 'race question' (Rassenfrage)

For Sophie Rogge-Börner, solving the 'gender question' through the re-establishment of original gender equality would regenerate, that is to say 'de-Jewify', the descendant peoples of the Nordic-Germanic 'race'. In other words, the restoration of original gender equality through female emancipation was the necessary pre-condition for the renewal of the purity and the superiority of the Nordic-Germanic 'race'. Consequently, Sophie Rogge-Börner tried to found a *völkisch* women's movement as an alternative to both the traditional strands of the German women's movement and national-socialist female organisations. While criticising a tendency towards 'Jewification', which, for example, manifested in some feminist associations or personalities' internationalist, pacifist, and liberal-democratic engagement, she claimed that the German women's movement was originally a racially motivated response to male dominance and an instinctive revolt of the Nordic-Germanic blood against an unnatural social organisation (Rogge 1924, 54–55; Rogge-Börner 1928, 30–31). Thus, Sophie Rogge-Börner praised the struggle of first-wave feminists like Auguste Schmidt, Louise Otto-Peters, Marie Calm, and Ottilie von Steyber (Rogge-Börner 1933a, 99), but it has not escaped the reader's notice that her list of so-called 'essentially German women' deliberately concealed the central role played by Henriette Goldschmidt, a famous Jewish pedagogue, Friedrich Froebel's follower, and wife of

Leipzig's rabbi, in the foundation of the *Allgemeiner Deutscher Frauenverein* (General German Women's Association) in 1865. Since emancipation could only be reached by women of Nordic-Germanic 'race', Sophie Rogge-Börner stated that Jewish women could not escape their 'racial' destiny and abolish Jewish patriarchy. In doing so, she exacerbated the discrimination and exclusion that Jewish women had already experienced within the German women's movement for decades (Dürkop 1984; Kaplan 1984, 1993, 2004; Kohn-Ley and Korotin 1994; Bereswill and Wagner 1998).

Sophie Rogge-Börner's ambition to carry the partial legacy of historical but 'de-Jewified' German feminism, and her constant criticism of Nazi women's policies, made a cooperation with the *NS-Frauenschaft* and the *Deutsches Frauenwerk*, whose primary goals were to gain recognition for women's participation in and contribution to National-Socialism rather than achieve gender equality, thoroughly impossible. She had an explicit argument with *Bund Deutscher Mädel*-leader Lydia Gottschewski, who claimed in her book *Männerbund und Frauenfrage: die Frau im neuen Staat* (Men's league and women's question: The woman in the new state) that the new national-socialist women's associations were rooted in the national-socialist ideology and had nothing in common with the old women's movement (Davies 2007, 111). Earlier, she was denounced after a speech she held in front of several associations of housewives for having criticised Adolf Hitler who asked German women to quit their careers to bear numerous children while remaining childless himself. According to Katharina Ruppin's denunciation letter, she also called in a very provocative manner for the right of women of working as judges, taking an active and equal part in political decision-making, and even getting a military education. As a result, the regime began monitoring Sophie Rogge-Börner from 1933 onwards, and eventually banned her mouthpiece *Die Deutsche Kämpferin*. Despite its violent anti-Semitism, the journal was forbidden by the Gestapo on 13 May 1937 for the foreign and exile press had interpreted some of its articles, rather positively, as a 'smear campaign' against Nazi Germany. While the only document conserved in the German National Archives does not reveal any further detail about the Gestapo's decision nor about the mentioned articles, it is to be noted that 1937 marked a break in the regime's politics regarding allies such as the various nationalist Christian movements or völkisch ideologues. The ban of *Die Deutsche Kämpferin* resulted from both the Gestapo's four-year-long surveillance and the regime's general attempt to silence the last few critical, or rather not totally favourable, voices.

Sophie Rogge-Börner and her journal's contributors called for full equality between spouses, sharing of parental authority, a gender-equal children's education within the family, a profound reformation of the school and university system to guarantee girls' and women's access to education and professional careers, the fight against gender discrimination in work legislation and against gender income inequality, and women's access to all military career ladders and active participation in the armed forces. While openly criticising democracy and parliamentarianism, Sophie Rogge-Börner demanded the realisation of political gender equality on behalf of the German people's 'natural and inalienable right to be led by the best, the purest, and the strongest among them' (Rogge-Börner 1933–34, 340).[4] Furthermore, she criticised the androcentric bias in science and supported feminist claims in favour of a rewriting of German and European history. This new history would have, on the one hand, included the many ignored stories and accomplishments of female personalities, and, on the other hand, adopted a gender-neutral – or, as she sometimes refers to it, 'androgynous' – point of view.

## The racial-feminist philosophy of education

Rejecting a 'universalistic' conception of gender that did not take racial specificities into account, Sophie Rogge-Börner called for the total overhaul of the German school and university system to correspond to her Nordic-Germanic ideal of both gender equality and elitism. In December 1933, she published a programmatic article entitled *Mädchenbildung nach deutschem Artgesetz* ('Education of girls according to the German racial law') in *Die Deutsche Kämpferin* aimed at weighing in on the Nazi education policy. This article summarised her arguments in favour of gender-equal education, which she also discussed in various books.

### Measuring intelligence. Does gender matter?

In the second half of the nineteenth century, the majority of German women's associations concentrated mostly on (bourgeois) women's right to education and work (Gerhard, Klausmann, and Wischermann 2001). Opposing the widespread idea inherited from Rousseau's conceptions that (higher) education endangered femininity and motherhood, and, therefore, should stay a male privilege, many German feminists founded their claims on the thesis of 'spiritual motherhood' developed by kindergarten's creator Friedrich Fröbel. Since 'motherly' qualities such as nurturing and caring were present in every woman, but detached from effective motherhood, women appeared to be predestined to become teachers or social workers (Gerhard 2009, 62–63 and 86–90). 'Spiritual motherhood' also provided an answer to the 'surplus women' debate in supporting bourgeois unmarried women's educational training and access to remunerated occupations. James Albisetti underlined that:

> For some women, this emphasis on the motherly role became a means for reforming society. In their view, women had retained more harmonious personalities than had men, who, in pursuing their careers, had become overly specialized and rationalistic. By exercising "spiritual motherhood" in teaching and social work, women could provide an antidote to the evils produced by the male-inspired industrialization and urbanization of Germany. (Albisetti 2014, 98)

While overruling the formerly asserted incompatibility between education and femininity, and promoting women's necessary contribution to society, this argumentation also tended to reformulate the idea that gender differences were essential, natural, and complementary. Although most feminists insisted on the fact that feminine qualities were as valuable as masculine ones, in practice, the differentialist – or complementarian – perspective worked to expand women's opportunities without challenging male dominance in depth. Very few radical feminists, such as Hedwig Dohm, adopted a universalistic – or egalitarian – perspective to claim women's rights as human rights and argue on behalf of the principle of the equality of all persons.

    Aware that this concept was directly associated with the French Revolution, democracy, individualism, and universalism, Sophie Rogge-Börner chose to reformulate it within a racist frame. In other words, 'race' replaced 'humankind' as the frame of reference to elaborate the definition of genders and to evaluate the power relations between them. That is why she could assert that, for people of Nordic-Germanic 'race', gender played no role in intelligence '(s)ince predispositions and capacities are the same in girls and boys, but they are differently distributed to each individual' (Rogge-Börner 1951, 85).[5] Considering gender dimorphism as the result of (and not the cause for) sexism, Sophie Rogge-Börner believed that men and women of one race had to be treated the same based on a common racial belonging, which transcended their gender. The primacy of the category of 'race' seemed to override the potential social implications of the category of 'gender'. As a consequence, the irrelevance of gender was the primary justification for gender-equal education:

> Women and men of *one* race are blessed with the same intellectual capacities which are differently distributed, regarding their density and dimension, to each person *individually*. This is why both sexes have the right to the same education of the mind; because both want to serve one community. (Rogge-Börner 1933c, 174)[6]

But this individualistic argumentation within a racist frame also founded the call for educational policies aimed at realising full gender equality.

### Gender equality as German 'de-Jewified' schools' primary educational goal

According to Sophie Rogge-Börner, gender equality needed to become the founding principle *and* the goal of the German education system, which was supposed to strengthen the gender-equal socialisation that boys and girls experienced within their families (Dafflon Novelle 2006). She criticised school education for transmitting normative gender expectations based on a negative conception of femininity, which forced young girls to conform to the social norm and, therefore, uncritically accept male dominance:

> The young girl has not been taught self-assertion, performance and own formation of the will but only passive commitment to endure and to serve. (Rogge-Börner 1933c, 171)[7]

Therefore, school must not only provide students with the necessary knowledge and skills for their future lives and careers, but also influence their personalities and characters in order to abolish formerly prevailing gender expectations and societal norms. Sophie Rogge-Börner stated that:

> The central task of every school stays the transmission of *knowledge* [...], as well as the formation of the *character* that has basically been ignored until today and whose entire importance has eventually been recognised now. The fatal scale of egocentrism has to fall down as the first condition for the male formation of the character; and the female youth should not be burdened with dependency and inferiority complexes anymore. (Rogge-Börner 1933c, 174)[8]

Convinced that intelligence had no gender and that women's inferiority complex (as well as men's superiority complex) could be prevented through gender-equal character education, Sophie Rogge-Börner saw the introduction of coeducation as a necessity, an idea that she continued to defend in her final book in 1951:

> But none of the many school reformers from different traditions of thought (apart from the Nordic countries and a few North American states) saw the light yet that it is against nature to separate children during their schooling by gender. Following this ominous tradition, the

division of humankind into two deficient halves, which already begins in the nursery, pro-
gresses; an evolution that will be of indelible consequences for the entire philosophy of life
of humankind. Here, the ground has been laid for the superiority complexes of the man
and the inferiority feelings of the woman (…). (Rogge-Börner 1951, 64)[9]

In this case too, Sophie Rogge-Börner's arguments had more in common with the egalitarian conceptions praised by radical (bourgeois) feminists, such as *Frauenverein Reform*'s
founder and coeducation advocate Hedwig Kettler, than with difference feminists like
Helene Lange, who was one the most popular and vocal campaigners for women's
rights to education, but did not challenge gender-segregated schools and curriculums.

According to Sophie Rogge-Börner, German philosophy of education's and education
policy's in-depth transformation could only occur through 'de-Jewification' – or, as it
has also been called, 'Germanisation', that is, 'Aryanisation'. Following nineteenth-
century education reform based on the Humboldtian model, school programmes
focused on teaching the history, philosophy and languages of classical antiquity, which
caused an uproar within *völkisch* and nationalistic circles, especially among Nordicists.
Sophie Rogge-Börner thought that school should revive Nordic and Germanic history,
teach Northern-European languages instead of (Old) Latin, (Ancient) Greek or French,
and transmit Nordic mythology rather than Christian values. In other words, the education
system had to comply with Germany's 'racial law'. Sophie Rogge-Börner stated:

> It [the German state] is facing the indubitable necessity of building the methods, the content
> and the aim of *all* higher school education on a foundation that is not based on the Mediter-
> ranean cultural sphere and a middle-eastern valuation of the sexes anymore, but corresponds
> to the *German racial law* that grew from the Nordic original substance, and consequently
> brings the educational pathways of both sexes very close to each other. (Rogge-Börner
> 1933c, 172)[10]

Akin to her position towards feminism and women's rights, Sophie Rogge-Börner's statements represented a paradoxical symbiosis of very different approaches expressed during
the 'education reform debate' in the first decades of the twentieth century. She re-appro-
priated liberal and feminist ideas such as equal opportunity, especially between boys and
girls, and coeducation, while supporting a highly ideological orientation of the curriculum.
In her eyes, this was the only way to allow children of both genders to reach their full
potential, send the most qualified individuals to the labour market, re-establish social
harmony between the (highly educated) gender-equal 'elite' and the 'mass', and, eventually, contribute to restore the Nordic-Germanic community's well-being and racial
supremacy.

## A feminist education for German girls?

As a virulent opponent to feminism, which he considered 'Jewified', Adolf Hitler already
stated in *Mein Kampf* that education's primary goals were to provide Germany with 'racially
pure' future (male) soldiers and, eventually, leaders. Thus, from a very young age, boys had
to learn to be nationalistic patriots, willing to die for their fatherland, while girls had to be
taught how to become (house)wives and mothers, preferably of sons. As a result, voices in
favour of girls' rights to (higher) education, coeducation, or equal opportunity had been
silenced in 1933. However, in practice, many young women enrolled in the *Bund Deutscher
Mädel* experienced autonomy, gained leadership competencies, and fulfilled their career

ambitions (Reese 1997). Recent research on women's complicity within the Third Reich has shown that women profited from similar opportunities in official national-socialist women's organisations, as doctors and nurses in eugenics institutions, and even as SS-guards in various concentration camps. From its first edition, *Die Deutsche Kämpferin* criticised the *'Gleichschaltung'* of all feminist and/or women's associations, which must either disintegrate or be incorporated into the *Deutsche Frauenfront* (later renamed *Deutsches Frauenwerk*). By choosing to incorporate, the associations had to unconditionally accept four rules: be placed under NSDAP (male) leadership, recognise the tasks the national-socialist ideology attributed to women, exclude their 'non-Aryan' members from leadership positions, and elect national-socialist women to replace them. While supporting the exclusion of 'non-Aryan' members as a necessary pre-condition to 'racial' renewal, *Die Deutsche Kämpferin*'s authors refused to agree to the national-socialist conception of genders. By May 1933, Gertrud Kühn had already deplored the sole goals of girls' education to become good wives, mothers, and householders. She made very clear that maintaining this state of affairs, like the National-Socialists planned to, was contrary to the German 'racial law':

> It does not result from organic thinking to see household and child care as the tasks of the woman only. However, the woman often is experienced in these tasks because her education has mostly focused on these fields for centuries. (Kühn 1933, 30)[11]

Convinced that Germany needed as many 'high-quality' women as men to regain racial supremacy, Sophie Rogge-Börner even contradicted the idea that 'spiritual motherhood', or motherliness, was shared by all girls and women. Therefore, she firmly opposed Adolf Hitler's assertion that school education's primary goal was to teach girls to become mothers, since it would be a waste of many girls' potential:

> It is not the task of the school to teach motherliness to the girls or e.g. to choose the teaching content from this perspective. The female person is or is not maternal. By no means is every woman maternal; the Creation in its (…) diversity allows the existence of high-quality, and therefore indispensable women, whose primary attributes are in other fields. A training of motherliness, aimed at its practical usefulness, is not taking place at school (…). (Rogge-Börner 1933c, 173)[12]

Given that intelligence was equally distributed across genders, and motherliness was not a quality natural to all women, higher education's goal was to raise young 'high-quality' women who could become well-educated mothers and/or would be fully prepared for study and work:

> The task of higher education for girls is to form women of high intellectual quality; on the one hand, in order to create mothers of high quality who will then educate a selection of young Germans for the State; on the other hand, in order to send a selection of young women to university and all professions. (Rogge-Börner 1933c, 175)[13]

As a result, Sophie Rogge-Börner demanded that schools and universities provide girls and boys, women and men, with the same curriculum. She emphasised the need for girls and women to catch up in former 'male' disciplines, like mathematics, natural sciences, or physical education.

However, Sophie Rogge-Börner's claim in favour of women's unrestricted access to university and the labour market was not rooted in the idea of equality of all persons, regardless of their gender, but in a strong belief in social determinism and elitism. Like most *völkisch* supporters who belonged to the bourgeoisie and feared its progressive decline, the writer believed that only a few exceptional individuals with high intellect, outstanding skills, and intrinsic leadership abilities could set up the country's intellectual, economic, and political elite. Sophie Rogge-Börner's call for a renewed aristocracy, whose constitution was based on talent and merit instead of birth and wealth, confirmed the profound anti-democratic and anti-modern orientation of the *völkisch* movement. The main difference lied in her claim that this elite had to be gender-equal, that is to be made up of half men and half women, and gender-neutral, that is to not distribute tasks and posts based on the elite member's gender.

Therefore, Sophie Rogge-Börner severely criticised the passing of the law against the overcrowding of German schools and universities in April 1933, which limited the amount of women among the newly admitted students to ten per cent beginning in 1934 (Thalmann 1984, 104), and prevented women's access to professional equality:

> Only the persons from both sexes who are outstanding due to their talent and their character may be admitted to university. To exclude women again from university if possible or to introduce a numerus clausus for them is out of the question. (Rogge-Börner 1933c, 175)[14]

The fact that the law's primary goal was to target Jews was even an aggravating factor in Sophie Rogge-Börner's eyes. As a radical anti-Semite, she fully supported the restrictions introduced by the regime in 1933 that prevented Jews from studying, holding civil service posts, and working as doctors or lawyers. However, she regularly denounced what she claimed to be a similar treatment between Jews and ('racially pure') German women, and asked the regime to endorse her interpretation of Germany's original 'racial law' in re-establishing gender equality.

### The call for a 'new male ethics'

Following its new gender-equal principle, the reformed school education should not only increase girls' intellectual, psychological, and physical development, but also encourage the formation of a 'new male ethics' (Rogge-Börner 1935, 10),[15] as opposed to education's former 'materialistic' approaches:

> Here, the male school formation has to ensure that the derelict sections of the male soul are taken care of and nurtured again, while the female school formation has to ensure that the neglected forces of reason and knowledge can grow properly. Only this makes it possible for the German human being to rise again, for us, in the way the Creator wanted them (…). (Rogge-Börner 1933b, 130)[16]

Against the national-socialist conception that German women were the primary bearers of racial purity and honour, Sophie Rogge-Börner claimed that boys and men had to follow the same moral principles. They should be taught about their (biological) responsibility towards the community, and needed to learn to abstain from sex before marriage, live in a monogamous relationship, avoid adultery, condemn prostitution, and become good fathers. However, this moralisation of male education implied the transformation of society as a whole. Sophie Rogge-Börner saw young men's sexual desires stimulated by their fathers' behaviours and conceptions, by fictional and scientific literature, by medical discourse, and by encounters in homosocial spaces, where they learned to consider women as a 'creature of lower worth' and an 'object of sexual exploitation' (Rogge-Börner 1935, 11).[17] She especially denounced the propaganda work of 'Jewish' doctors through sex education, who allegedly encouraged young men to have sexual intercourse with many partners, even with prostitutes. To fight this state of affairs, male education should include courses to revaluate fatherhood and moralise sexuality. The president of the *Rechtsschutzverein für Frauen* (Association of legal protection for women) Agnes Martens-Edelmann defended similar ideas in an article entitled 'Education to Marriage and Fatherliness' published in *Die Frau* in 1928/29 and again in *Die deutsche Kämpferin* in 1933 (Martens-Edelmann 1933a, 1933b). Praising the formations offered by the American Home Economics Association and various Swiss schools, which taught students about childcare, housekeeping, and marriage law, Agnes Martens-Edelmann followed a feminist agenda. Since society was meant to mirror the family, introducing equality between the spouses, instead of the husband's 'absolutism', was the first step in promoting gender equality and abolishing male dominance (Martens-Edelmann 1933b, 23).

## Conclusion

As a German, middle-class, nineteenth-century-born woman with restricted access to education and to professional self-realisation, Sophie Rogge-Börner was not authorised to go to university. Before German women obtained the right to study in 1908, the only way was to go abroad, for example to Switzerland, which often put a heavy financial burden on the families. Like many other middle-class young women, Sophie Rogge-Börner had to renounce her ambitions. She passed the state exam for higher education and worked as a teacher, before opting for a writer's and journalist's career. As a result, her life was profoundly shaped by the increasing visibility of the women's movement, formed originally as an 'education movement', and its concrete successes. But it was also influenced by her monarchist and nationalist family, her admiration for her father who was an officer, and the widespread revanchism after Germany's defeat in 1918. This may explain why her political engagement in favour of women's rights and her fight for 'racial' renewal seem to combine many contradictory elements.

This article showed that racial-feminist thought was based on three key aspects. First, racial-feminism proceeded to the naturalisation and racialisation of power relations between genders, in ascribing a 'Nordic-Germanic' character to gender equality and a 'Jewish' character to patriarchy. By doing so, it provided a new anti-Semitic argumentation contradictory to the radical right's criticism of a 'Jewified' feminist movement and its anti-feminist ideology. Secondly, racial-feminism explained the advent of male dominance in Nordic-Germanic societies as a result of racial mixing and degeneration. As a consequence, this argumentation postulated a link between 'racial' renewal and the re-establishment of gender equality, which should legitimate the feminist agenda of 'racially pure' women. The article's second section took a closer look at Sophie Rogge-Börner's claims for a reform of the German education system towards gender-equal and gender-neutral education. It showed first, that her arguments were based on an egalitarian conception of intelligence as a genderless attribute, but which only applied to people of Nordic-Germanic 'race'. In other words, Sophie Rogge-Börner limited her egalitarian conception of gender, which was traditionally defended by radical, universalist feminists, within racial borders.

Profoundly anti-Semitic, she linked the abolishment of gender-segregation to the 'de-Jew-ification' of education. The narrative of a racially superior but gender-equal Nordic-Germanic 'race' supported claims for equal opportunities, starting from coeducation, identical school programmes for girls and boys, and finally, women's access to higher education and elite careers.

In conclusion, by bringing to light this particular articulation of feminism, racial anti-Semitism, and elitism, this article underlines the necessity to question the racial preconceptions of feminist discourse in adopting an intersectional perspective.

## Notes

1. All translations from German into English are by me. Italics, which were used as a form of emphasis, have been kept as in the original writings.
2. Ralf Rogge was born on 20 May 1911 in Rüstingen-Wilhelmshaven and studied medicine in Berlin. He was a member of the NSDAP, unlike his parents, and joined the SS in November 1933 as well as the Waffen-SS in 1939. After a brief career as a doctor, he worked for diverse national-socialist administrations as well as second camp doctor in Buchenwald from January to August 1944. Ralf Rogge was married twice: first, and very briefly, to Gerda Exner, and second to Eva Wigankow. From 1945, Ralf Rogge and his family lived in Wurzeldorf (Kořenov in modern Czech Republic) with his parents, before moving to Wernigerode where he was arrested on 11 February 1947. He died in November the same year in the special camp Bautzen.
3. Also called a 'movement', the *Deutschvölkische Freiheitspartei* (or DVFP) was founded in 1922 and gathered former members of the *Deutschnationale Volkspartei* like Ernst Graf zu Reventlow, Albrecht von Graefe, Wilhelm Henning, and Reinhold Wulle as well as former members of the *Deutschvölkischer Schutz- und Trutzbund*. In 1924, radical DVFP members merged with former NSDAP members to found the *Nationalsozialistische Freiheitsbewegung* (National Socialist Freedom Movement) which was represented in the Reichstag by, among others, Erich Ludendorff. See Breuer 2010.
4. 'unveräußerlichen, natürlichen Anspruch auf Führung durch seine Besten, Reinsten und Stärksten'.
5. 'Denn Anlagen und Fähigkeiten sind die gleichen in Mädchen und Knaben, sind nur individuell unterschiedlich verteilt.'
6. 'Weib und Mann *einer* Rasse sind mit den gleichen geistigen Potenzen begabt, die nach Dichtigkeit und Räumigkeit *individuell* verschieden verteilt sind. Daher haben beide Geschlechter Anspruch auf gleiche Geistesschulung; denn beide wollen einer Gemeinschaft dienen.'
7. 'Nicht zu Selbstbehauptung, Leistung und eigener Willensbildung, sondern allein zur passiven Verpflichtung des Duldens und Dienens wurde das Jungmädchen erzogen.'
8. '*Wissen*übermittlung […] bleibt die zentrale Aufgabe jeder Schule, neben der nun endlich auch in ihrer ganzen Bedeutung anerkannten *Charakter*bildung, die bislang einfach gefehlt hat. Als erste Voraussetzung zur männlichen Charakterbildung muß der unheilvolle Maßstab der Ich-Bezogenheit fallen; und die weibliche Jugend darf nicht mehr belastet werden mit den Komplexen der Abhängigkeit und Zweitklassigkeit.'
9. 'Aber noch keinem der zahlreichen Schulreformer unterschiedlicher Richtungen ist (abgesehen von den nordischen Staaten und einzelnen Staaten der nordamerikanischen Union) die Erleuchtung gekommen, daß es widernatürlich ist, Kinder in ihrer Schulzeit nach Geschlechtern zu trennen. Mit diesem unheilvollen Brauch nimmt die Spaltung des Menschen in zwei unzulängliche Halbe, die schon in der Kinderstube beginnt, einen Fortgang, der von unauslöschbaren Folgen für die gesamte Lebensanschauung des Menschen wird. Hier wird der Grund gelegt für die Überlegenheitskomplexe des Mannes und die Minderwertigkeitsgefühle der Frau […].'

10. 'Er [Der Staat] steht aber vor der unanzweifelbaren Notwendigkeit, Methode, Stoff und Ziel *aller* höheren Schulbildung auf eine Grundlage zu stellen, die nicht mehr im mittelländischen Kulturkreis und in vorderasiatischer Geschlechterwertung ruht, sondern dem aus nordischer Ursubstanz erwachsenen *deutschen Artgesetz* entspricht und daher den Bildungsweg der beiden Geschlechter ganz nahe aneinander rückt.'
11. 'Es zeugt nicht von organischem Denken, Hauswirtschaft und Kindererziehung lediglich als Aufgabe der Frau anzusehen. Die Frau ist allerdings durch die jahrhundertelange Erziehung meistens auf diesen Gebieten erfahren.'
12. 'Die Schule hat auch nicht die Aufgabe, die Mädchen zur Mütterlichkeit zu erziehen oder von diesem Gesichtspunkt aus etwa den Lehrstoff auszuwählen. Das Weibwesen ist mütterlich oder ist es nicht. Durchaus nicht jede Frau ist mütterlich; die Schöpfung in ihrer (…) Vielfalt läßt hochwertige und daher unentbehrliche Frauen zu, deren primären Komponente auf andern Gebieten liegt. Eine Ausbildung der Mütterlichkeit zu praktischer Verwertbarkeit liegt außerhalb der Schule (…).'
13. 'So hat die höhere Mädchenbildung die Aufgabe, geistig hochwertiges Frauentum heranzubilden; einmal um hochwertige Mütter ins Leben zu schicken, die dem Staate wieder eine Auslese deutscher Jugend zu erziehen vermögen; zum andern, um auch auf die Hochschulen und in alle Berufe eine Auslese jungen Frauentums zu entsenden.'
14. 'Zum Hochschulstudium ist in beiden Geschlechtern nur das nach Begabung und Charakter Überdurchschnittliche zuzulassen. Die Frau womöglich wieder auszuschließen von der Universität oder einen numerus clausus für sie einzuführen, ist nicht erwägbar.'
15. 'neuen Ethik des Mannes'
16. 'Dabei hat männliche Schulbildung ihr Hauptaugenmerk darauf zu richten, daß die verödeten Seelenbezirke des Mannes wieder Pflege und Nahrung bekommen, weibliche Schulbildung darauf, daß die vernachlässigten Verstandes- und Erkenntniskräfte sich gesund entwickeln können. Nur so erwächst uns wieder der deutsche Mensch, wie der Schöpfer ihn wollte […].'
17. 'Wesen minderen Grades'; 'sexuelles Ausbeutungsobjekt'

## Disclosure statement

No potential conflict of interest was reported by the author.

## References

Albisetti, James C. 2014. *Schooling German Girls and Women*. Princeton, NJ: Princeton University Press. (originally published in 1989).

Allal, Marina. 2006. "Antisémitisme, hiérarchies nationales et de genre: reproduction et réinterprétation du rapports de pouvoir." *Raisons politiques* 24: 125–141.

Baden, Jennifer. 2009. "Nordische Mythen für Schule und Volk. Mythologisches Wissen im Kontext der Diskussion um die Schulreform im Deutschen Kaiserreich." In *"Sang an Aegir". Nordische Mythen um 1900*, edited by Katja Schulz, and Florian Heesch, 73–96. Heidelberg: Universitätsverlag Winter GmbH.

Bereswill, Mechthild, and Leonie Wagner, eds. 1998. *Bürgerliche Frauenbewegung und Antisemitismus*. Tübingen: Edition Diskord.

Braun, Christina von. 1992. "'Der Jude' und 'Das Weib'. Zwei Stereotypen des 'Anderen' in der Moderne." *Metis: Zeitschrift für historische Frauen- und Geschlechterforschung* 2: 6–28.

Braun, Christina von. 1994. "Zur Bedeutung der Sexualbilder im rassistischen Antisemitismus." In *Jüdische Kultur und Weiblichkeit in der Moderne*, edited by Inge Stephan, Sabine Schilling, and Sigrid Weigel, 23–49. Köln: Böhlau Verlag.

Breuer, Stefan. 2008. *Die Völkischen in Deutschland. Kaiserreich und Weimarer Republik.* Darmstadt: Wissenschaftliche Buchgesellschaft.

Breuer, Stefan. 2010. *Die radikale Rechte in Deutschland 1871-1945. Eine politische Ideengeschichte.* Stuttgart: Reclam.

Crips, Liliane. 1990. "Une revue 'national-féministe': Die deutsche Kämpferin. 1933–1937." In *La tentation nationaliste. Entre émancipation et nationalisme. La presse féminine d'Europe 1914-1945*, edited by Rita Thalmann, 167–182. Paris: Editions Deuxtemps Tierce.

Dafflon Novelle, Anne. 2006. *Filles – garçons. Socialisation différenciée?* Grenoble: Presses Universitaires de Grenoble.

Davies, Peter. 2007. "'Männerbund' and 'Mutterrecht': Herman Wirth, Sophie Rogge-Börner and the *Ura-Linda-Chronik*." *German Life and Letters* 60: 98–115.

Davies, Peter. 2009. "Women Warriors, Feminism, and National Socialism: The Reception of J. J. Bachofen's View of Amazons among German and Austrian Right-Wing Women Writers." In *Warlike Women in the German Literary and Cultural Imagination since 1500*, edited by Sarah Colvin, and Helen Watanabe-O'Kelly, 45–58. New York, NY: Camden House.

Dürkop, Marlis. 1984. "Erscheinungsformen des Antisemitismus im Bund Deutscher Frauenvereine." *Feministische Studien* 1: 140–149.

Evans, Richard J. 1986. "The Concept of Feminism. Notes for Practicing Historians." In *German Women in the Eighteenth and Nineteenth Centuries: A Social and Literary History*, edited by Ruth-Ellen B. Joeres, and Mary Jo Maynes, 247–268. Bloomington: Indiana University Press.

Gehmacher, Johanna. 1998. "Die Eine und der Andere. Moderner Antisemitismus als Geschlechtergeschichte." In *Bürgerliche Frauenbewegung und Antisemitismus*, edited by Mechthild Bereswill, and Leonie Wagner, 101–120. Tübingen: Edition Diskord.

Gehmacher, Johanna. 2001. "Nachfolgeansprüche. Deutschnationale und nationalsozialistische Politik und die bürgerliche Frauenbewegung. Österreich 1918-1938." In *Feminismus und Demokratie. Europäische Frauenbewegungen der 1920er Jahre*, edited by Ute Gerhard, 159–175. Königstein im Taunus: Ulrike Helmer Verlag.

Gerhard, Ute. 2009. *Frauenbewegung und Feminismus. Eine Geschichte seit 1789.* München: Beck.

Gerhard, Ute, Christina Klausmann, and Ulla Wischermann. 2001. "Neue Staatsbürgerinnen – die deutsche Frauenbewegung in der Weimarer Republik." In *Feminismus und Demokratie. Europäische Frauenbewegungen der 1920er Jahre*, edited by Ute Gerhard, 176–209. Königstein im Taunus: Ulrike Helmer Verlag.

Grossmann, Atina. 1991. "Feminist Debates about Women and National Socialism." *Gender & History* 3 (3): 350–358.

Heinsohn, Kirsten. 2000. "Im Dienste der deutschen Volksgemeinschaft: Die "Frauenfrage" und konservative Parteien vor und nach dem Ersten Weltkrieg." In *Nation, Politik und Geschlecht. Frauenbewegungen und Nationalismus in der Moderne*, edited by Ute Planert, 215–233. Frankfurt: Campus Verlag.

Heinsohn, Kirsten. 2007. "Kampf um die Wählerinnen. Die Idee von der "Volksgemeinschaft" am Ende der Weimarer Republik." In *Volksgenossinnen. Frauen in der NS-Volksgemeinschaft*, edited by Sybille Steinbacher, 29–47. Göttingen: Wallstein Verlag.

Heinsohn, Kirsten, Barbara Vogel, and Ulrike Weckel, eds. 1997. *Zwischen Karriere und Verfolgung. Handlungsräume von Frauen im nationalsozialistischen Deutschland.* Frankfurt: Campus Verlag.

Junginger, Horst. 2004. "Sigrid Hunke (1913-1999). Europe's New Religion and its Old Stereotypes." In *Antisemitismus, Paganismus, Völkische Religion*, edited by Hubert Cancik, and Uwe Puschner, 151–162. München: Saur.

Kallenberg, Vera, Johanna M. Mueller, in collaboration with Meyer, Jennifer. 2013. "Introduction. Intersectionality as a Critical Perspective for the Humanities." In *Intersectionality und Kritik. Neue*

*Perspektiven für alte Fragen*, edited by Vera Kallenberg, Jennifer Meyer and Johanna M. Mueller, 15–35. Wiesbaden: Springer VS.

Kandel, Liliane. 2004. "Femmes, féminismes, nazisme ou: on ne naît pas innocent(e), on le devient." In *Féminismes et nazisme*, edited by Liliane Kandel, 8–26. Paris: Odile Jacob.

Kaplan, Marion. 1984. "Schwesterlichkeit auf dem Prüfstand. Feminismus und Antisemitismus in Deutschland, 1904-1938." *Feministische Studien* 1: 128–139.

Kaplan, Marion. 1993. "Jüdische Frauen im Nazi-Deutschland 1933–1939." In *Lektüren und Brüche. Jüdische Frauen in Kultur, Politik und Wissenschaft*, edited by Mechthild M. Jansen, and Ingeborg Nordmann, 196–214. Wiesbaden: HLZ.

Kaplan, Marion. 2004. "Les femmes juives et l'expérience du féminisme dans les années 30." In *Féminismes et nazisme*, edited by Liliane Kandel, 29–41. Paris: Odile Jacob.

Kohn-Ley, Charlotte, and Ilse Korotin, eds. 1994. *Der feministische "Sündenfall"? Antisemitische Vorurteile in der Frauenbewegung*. Wien: Picus-Verlag.

Kühn, Gertrud. 1933. "Die 'Aufgabe' der Frau." *Die deutsche Kämpferin* 1 (2): 30–31.

Laffont, Hélène. 2006. "Zur Rezeption Bachofens im Nationalsozialismus." In *Philosophie und Zeitgeist im Nationalsozialismus*, edited by Marion Heinz, and Goran Gretić, 143–162. Würzburg: Königshausen & Neumann.

Martens-Edelmann, Agnes. 1933a. "Erziehung zur Ehe und Vaterschaft." *Die Deutsche Kämpferin* 1 (1): 5–6.

Martens-Edelmann, Agnes. 1933b. "Erziehung zur Ehe und Vaterschaft." *Die Deutsche Kämpferin* 1 (2): 21–23.

Meyer, Jennifer. 2013. "Mouvement völkisch et féminismes en Allemagne. Une approche intersectionnelle à partir de l'exemple de Sophie Rogge-Börner (1878-1955)." In *Le premier féminisme allemand 1848-1933. Un mouvement social de dimension internationale*, edited by Patrick Farges, and Anne-Marie Saint-Gille, 77–90. Villeneuve d'Ascq: Presses Universitaires du Septentrion.

Reese, Dagmar. 1997. "Verstrickung und Verantwortung. Weibliche Jugendliche in der Führung des Bundes Deutscher Mädel." In *Zwischen Karriere und Verfolgung. Handlungsräume von Frauen im nationalsozialistischen Deutschland*, edited by Kirsten Heinsohn, Barbara Vogel, and Ulrike Weckel, 206–222. Frankfurt: Campus Verlag.

Rogge, Pia Sophie. 1924. "Ist in Deutschland eine nationale Frauenbewegung nötig?" *Frau und Nation. Monatsschrift für die Mitarbeit der Frau am nationalen Wiederaufbau* 1 (2): 51–55.

Rogge-Börner, P. Sophie. 1928. *An geweihtem Brunnen. Die deutsche Frauenbewegung im Lichte des Rassegedankens*. Weimar: Verlag 'Deutscher Aufbau'.

Rogge-Börner, Sophie. 1933a. "Liberalismus." *Die Deutsche Kämpferin* 1 (6): 97–101.

Rogge-Börner, Sophie. 1933b. "Trennung oder Ganzheit." *Die Deutsche Kämpferin* 1 (7): 129–130.

Rogge-Börner, Sophie. 1933c. "Mädchenbildung nach deutschem Artgesetz." *Die Deutsche Kämpferin* 1 (9): 169–175.

Rogge-Börner, Sophie. 1933–34. "Volksgemeinschaft als Blutsgebot." *Die Frau* 41: 335–340.

Rogge-Börner, Sophie. 1935. *Der neue Mensch aus deutschem Artgesetz*. Berlin-Tempelhof: Hans Bott Verlag.

Rogge-Börner, Sophie. 1951. *Planet im Absturz?* Göttingen: Göttinger Verlagsanstalt.

Streubel, Christiane. 2006. *Radikale Nationalistinnen. Agitation und Programmatik rechter Frauen in der Weimarer Republik*. Frankfurt: Campus Verlag.

Thalmann, Rita. 1984. *Frausein im Dritten Reich*. Münich: Carl Hanser Verlag.

Volkov, Shulamit. 2000a. "Antisemitismus als kultureller Code." In *Antisemitismus als kultureller Code. Zehn Essays*, 2e ed., edited by Shulamit Volkov, 13–36. München: Verlag C. H. Beck.

Volkov, Shulamit. 2000b. "Antisemitismus und Antifeminismus: Soziale Norm oder kultureller Code." In *Das jüdische Projekt der Moderne. Zehn Essays*, edited by Shulamit Volkov, 62–81. München: Verlag C. H. Beck.

Wiedemann, Felix. 2009. "Der doppelte Orient. Zur völkischen Orientromantik des Ludwig Ferdinand Clauß." *Zeitschrift für Religions- und Geistesgeschichte* 61: 1–24.

Wobbe, Theresa. 1994. "Mathilde Vaerting (1884-1977). 'Es kommt alles auf den Unterschied an (…) der Unterschied ist das Grundelement der Macht'." In *Frauen in den Kulturwissenschaften. Von Lou-Andreas-Salomé bis Hannah Arendt*, edited by Barbara Hahn, 123–135. München: Verlag C. H. Beck.

Wobbe, Theresa. 1998. "Mathilde Vaerting (1884-1977). Die Macht des Unterschiedes." In *Frauen in der Soziologie. Neun Portraits*, edited by Claudia Honegger, and Theresa Wobbe, 178–202. München: Verlag C. H. Beck.

Ziege, Eva-Maria. 1997. "Sophie Rogge-Börner – Wegbereiterin der Nazidiktatur und völkische Sektiererin im Abseits." In *Zwischen Karriere und Verfolgung. Handlungsräume von Frauen im natio-nalsozialistischen Deutschland*, edited by Kirsten Heinsohn, Barbara Vogel, and Ulrike Weckel, 44–77. Frankfurt: Campus Verlag.

# The 'obnoxious mobilised minority': homophobia and homohysteria in the British national party, 1982–1999*

George J. Severs

**ABSTRACT**

This article examines the British National Party (BNP)'s opposition to gay men during the 1980s and 1990s. Drawing on the sociological concept of 'homohysteria', it examines written material from BNP publications during those decades, looking specifically at the AIDS crisis, the party's belief in a 'queer conspiracy', and the role which homosexuality played in the decline of the National Front and the birth of the BNP. The first study dedicated to British fascism's anti-gay prejudice, this article argues that the existing scholarship fails to understand the degree and nature of anti-gay sentiment in the BNP, concluding that the party was homohysteric from its inception.

## 1. Introduction

> I took a party ten years ago which said that homosexuality should be outlawed, people should be driven underground and persecuted. The British National Party position now is that what people do in the privacy of their own homes is absolutely up to them …

These were some of the last words spoken by Nick Griffin, then a Member of the European Parliament and leader of the British National Party (BNP) (1999–2014), on the BBC's flagship political programme *Question Time* on 22 October 2009. This, along with the rest of Griffin's speech against 'militant homosexuals', led many commentators to label him and his party homophobic (Czyzselska 2009). However, this statement did not spark the scholarly attention it warranted, which is surprising given the major question it arouses: how did the BNP go from being a party unashamed and unreserved in its opposition to homosexuality to one content for homosexuals to exist in private? This article aims to establish the party's attitude towards gay men under John Tyndall, former leader of the National Front (NF) and the BNP's founding leader (1982–1999), thus serving as a starting point for those seeking to answer this question. In that vein, it will examine anti-gay sentiment in the 'early' BNP, from its founding in 1982 to Griffin's election as leader in 1999, at which point, a period of 'modernisation' began (Thompson 2004; Copsey 2007; Rhodes 2009).[1]

Not to be confused with the BNP founded in 1960 by John Bean, a group which went on to merge with several other fascist parties to form the NF in 1967, the 'modern' BNP with which this article is concerned emerged from the NF. Founded in 1982 by John Tyndall, the

---

*The title is taken from the caption of a picture of gay men kissing on a demonstration: *Obnoxious mobilised minority* (1996)

party situated itself on the extreme right wing of British politics. Among its key concerns was a committed opposition to immigration (and the integration of migrant/minority ethnic people with what it saw as 'indigenous white British' communities), feminism, and homosexuality. The party remained belligerently nostalgic towards the British Empire, advocated a policy of compulsory repatriation, and constantly articulated passionate support for the nuclear family as a bastion of national reproduction. Whilst it is true that, following its emergence from the NF, many BNP leaders and members were concerned with distancing themselves from previous fascistic associations, the party remained part of a neo-Nazi ideological tradition (Eatwell and Mudde 2004, 65).

The BNP has received a great deal of scholarly attention over the last few decades, and there now exists a wealth of secondary literature on the party, ranging from broad surveys of its ideology and political activity, to comparative and transnational studies (Copsey 2008; Goodwin 2011; Mammone, Godin and Jenkins 2012; Trilling 2013). Far fewer in number, however, are studies concerning British fascism's explicit and trenchant opposition to homosexuality. Julie V. Gottlieb provides a thoughtful analysis of 'Britain's new fascist men', in a refreshing contribution which successfully seeks to 'gender the history of British fascism' by examining the levels and depictions of male hegemony in the propaganda of early British fascism (Gottlieb 2004, 83). Gottlieb's work provides a framework for understanding the gender history of early British fascism, specifically focusing on the British Union of Fascism (BUF) led by Sir Oswald Mosley (b. 1896 – d. 1980). Specifically, we glean that the BUF held a materialist, physical conception of masculinity, centred on the male body and framed by what Gottlieb terms the 'fascist-Futurist paradigm', that is, one which married fascism's propensity for seeking examples of the ideal masculine form in the past with its newly discovered penchant for science, technology and 'progress' (Gottlieb 2004, 90). Whilst the BUF operates largely outside the scope of this article, it is worth noting that the Union's gender politics operated within a sexual binary, with male and female bodies existing in political opposition to one another. Fascist new men were recognised as such through their 'healthy male bodies', whilst women, though often depicted as strong defenders of the fascist cause, were confined to 'single-sex gang formation' and often sexualised in propaganda in order to recruit young men (Gottlieb 2004, 91–92). There is a necessary lack of emphasis on the sexuality of fascist new men, but Gottlieb makes it clear that, from its inception, British fascism was inherently concerned with masculinity and the binary relationship between masculinity and femininity. This gendered conception of fascist masculinity has been central to the political and gendered identity of individual fascist men, as well as to ideological fascism itself.

Similar themes emerge in Martin Durham's article 'Gender and the British Union of Fascists' (Durham 1992). By examining how a future fascist Britain was being imagined by, and in the 'interests' of women, Durham's study reveals that early British fascism was indeed engaging in discourses which propagated a sexual binary, though this is not discussed explicitly by the author. There was a place for women in the BUF during the 1930s; yet, Mosely was keen to emphasise that their roles would 'be different from that of the men: *we want men who are men and women who are women*' (Durham 1992, 515). Though not concerned with sexuality, this article does begin to highlight a nascent fear of forces which might blur these gendered sexual boundaries, as well as a dislike for the individuals who did not embody the ideologically prescribed sexual norms. James Drennan, an early fascist chronicler of the BUF, singled out 'the womanish man' as a particularly urban phenomenon and as an obvious group for the movement to oppose (Durham 1992, 522). Alexander Raven Thompson, editor of the BUF periodical *Action*, believed that democracy bred 'more sissies than it does Empire builders', echoing Drennan's statements about the effect of liberal democratic modernity on the masculinity of British men (Durham 1992, 523). Though Durham was not interested himself in the dynamics of the sexual binary fostered by this discourse, it is clear that there was one, and that evidence of gendered lines becoming blurred was opposed by the BUF, even 30 years before the Sexual Offences Act 1967 partially legalised homosexuality in Britain.

More attention has been paid to twenty-first century fascism's engagement with sexuality. Matthew J. Goodwin includes an analysis of homophobia in the BNP in his book *New British Fascism*, whilst studies from the University of Oregon and *Expo* have given the issue independent evaluation in a European and North American context (Goodwin 2011; Commerer 2010; Hannus 2012). Most recently, the journal *Patterns of Prejudice* released a special issue in 2015 dealing with 'gender and the populist radical right'. All of these have proved useful and illuminating contributions to our understanding of contemporary far right European and North American parties, yet they do little to aid our understanding of fascism's thinking about gay men during the 1980s and 1990s. The *Patterns of Prejudice* special issue, for example, tracks the tendency of contemporary fascists to defend homosexual rights in order to add to their arsenal of Islamophobic rhetoric. Tjitske Akkerman writes that '[a]lthough radical-right parties may generally not be very much inclined to defend the rights of homosexuals, in some cases they may do so in the context of immigration', whilst the editors point out that post-9/11 far right parties in Europe have argued 'that Islamic values are at odds with liberal democratic values, such as … emancipation of homosexuals and women … ' (Akkerman 2015, 43; Spierings, Zaslowe, Mügge and de Lange 2015, 8–9). Attention is starting to be paid to the ways in which far right parties engage with issues of sexuality, though they remain overwhelmingly confined to the contemporary political scene.

Homosexuality's place within late-twentieth-century British fascism was briefly discussed in Nigel Copsey's recent chapter concerning the representation of the British far right in popular culture. Copsey uses the novel *Children of the Sun* by Max Schaefer to highlight the presence of gay British neo-Nazis within the popular press, as the book 'intersperses narrative text with actual cuttings from far right periodicals and newspaper reports' (Copsey 2015, 115). This is just one of Copsey's contributions to the beginnings of a wider understanding of the British far right's engagement with homosexuality in the post-war period, upon which this article is able to build.

This article seeks to fill the vacuum of historical attention paid to British fascism's interaction with homosexuality. By examining the documents produced by the NF and the BNP from 1981 (the year before the party's founding) and 1999 (the year in which Griffin defeated Tyndall to become party leader), this article will address the themes of anti-gay sentiment prevalent in party discourse and policy. It focuses specifically on the material published by the BNP during this period, namely *Spearhead* and *British Nationalist*, though the former is Tyndall's own publication used for party political purposes. Other sources were consulted during the research process, such as *The Thunderer: The Newsletter of the British National Party Christian Fellowship*. However, this article is overwhelmingly concerned with the two major party publications of the period as, by engaging with the anti-gay rhetoric evident within them, it is possible to begin to discern the prejudicial attitudes being articulated and consumed by BNP writers and readers.

Specifically, it aims to make three central arguments. First, that the BNP emerged from a homohysteric milieu and thus established itself as a homophobic party (the differences between these two terms are discussed below). The party's unique selling point to members in 1982 was that it was opposed to (and supposedly devoid of) gay men – it became *the* anti-homosexuality party of choice for would-be fascist members in the early 1980s. Second, that homophobia and homohysteria operated symbiotically through-out the period, largely due to the party's response to the HIV/AIDS epidemic. Third, that the BNP's anti-gay sentiment manifested itself in positioning gay men within fascism's tra-ditional conspiratorial discourse. The Jewish–Bolshevik–Masonic conspiracy was made to accommodate gay men.

Though the party was vocally opposed to lesbianism in its literature throughout the period, the vast majority of its attention was paid to gay men, stemming from the party's belief that the 'conspiratorial' nature of gay men threatened the British nationalist move-ment, as well as a perceived biological threat posed by HIV/AIDS. For this reason, the over-whelming majority of what follows will focus on the BNP's opposition to gay men.[2] Fascist writers are varied in their terminology when referencing sexual minorities, with 'gay', 'queer', and 'homosexual' being the most common. In what follows, I refer to both 'homosexuality' and 'gay men'. 'Homosexuality' because often the party uses this (and 'queer') as a 'catch all' term for sexual minorities, including, but not limited to, gay men. I endeavour to refer to 'gay men' when it is this group specifically being targeted or discussed by the sources.

## 2. Homophobia and homohysteria

Insofar as the BNP's opposition to gay men is mentioned in the secondary literature, two assumptions are made: that it existed as a present, though peripheral force in the minds of the party's leaders and members, and secondly, that it can be described as 'homophobia'. This article argues that both of these presuppositions are largely inaccurate and betray the glib indifference with which anti-gay sentiment in the British far right has been treated to date. Even Commerer's laudable work which focuses exclusively on Europe's far right opposition to homosexuality makes the mistake of narrowly discussing the attitude in terms of 'homophobia' (Commerer 2010).

The reason that 'homophobia' is unsatisfactory as a term to describe the attitudes and behaviour of the BNP towards gay men during the period becomes apparent when it is defined alongside 'homohysteria'. The common sense (and widely accepted) definition of 'homophobia' is a fear or hatred of homosexuals, and it seems that writers such as Tril-ling and Goodwin accept this definition in their employment of the word (Trilling 2013, 70; Goodwin 2011, 116). A cursory glance at almost any BNP publication which discusses homosexuality, however, suggests that this term is insufficient given the party's opposition to homosexuality both socially and politically. The BNP was arguing that homosexuality should be outlawed, rather than simply articulating an aversion towards an 'alternative sexuality'. In short, the party demonstrated more than just a general disdain for homosex-uals, but rather a desire to see their erasure from Britain.

Homohysteria, however, is far more applicable. Coined by the sociologist Eric Anderson, homohysteria 'is characterized by the witch-hunt to expose who they [homosexuals] are.

When one adds homophobia, to the social understanding that homosexuality exists in great numbers … we have homohysteria' (Anderson 2012, 86). Anderson points out that homohysteria was at its 'apex' in the 1980s, writing that '[t]he public's awareness that homosexuals looked normal (even if still believing that they were not), and that they lived among us' was most pronounced during that decade, not least because of the outbreak of HIV/AIDS which, during the early 1980s, appeared to be affecting gay men in isolation (Anderson 2012, 86; Berridge 1996, 5–6).

There has been some confusion about the term 'homohysteria'. Two of the leading scholars working on studies of homohysteria set out to clarify it more concretely in 2014, and these definitional efforts serve to lay some of the theoretical foundations of this article (McCormack and Anderson 2014). The authors were keen to emphasise that homohysteria is a sociological measure of the impact of changing levels of homophobia on heterosexual men's gendered behaviour, especially towards each other (McCormack and Anderson 2014, 154–155). When levels of homophobia spiked, and when gay men were obvious *en masse* rather than erased from society because of a homophobic culture, then homohysteria becomes more palpable. In short, 'homophobia conceptualizes the nature and effects of prejudice and discrimination on sexual minorities' whilst 'homohysteria conceptualises the contexts when homophobia effects (or is used to police) heterosexual men's gendered behaviours' (McCormack and Anderson 2014, 153).

It is just such a context that this article addresses. Namely, the homohysteric culture out of which the BNP was born. From its genesis, as we shall see, the party was engaged in what can be seen as a witch-hunt to expose gay members, as well as writing, organising and agitating in opposition to gay men. This, alongside the party's role in the homohysteric backlash, which accompanied the AIDS crisis, clearly marks out a shift in the behaviour and attitudes of the heterosexual men of the British far right, both at the top and at the grassroots. As these themes are expanded on below, the homohysteric credentials of the early BNP will become apparent. It will be argued that the BNP emerged from a culture of homohysteria, making homophobia a defining and central feature from its outset, whilst the AIDS crisis ensured that, for the rest of the period, homophobia and homohysteria coexisted in the party's policies and rhetoric.

## 3. Anti-gay sentiment in the British far right

The BNP was not alone on the far right in harbouring opposition to homosexuality. As will be outlined later, the BNP emerged out of a debate within the NF about the 'problem' of homosexuality, and how best to deal with it. There was, though, an historical pedigree out of which this debate, and indeed the BNP itself, emerged.

It is worth remembering that homosexuals, and gay men in particular, were victims of the Holocaust. Arrests of gay men began in 1933, the year Hitler became Chancellor of Germany, with these numbers increasing following the extension of state powers to persecute homosexuals in June 1935. In all, 100,000 men were arrested in the period leading up to 1945, with between 5000 and 15,000 ending up in concentration camps (United States Holocaust Memorial Museum 2016). This is significant because a great many post-war British fascists maintained a passionate nostalgia for Nazi Germany. Historians have noted that Hitler was often seen 'as a divine being within a cosmic order', whilst Combat 18's connection to Hitler has been well noted ('1' and '8' referring to Hitler's initials, 'A' being the first letter of the alphabet and 'H' the eighth) (Jackson 2015, 91; Shaffer 2015, 149). BNP sources from the period do not tend to use the Nazis' assault against homosexuality as a form of historical justification, though this early example of fascist opposition to gay men should not be ignored. Whether the 'gay holocaust' should be spoken of as homohysteria requires attention elsewhere. For the purposes of this article, it suffices to say that there was a precedent of far right anti-gay sentiment taken to its most violent extreme, one which many BNP members and leaders were aware of.

Before homosexuality was largely decriminalised in Britain in 1967, fascist parties were less concerned with issues of sexuality than those of the later post-war period. A cursory glance at the publications of the British Union of Fascists (BUF) or its leader Sir Oswald Mosley betrays this, with party concerns being much more centred on issues of empire and race (Mosley 1970). This is unsurprising, given the fact that homosexuality's criminalised status necessarily confined gay and lesbian activity to 'underground' cultural spaces, resulting in a blinkered visibility of homosexuals both to contemporaries and to historians of the period (Houlbrook 2005, 19–21).

Absence of evidence, though, is not evidence of absence, and historians of British fascism would be wrong to assume that the writings of early British fascists were not gendered. Indeed, the BUF's 'new man' has significant implications for notions of masculinity within official party dogma. Early British fascism, though gendered, was not overly concerned with questions of sexuality. As the period went on, especially into the 1970s, this began to change. There were, for example, smaller parties on the far right which became especially concerned with opposing homosexuality. The National Democratic Freedom Movement (NDFM), active in Leeds in the mid- to late-1970s, is particularly worthy of note here, not least because there are anti-fascist activists who initially opposed the NDFM because of the party's intense anti-gay stance.[3]

Though homosexuality was not necessarily the central issue of the NDFM, accounts from former members do emphasise both the revulsion they felt at the perceived homosexuality within the NF, as well as their street-based opposition to gay anti-fascists. In particular, Eddy Morrison, a prominent figure in the British far right having been involved in the NF, New National Front and the BNP before establishing his own short-lived National Action Party, mentions the party's opposition to 'Transsexuals against Nazis', as well as 'a bunch of red weirdos' (Malatesta 2010; Morrison 2013). Of course, this group did not attract the hatred of people like Morrison based solely on their sexualities. Their anti-fascist politics was always going to be a source of conflict with members of the far right. What is crucial, though, is Morrison's description of the group as 'weirdos' and later as 'filth' (Morrison 2013). It seems that the 'different' genders and sexualities of this group aroused a particular kind of attention in Morrison and others like him in the NDFM, and he singles them out for that reason. In short, the sexual identity of this particular anti-fascist group generated an additional layer of hatred from the far right groups with which it was already in conflict.

Furthermore, the NDFM's co-founder David Myatt's written work is believed to have influenced the right-wing bomber David Copeland, who targeted the gay district of London, blowing up the Admiral Duncan pub in Soho in April 1999, as well as black and Asian areas in the same year. Following the explosion, a copy of Myatt's *A Practical Guide to Aryan Revolution* was discovered in Copeland's flat, a fact which, though arguably tenuous, does link the leaders of the NFDM to a right-wing terrorist who targeted gay men (Kapiris 2014).

Copeland himself clearly represents a special case of far right hatred for gay men, and one of the most active examples of homohysteria. Graeme McLagan and Nick Lowles argue that his attack on the Admiral Duncan, and on gay men especially, was more 'personal' than his other targets, due to frequent assumptions from his family and peers that he might not be heterosexual. 'In denying any homosexual leanings', they write, 'his hatred towards gay men became even more bitter' (McLagan and Lowles 2000, 149–150). Here, we see a particularly extreme example of the way in which homohysteria can (and does) affect male behaviour. Copeland is useful here in demonstrating that the BNP was not alone during the period in harbouring an extreme hatred for gay men, though it should be noted that he was a member of the party (McLagan and Lowles 2000, 20). This far more extreme example of homohysteria, stemming from Copeland's belief that 'homosexuals were degenerates, with no place in society', his desire to 'kill and maim' gay men, as well as to terrify others into heteronormative conformity, ought to be born in mind during discussion of the BNP's homohysteric polemic which follows, as one possible result of this particular brand of political rhetoric (McLagan and Lowles 2000, 150).

Finally, the NF's 'homosexuality debate' requires attention. Though this period of internal in-fighting has been well studied, the centrality of homosexuality to the schism often goes unappreciated. Nigel Copsey is one notable exception to this, having identified the link between the 'schism at the "gay" National Front and the birth of the British National Party', though it remains surprising how limited the attention has been to homosexuality as a factor in the history of this dispute (Copsey 2008, 21).

NF publications from the period demonstrate homosexuality's centrality to the party division. Initially latent, as the party leadership appear to have been keen to underemphasise its importance for fear of alienating its membership, homosexuality soon became the major piece of political capital in use between rival factions in the NF. Andrew Fountaine, a founding member of the NF, became a prominent critic of the party elite and led a faction in leaving the party after failing in his bid to challenge Tyndall for the NF leadership, citing endemic homosexuality within the party elite and the 'symbiotic' relationship between Tyndall and Martin Webster, National Activities Organiser for the NF and himself a gay man, as his primary motivation (Copsey 2008, 21). This is perhaps most clear in John Tyndall's discussion of homosexuality in *Spearhead*. In the December 1979 edition, one which was keen to emphasise the party's unity and to foster the notion that the schism had ended, Tyndall was asked in a printed interview whether allegations made by Fountaine 'that he attempted to bring certain matters of members' misconduct, including matters of a homosexual nature, to the attention of the Directorate and that [Tyndall] would not allow this' were true. Tyndall dismissed the claims as nonsense, though he claimed that Fountaine was interested in the issue 'as one to be exploited so as to *cause* embarrassment to the party (*Spearhead* December 1979: 6-7, 20)'. In the next edition (January 1980), however, Tyndall resigned from the NF, offering a whole-page explanation in which he clarified:

> As I predicted to the Directorate, its failure to remove the taint of homosexuality from the party's leadership has caused widespread defections from the party, particularly in the West Midlands (Tyndall 1980, 18).

Clearly, then, whether it was suppressed or highlighted, homosexuality was the major 'political football' of the internal debate, largely capitalised on by Fountaine and his fellow defectors. The gay men at the top of the Directorate, largely assumed to be led by (or exclusively) Webster, were discussed in a wholly pejorative discourse and positioned as the 'enemy' within this Manichean narrative.

In his analysis of the schism, Copsey notes the fact that homosexuality within the NF was used by Tyndall (amongst others) for the purposes of political point scoring, but maintains that the split can be more aptly attributed to the dispute between Tyndall and the NF Directorate, the former having resigned following the Directorate blocking multiple attempts to vest 'dictatorial powers' in himself. The New National Front, he argues, was essentially Tyndall's 'pressure group for wrestling control from the NF Directorate', and as a result 'remained committed to the political ideas of the original NF ... [whilst offering] an alternative leadership to disaffected Front members' (Copsey 2008, 23). Of course, Copsey is right to emphasise the point that homosexuality was not the only issue at play during the schism, and that the power rivalry between Tyndall and the Directorate could more aptly be described as 'the reason' for the NF's split. However, the fact that opposition to homosexuality was used as the political tool of those leaving the NF (from Fountaine in November 1979 to Tyndall in January 1980) cannot be overlooked. Even if homosexuality was not the overwhelming reason for Fountaine's exit, the fact that he broadcasted it in such terms set the tone of future discussions of the movement's direction. Party publications from the period consistently discussed the schism in these anti-gay terms, both in leading articles and in members' contributions (*Spearhead* February 1982, 7; *Spearhead* May 1982, 6). Thus, though the NNF and later the BNP may have nominally subscribed to the same political project as the NF, the schism which marked the split between them ushered in a new culture of anti-gay sentiment. The BNP inherited the homophobic culture of the NF (Copsey 2008, 22), but was established during a period of intense opposition to gay men, and one in which they were being actively sought out and removed.

With this in mind, it is fair to say that the BNP was established within a culture of homohysteria. The British far right at the time was concerned with the reality of the presence of gay men within its midst and were organising new political organisations which would exclude them. Take, for example, Eddy Morrison's article for *Spearhead* in February 1982 'Time for a Name Change' in which he writes '[l]et's face it, members of the New National Front – Webster's NF, with all its stigmas of homosexuality and punk nationalism is not going to pack up and go home!' (7). Indeed, in the edition of *Spearhead* published in March 1982, a month before the BNP was founded, one commentator described the NF leadership as 'that preposterous collection of clowns, babies, queers and crypto-marxists', once again placing homosexuality at the centre of the schism between the NF and the BNP, though as this quote suggests, homosexuality within the NF was not the only reason for the split. The conclusion of these articles and many like them from the time was that homosexuality within the NF had been too widely reported in the mass media and was too embedded in the party elites for the NF to ever 'recover'. A new party was needed, one which would not tolerate homosexuality.

The BNP, therefore, came into being both during and because of the far right's homohysteric culture, and could justly be described as a homohysteric party. If we revisit Anderson's definition from *Inclusive Masculinity* this seems much clearer:

> fundamental to the creation of a culture of homohysteria is the necessity of public awareness
> that reasonable and 'normal' people could also be gay. [...] When one adds homophobia to

the social understanding that homosexuality exists in great numbers, and that it is not easily identifiable … we have a culture of homohysteria. (Anderson 2012, 86)

The BNP became a political necessity for people like Morrison and other members because of the recognition that homosexuality existed within the existing hierarchies of the British far right and the desire not to coexist with them. What follows will discuss the ways in which homophobia and homohysteria operated symbiotically within BNP discourse and policy orientation during the period. The point remains, however, that the party was born out of a homohysteric culture, and that homohysteria was therefore at the heart of the party at the moment of its founding.

It is crucial to note, moreover, that this was not only an issue for the BNP at the moment of its founding, but was continuously central to the party's rhetoric for the entirety of the period. Before he became leader of the party, Nick Griffin had contributed to many BNP publications, and in one notable *Spearhead* article from June 1999, wrote about David Copeland and the nail bombs he had planted across London. Concerning the bomb placed in the Admiral Duncan gay pub in Soho, Griffin wrote that '[t]he TV footage of dozens of "gay" demonstrators flaunting their perversion in front of the world's journalists showed just why so many ordinary people find those creatures so repulsive'. Much can be extrapolated here, from Griffin's dehumanising of gay men by describing them as 'creatures', to his positioning of homosexuals as a group separate from 'ordinary people'. What is of immediate importance, though, is that the anti-gay polemic represents an escalation from the 1982 discourse. Rather than arguing for political organisations devoid of gay men, Griffin was revelling in the fact that a far right bomber had succeeded in killing several homosexuals. Removing gay men from far right political parties had been the primary objective in 1982; the homohysteric scope seems to be broader and more insidious at the end of the period. Indeed, a special April 1994 issue of *British National-ist* in preparation for the local elections in May listed as its penultimate election promise:

OUTLAW HOMOSEXUALITY: The BNP believes that homosexuality should be outlawed, to prevent the further spread of AIDS, and to protect our young people from corruption.

This is quite clearly the language of homohysteria, and can be situated comfortably in the party's discourse on homosexuality.

When the BNP was founded, the polemic against gay men was specific to those within its own ranks and looked towards an internal purge. The language evident in publications from 1994 and towards the end of Tyndall's tenure, however, speaks of proscribing homo-sexuality nationally. Interestingly, there is one article in *Spearhead* from the period (June 1996) which does not call for express outlawing of homosexuality, though the Australian author does recommend that it 'should be firmly, though compassionately, discouraged in society' (Jackson 1996). With this in mind, it is not without grounding to define the polemic of the BNP as homohysteric, given that it was this language which founded the party and which remained consistent throughout the period.

## 4. HIV/AIDS and the BNP

When attempting to understand the AIDS crisis and the BNP, 1982 is a seminal year. Firstly, as we have seen, the BNP formed in 1982 and was actively seeking out gay members in something of a purge after splitting with the NF and identifying themselves in opposition to the NF's 'gay' image. Yet, 1982 was also the year in which cases of HIV/AIDS were first identified in the UK. The leading historian of the British AIDS crisis, Virginia Berridge, writes that, thanks to the crisis, '[g]ay men were more publicly visible, their sexuality more discussed and accepted than ever before' (1996, 56). Of course, Berridge is not concerned with the far right here, and though her assertion that gay men became more accepted during the epidemic is contentious, the point that gay men became increasingly obvious (if not ubiquitous) is vital in understanding the climate of popular homohysteria which fostered the BNP's attitudes towards them.

BNP literature from the period consistently conflated male homosexuality and the AIDS virus, a trait by no means exclusive to the BNP but one which it in particular capitalised on. Indeed, there was an explicit polemic of homohysteria present in BNP publications throughout the period which drew heavily on the AIDS epidemic. Writing retrospectively in his autobiography, John Tyndall described the 'effeminate looking men' he encountered in London in 1954 as 'the advance guard of the "gay" plague that was later to sweep through society like a poisonous virus', clearly referencing the virus in this polemic against gay men (Tyndall 1998, 42). Indeed, once this 'plague' became apparent to the party, as it did to Britons in general in 1984–1985, the BNP placed AIDS at the heart of its homohysteric discourse (Berridge 1996, 56). The party began anchoring its commitment to 'outlawing' homosexuality to a belief that the logical conclusion of such a policy would be the 'wiping out of AIDS', and printed this as official policy every month in *British Nationalist*, a trend which was only curtailed with the advent of Griffin's modernisation process. Even when lamenting the state of the education system, party authors included homohysteric arguments prejudiced on a conflation of gay men as necessarily being HIV/AIDS carriers. 'Now the Labour Government is making it legal again for education authorities to promote and encourage homosexuality', wrote Carol Garland, a BNP lay member, in a *Spearhead* article in December 1999, 'not seeming to understand that the best possible protection against AIDS is not to indulge in it'. Here, as with other examples, Garland is writing under the assumption that gay sex necessarily leads to AIDS, a belief which was central both to her thinking and the homohysteric attitudes of the BNP more widely.

For much of the period, it was possible for supporters to purchase stickers from the party which read '[p]rotect us from AIDS: Outlaw homosexuality!' (see Plate 1). Party material such as this suggests that the BNP was involved in an active campaign against homosexuality. Though not as active as 'gay bashing', a tactic which had been favoured by the NF (Kelly 2013), the process of displaying such a sticker was by no means passive. It required its user to make a public declaration that they were both against homosexuality being tolerated (agreeing that it ought to be 'outlawed') and that they believed male homosexuality to be the cause of the AIDS virus (Plate 1). Of course, the sticker alone is not reflective of when and by whom it was displayed, the data for which would be virtually impossible to accrue. However, it permits historians of the BNP to determine that the party was campaigning actively against gay men, that the party leadership was aiming to disseminate homohysteric material to grassroots activists (potentially because of demand, though this is unclear), and that the outlawing of homosexuality, specifically male homosexuality, was a central tenant of the BNP agenda 1982–1999, primarily because of the AIDS crisis.[4]

# Protect us from AIDS

# Outlaw
# homosexuality!

## BRITISH NATIONAL PARTY
PO Box 117, Welling, Kent DA16 3DW

**Plate 1** BNP Sticker, dating from the 1990s. Source: The *Hope Not Hate* private archive.

Much of the language employed around the issue of homosexuality in BNP publications from the period can be read as implicitly linking gay men with the spread of AIDS. Articles were consistently published describing homosexuals as 'destructive' and 'threatening', with 'ordinary' people posited as in need of protection from this group. Many of these referenced AIDS explicitly, but we can clearly see the virus' influence on the authors who do not anchor their argument in it. In May 1994, Linda Miller, a BNP organiser based in London, wrote in *Spearhead* of homosexuality: 'today it is one of the most sinister and destructive forces in society', going on to suggest that homosexuals were 'more likely to wage psychological warfare against the family and heterosexual society'. Clearly, Miller was not concerning herself with a discussion of the AIDS crisis, but she buys into the language and view of gay men as posing a biological threat to nuclear white 'indigenously British' families. Indeed, she goes on to compare heterosexual and homosexual men with red and grey squirrels in Britain, making her belief in a biotic danger emanating from the gay community palpable. Homohysteria from the period which did not explicitly reference AIDS, then, was clearly influenced by the discourse of homohysteria which did associate gay men with AIDS, suggesting just how pervasive this conflation was in party discourse.

As a case study of party attitudes towards gay men, the AIDS crisis is useful in demonstrating the ways in which homophobia and homohysteria functioned symbiotically during the period. As has been argued above, the BNP emerged in a culture of homohysteria, but this did not necessarily mark it out as a homohysteric party by default. With gay men seemingly erased from party ranks, the BNP could have become a quietly homophobic party; one which was not supportive of homosexuality or gay rights but not one involved in active anti-gay politics. The advent of AIDS in Britain, though, ensured that the BNP was a homohysteric party throughout Tyndall's premiership. Anderson has argued that HIV/AIDS ushered in a heightened wave of homohysteria as it meant that the 'ubiquitous presence of gay men could no longer be denied', as well as pathologising gay men as a biological threat (Anderson 2012, 87). This seems to have been the case in the BNP. Homophobia was an underlying current in the BNP since its founding as the anti-gay far right party, yet the AIDS crisis meant that homohysteria operated alongside homophobia throughout the period.

## 5. The 'Queer Plot'

These two examples (the origins of the party and HIV/AIDS) are vistas into the homohysteria of the BNP, but they should not be viewed in isolation. Homohysteria was not just a factor of the BNP during its genesis or in reference to the AIDS crisis, but was instead a consistent train of thought throughout the period. This becomes most clear when one realises that the BNP viewed homosexuals as a conspiratorial people, placing them alongside Jews, Masons and communists who are the traditional groups believed to be working against nationalists and/or the state by fascist groups, usually termed the 'Jewish-Masonic-Bolshevik conspiracy'. In one notable *Spearhead* article in May 1994, Linda Miller made the case for viewing gay men in the same light as the party's traditional conspiratorial 'enemies'. In it, she argued that a parallel existed between gay men and Masons, both being a 'society, which excludes women, and which has some odd rituals of the kind that only certain types of men would find particularly appealing'. A tenuous link, perhaps, but the connection is one with particular resonance in BNP thought. Miller goes so far as to compare gay men with Jews, a traditional enemy of the 'old' BNP and their Mosley-led predecessors, arguing that homosexuals were infiltrating powerful Zionist groups, whilst the Zionists thereafter blackmailed gay men into adhering to their global programme for fear of being 'outed'. The 'queer plot', therefore, is aptly named, as BNP writers placed gay men at the heart of fascism's traditionally conceived conspiratorial network.

Another explicit link drawn between homosexuals and a conspiratorial 'underground' movement was made by Ellen Strachan, described by Anti-Fascist Action in 1997 as the BNP's 'in-house "trained psychologist"' (*Fighting Talk* March 1997, 16). In September 1996, Strachan argued in *Spearhead* that gay men tended to be 'free market internationalists' (an obvious enemy of the British nationalist movement, especially one with its roots in National Socialism) because of their 'strong group loyalty and high disposable income'. Though not as trenchant in her homohysteric rhetoric as Miller, Strachan clearly believed that gay men were involved in a conspiratorial agenda which was mobilising against nationalism in a manner particular to homosexuals. This article was so well received by the BNP that John Tyndall gave it outright endorsement in an article written for the same edition of *Spearhead* on the subject of 'authority's collapse', alluding to both the omnipresence and legitimacy of this idea within the party.

Moreover, as with many homophobes, the BNP saw gay men as paedophiles. The aforementioned 1994 election promise that '[t]he BNP believes that homosexuality should be outlawed, to prevent the further spread of AIDS and to protect our young people from corruption' is relevant here also. This quote is one of many which suggest that much of the BNP's homohysteria was grounded in a belief that gay men were predatory and paedophilic. Indeed, this election promise was juxtaposed with a caricatured election promise of the 'main parties': '[t]he Lib/Lab/Con parties have legalized queer sex at 18, and are now press-ing for it to be practised by 16-year-olds', and later in the same April 1994 edition of *British Nationalist*:

> [i]t is no coincidence that many Lib/Lab/Con politicians are campaigning for sex with sixteen-year-old boys. Many are queers themselves! The Establishment is riddled with queers and pae-dophiles who would love to indulge their filthy practices with our children.

Quite clearly, the polemic of homohysteria here is one which attempted to establish a link between gay men and paedophilia, paedophilic homosexuality and the main parties and gay men as a direct and impending threat to the children of British families, furthering the assertion of gay men as a threatening 'other' or outsider group.

Throughout the period, gay men were viewed by the BNP as an enemy in a number of ways. The biological example has already been discussed in reference to HIV/AIDS, yet party authors were notably concerned about the political threat they believed gay men posed to their movement. In her May 1994 *Spearhead* article, Miller concluded that '[w]hen the BNP achieves victory, we must remember that the queers will always be a fifth column. They must be found out and removed from any position of influence.' This extreme passage situates gay men (to whom the word 'queer' invariably refers throughout the literature) in direct political opposition to the BNP. Indeed, description of them as a 'fifth column' conjures imagery of an 'enemy within' during wartime, a point with stark connections to the BNP's conception of gay men as a threat to both themselves and to the nation, but also to the way in which the AIDS virus attacks the body. It is uncertain whether Miller was aware of this connection, as her article does not appear to be reflective of the nuanced authorship that such a subtle comparison would require. However, as we have seen, other BNP authors certainly do make the connection, often unwittingly. Gay men were not only being written about by BNP authors as part of the Jewish–Bolshe-vik–Masonic conspiracy during the period, but also as an organised group threatening British nationalism in particular.

It is clear to see that contributors to BNP publications throughout the period accepted the view of gay men as a minority which existed outside the national 'norm', which goes some way in explaining the small but regular articles which vent a degree of anger that gay men (and, less frequently, lesbians) were receiving 'special treatment' from govern-ment. One notable example from the December 1999 *Spearhead* had it that:

> [p]rostrate [*sic*] cancer kills 10,000 men a year in Britain, yet just £47,000 annually is spent on researching it. AIDS, on the other hand, kills a mere 400 a year. And how much is available for AIDS research? £18 million!

What this illustrates, besides the conflation of AIDS as a disease affecting and propagated by gay men (as has been outlined above), is the ubiquitous belief that homosexuals were receiving special treatment over the interests of the heterosexual 'British' populous. Accepting this parallel, the outcry that homosexuals were having more public funds spent on them unnecessarily which is so visible in the BNP literature, places homohysteria even more centrally into the BNP's agenda, so much so that it almost exactly mirrors one of the ways in which the party famously bemoaned asylum seekers (Schuster 2003; Kushner 2003; Trilling 2013, 94–99). Though this is less conspiratorial in the orthodox sense of the term, it does point to the BNP's belief that homosexuals were receiving special treatment from the government, a fact which undoubtedly contributed to the paranoia-fuelled sense of the group as an 'obnoxious mobilised minority' which was extracting more than its fair share from local and national government.

## 6. Conclusion

This article set out to challenge the pre-existing suppositions present within the literature regarding the BNP's engagement with gay men. Current scholarship contends that anti-gay attitudes were peripheral and that, where they were present, they could be defined as homophobia. Yet, by examining the ways in which the party wrote about gay men, and how it shaped its policies towards them, it is clear that these premises were inaccurate. The BNP itself was born out of a culture which anchored the party in opposition to gay men, opposition which extended to a belief that the group should be nationally pro-scribed. When AIDS became a major issue in Britain in the mid-1980s, the BNP's polemic against gay men took on a more vitriolic tone, one which adopted a viral dis-course and which conflated gay men with the dissemination of the disease. The party also placed gay men within its orthodox conception of the underground anti-nationalist conspiratorial movement, a fact which prompted more homohysteric rhetoric and which offers a new dimension to how the BNP viewed gay men, namely as a dangerous, mobilised minority. In short, a thorough reading of BNP documents 1980–1999 reveals that the party's opposition to gay men was a central and continuous doctrine.

Had it not been for the advent of the AIDS crisis, it is entirely possible that the BNP would have reverted to an NF model of intense homophobia. Yet, the backlash which the HIV/AIDS epidemic prompted cemented homohysteria's place in the party's policies and rhetoric for the duration of the period. Homophobia was extant from the outset of the BNP's political life, and the circumstances in which the party had come into being set its early days aside as homohysteric. What the AIDS epidemic and the accompanying backlash ensured was that homophobia and homohysteria operated symbiotically within the BNP. It was not enough to hate gay men; the party made it official policy to erase them.

Both the AIDS crisis and the widespread belief that gay men were organising against the nationalist movement by undermining the NF added weight to the notion that homo-sexuality was part of the anti-fascist underground conspiracy. This belief, developed by party writers during the period, situated gay men within the Jewish–Masonic–Bolshevik conspiracy, contributing to a mounting belief that gay men were a political enemy to the British nationalist movement. Not only does this add to our understanding of the way BNP prejudice operated against gay men, it also begins to question the rigidity of orthodox fascist discontents. As we increasingly recognise the extent to which modernity has disturbed received wisdoms of all kinds, it is crucial to continue to question the ways in which traditionally conceived prejudices functioned. As this example has shown, gay men can very easily be overlooked, despite their centrality within the BNP's particular worldview.

Though not alone in discussing the ways in which gender and sexual minorities have been engaged with by British fascism, this article has begun to fill a sizable lacuna of knowledge. Very little had previously been written about the ways in which British fascism located itself in opposition to homosexuality, nor the ways in which that prejudice operated. By analysing the BNP's anti-gay sentiment and policy in terms of homohysteria, this article has sought to challenge the current thinking on fascism's 'homophobia', and to set out some of the ways in which its anti-gay sentiment functioned in reality.

It is hoped that this study of the BNP's homohysteria will help to facilitate and stimulate future scholarly endeavours, and that it has, to a certain extent, challenged traditional notions of how the party situated itself in opposition to gay men. The gender history of British fascism has been well served over the last few decades; yet, despite a few brief but trailblazing efforts, its sexuality history has been overlooked. As one of the first studies dedicated solely to examining the ways in which British fascism engaged with homosexuality, it is hoped that others will see the merit in pursuing a sexuality history of fascism, and begin to question the place of homosexuality within their own histories of the far right.

## Notes

1. One should be cautious of the fact that the far right, especially in times of modernisation, was keen to change its image to the electorate, whilst not necessarily changing its core beliefs or fascist dogma. Cas Mudde has referred to this as 'the front stage of the extreme right parties' (Mudde 2000, 21).
2. Virtually nothing has been written on the BNP's opposition to gay or queer women. For initial primary material on this issue, see 'Labour Fat Cats Stalked by "equality"' and 'Queers on Top!', *British Nationalist* (August 1993), p. 2 and p. 4 respectively, and Nigel Jackson, the Australian fascist and supporter of the holocaust denier David Irving, 'In Search of Well-being', *Spearhead*, No. 328 (June 1996), pp. 12–13.
3. The NDFM was brought to my attention initially by one such activist, Terri, at the launch of Leplat (2015) in December 2015 at Housmans Book Shop, London. I am grateful to her for taking the time to enlighten me.
4. I am grateful to Mr Joe Mulhall (RHUL and *Hope Not Hate*) for sourcing these stickers for me. The interpretation of the source is my own.

## Acknowledgements

For their assistance in reading earlier drafts of this article, I wish to thank Sophie Syms, James Somper, Julie Severs, Ruby Ellis, Andrea Mammone, and especially Joe Mulhall. As this article deals primarily with men, I dedicate it to the women who have most encouraged me: Dr Elizabeth Batters, Roz Bundy, Julie Severs, Alison Severs, Ruby Ellis, Sophie Syms, Katie Ball and Sinéad Jein.

## Disclosure statement

No potential conflict of interest was reported by the author.

## References

Primary Material

*British Nationalist*. 1993, August. British Library: Zk.9.d.774.

*British Nationalist*. 1994, April. British Library: Zk.9.d.774.

Garland, C. 1999, December. "Wanted: A New Breed of Men with Old Ideas." *Spearhead* 370: 20–21. British Library: Rh.9x.23.

Griffin, N. 1999, June. "Stranger Things have Happened." *Spearhead* 364: 14–17. British Library: Rh.9x.23.

Jackson, N. 1996, June. "In Search of Well-being." *Spearhead* 328: 12–13. British Library: Rh.9x.23.

Miller, L. 1994, May. "A Queer Plot." *Spearhead* 303: 10–11. British Library: Rh.9x.23.

Morrison, E. 1982, February. "Time for a Name Change." *Spearhead* 160, British Library: Rh.9x.23.

Mosley, O. 1970. *My Life*. London: Thomas Nelson and Sons.

*'Obnoxious mobilised minority: Queers 'demonstrate' in London'*. 1996, June. *Spearhead* 328, p. 3.

*Spearhead* 133. 1979, December. British Library: Rh.9x.23.

*Spearhead* 161. 1982, March. British Library: Rh.9x.23.

*Spearhead* 163. 1982, May. British Library: Rh.9x.23.

*Spearhead* 370. 1999, December. British Library: Rh.9x.23.

Strachan, E. 1996, September. "Internationalism in the 1990s." *Spearhead* 331, British Library: Rh.9x.23.

The Thunderer: The Newsletter of the British Nationalist Party Christian Fellowship. 1994, July/August. British Library: Zk.9.a.3635.

Tyndall, J. 1982. "Resignation – A Personal Statement." *Spearhead* 134, British Library Rh.9x.23: 18.

Tyndall, J. 1996, September. "When Authority Collapses." *Spearhead* 331, British Library: Rh.9x.23.

Tyndall, J. 1998. *The Eleventh Hour: A Call for British Rebirth*. London: Albion Press. British Library: Yc.1993a.1613.


Secondary material

Akkerman, T. 2015. "Gender and the Radical Right in Western Europe: A Comparative Analysis of Policy Agendas." *Patterns of Prejudice* 49 (1–2: Special Issue: Gender and Populist Radical Right Politics): 37–60.

Anderson, E. 2012. *Inclusive Masculinity: The Changing Nature of Masculinities*. London: Routledge.

Berridge, V. 1996. *AIDS in the UK: The Making of Policy. 1981–1994*. Oxford: Oxford University Press.

Copsey, N. 2007. "Changing Course or Changing Clothes? Reflections on the Ideological Evolution of the British National Party 1999–2006." *Patterns of Prejudice* 41 (1): 61–82.

Copsey, N. 2008. *Contemporary British Fascism: The British National Party and the Quest for Legitimacy*. Basingstoke: Macmillan.

Copsey, N. 2015. "When Popular Culture met the Far Right: Cultural Encounters with Post-war British Fascism." In *Cultures of Post-war British Fascism*, edited by N. Copsey and J. E. Richardson, 108–127. London: Routledge.

Durham, M. 1992. "Gender and the British Union of Fascists." *Journal of Contemporary History* 27 (3): 513–529.

Eatwell, R., and C. Mudde, eds. 2004. *Western Democracies and the New Extreme Right Challenge*. London: Routledge.

Goodwin, M. J. 2011. *New British Fascism: The Rise of the British National Party*. London: Routledge.

Gottlieb, J. V. 2004. "Britain's New Fascist Men: The Aestheticization of Brutality in British Fascist Propaganda." In *The Culture of Fascism: Visions of the Far Right in Britain*, edited by J. V. Gottlieb and T. P. Linehan, 83–99. London: I. B. Tauris.

Houlbrook, M. 2005. *Queer London: Perils and Pleasures in the Sexual Metropolis, 1918-1957*. London: University of Chicago Press.

Jackson, P. 2015. "British neo-Nazi fiction: Colin Jordan's Merrie England – 2000 and The Uprising." In *Cultures of Post-war British Fascism*, edited by N. Copsey and J. E. Richardson, 86–107. London: Routledge.

Kushner, T. 2003. "Meaning Nothing but Good: Ethics, History and Asylum-seeker Phobia in Britain." *Patterns of Prejudice* 37 (3): 257–276.

Leplat, F., ed. 2015. *The Far Right in Europe*. London: Resistance Books.

Mammone, A., E. Godin, and B. Jenkins, eds. 2012. *Mapping the Extreme Right in Contemporary Europe: From Local to Transnational*. London: Routledge.

McCormack, M., and E. Anderson. 2014. "Homohysteria: Definitions, Context and Intersectionality." *Sex Roles* 71 (3–4): 152–158.

McLagan, G., and N. Lowles. 2000. *Mr Evil: The Secret Life of Racist Bomber and Killer David Copeland*. London: John Blake.

Mudde, C. 2000. *The Ideology of the Extreme Right*. Manchester: Manchester University Press.

Rhodes, J. 2009. "The Banal National Party: The Routine Nature of Legitimacy." *Patterns of Prejudice* 43 (2): 142–160.

Schuster, L. 2003. "Common Sense or Racism? The Treatment of Asylum-seekers in Europe." *Patterns of Prejudice* 37 (3): 233–256.

Shaffer, R. 2015. "British, European and White: Cultural Constructions of Identity in Post-war British Fascist Music." In *Cultures of Post war British Fascism*, edited by N. Copsey and J. E. Richardson, 142–160. London: Routledge.

Spierings, N., A. Zaslove, L. M. Mügge, and S. L. de Lange. 2015. "Gender and Populist Radical-right Politics: An Introduction." *Patterns of Prejudice* 49 (1–2: Special Issue: Gender and Populist Radical Right Politics): 3–15.

Trilling, D. 2013. *Bloody Nasty People: The Rise of Britain's Far Right*. London: Verso.

Web links

Anti-Fascist Action. 1997, March. *Fighting Talk* 16: 1–24. Accessed September 15 2016. https://libcom.org/files/FIGHTING%20TALK%20-%2016.pdf.

"Asylum Seekers? Longer Hospital Waiting Lists? More Wage Cuts? More Homelessness? Enough is enough!" Accessed March 19 2015. http://web.archive.org/web/20010611211812/http://bnp.org.uk/resources/asylum.pdf.

Commerer, B. 2010. "Populist Radical Right Homophobia." APSA 2010 Annual Meeting Paper. Accessed July 18 2014. http://papers.ssrn.com/sol3/papers.cfm?abstract_id=1657658##.

Czyzselska, J. 2009. "I thought we Got Past this Homophobia." *The Guardian*. Accessed March 21 2015. http://www.theguardian.com/commentisfree/2009/oct/24/nick-griffin-bnp-homophobia.

Hannus, M. 2012. Expo: Threatening Visibility – Radical Right Homophobes in European Parliaments 2012. Accessed July 20 2014. http://expo.se/www/download/res_threatening_visibility_EN_w_1.2.pdf.

Kapiris, M. 2014. "Myatt: Theoretician of Terror?" Accessed January 15 2015. https://regardingdavidmyatt.wordpress.com/tag/a-practical-guide-to-aryan-revolution/.

Kelly, J. 2013. "Nicky Crane: The Secret Double Life of a Gay Neo-Nazi." *BBC News Magazine*. Accessed March 19 2015. http://www.bbc.co.uk/news/magazine-25142557.

Malatesta. 2010. "Eddy Morrison and the NF Split." Accessed September 12 2016. https://malatesta32.wordpress.com/2010/08/12/eddy-morrison-the-nf-split/.

Morrison, E. 2013. "Memoirs of a Street Soldier." Accessed January 10 2015. http://memoirsofastreetsoldier.blogspot.co.uk/.

Thompson, K. J. 2004. "All Change on the British 'Extreme Right'? Nick Griffin and the 'Modernization' of the British National Party (BNP)." PhD Diss., Univ. of Bath. Accessed February 25 2015. http://ethos.bl.uk/OrderDetails.do?uin=uk.bl.ethos.402101.

United States Holocaust Memorial Museum. 2016 (?). "Persecution of Homosexuals in the Third Reich." Accessed September 15 2016. https://www.ushmm.org/wlc/en/article.php?ModuleId=10005261.

Audio-visual sources

Question Time, [television programme, online], Prod. credit n.k., Prod. company n.k., Prod. country n.k., 22:35 22/10/2009, BBC ONE, 63mins. Accessed February 24 2015. http://bobnational.net/record/17143.

# Female leaders in a radical right movement: the Latvian National Front

Anita Stasulane

**ABSTRACT**

Gender is the central axis around which the transformation of radical right forces is taking place: a new type of movement is emerging which is not excessively masculine. Latvia is experiencing an increase in women's participation in the radical right, the Latvian National Front (LNF) being a vivid example. The development of the LNF was influenced by Jean-Marie Le Pen's National Front whose representatives visited Latvia in 1996. This article provides a detailed look into women's participation in the LNF, and a nuanced view of their activities. Although gender equality issues have not been a priority of right-wing radical movements, increased participation of women in socio-political developments and women's increased financial independence have changed both the gender proportion in the radical movements and traditional gender roles. The LNF case suggests that relations between gender and radicalism are dynamic and contextual. A determining factor of the LNF's attitude towards gender issues is the idea of a woman's mission explained through the lens of esotericism.

## Introduction

Although radical right movements have been characterised as strongly masculine (Stratigaki 2013) and women – when compared to men (Givens 2005, 58–60) – vote less frequently for far-right parties in elections, recently women have significantly influenced the strengthening of the political right wing (Fontana, Sidler, and Hardmeier 2006). Movements, initially dominated by men, now offer ways for women to realise their political engagement. Women in the Netherlands, Belgium, Hungary and Greece are visible on the right-wing radical political stage and, in Northern Europe, women even play a leading role. However, Marine Le Pen from the National Front is the best-known woman politician of the radical right. Her activity in France has shaped the meaning of far-right activism and contributed to the popularity of radical right ideology among women (Mayer 2013). It is argued here that this signals the emergence of a new type of radical right movement, which is not excessively masculine (Félix 2015, 168). It is argued, further, that gender is the central axis around which the transformation of radical right forces is taking place and that these changes are global, not local, in nature. This is demonstrated in this article through the discussion of the Latvian case, where an increase in women's participation in radical right movements is observed, of which the Latvian National Front (LNF) is a vivid example.

Although gender equality issues have not been a priority of right-wing radical movements, increased participation of women in socio-political developments and women's increased financial independence have changed the gender composition of radical movements as well as traditional gender roles, that is, women are no longer portrayed as responsible for the reproduction of their nation, but rather depicted as protecting it side by side with men. The LNF case suggests that relations between gender and radicalism are dynamic and contextual. A determining factor of the LNF's attitude towards gender issues is the idea of a 'woman's mission', explained through the lens of esotericism.

The chapter is based on research data collected during the FP7 collaborative research project 'Memory, Youth, Political Legacy and Civic Engagement' (MYPLACE[1]) on young people's social participation. The fieldwork on the LNF was carried out from September 2012 to March 2013 in Riga by employing a combination of ethnographic methods, including 30 semi-structured in-depth interviews, participant observation and by collecting audio-visual material. The sample comprised 66.7% women and 33.3% men who were recruited from the LNF. The majority of female respondents were 20–35 years old. All interviews were conducted in confidentiality, and the names of interviewees are withheld by mutual agreement. In order to preclude the possibility of unintentional coincidence and to guarantee the anonymity of the respondents completely, codes using the abbreviation of the *Latvian National Front* name (LNF) and an interview number (e.g. LNF1; LNF2; LNF3, etc.) were used as pseudonyms, rather than using people's names (e.g. Alberts, Anna, etc.).

## Radical right organisations in Latvia

Various historical factors, the political environment and social atmosphere have shaped the character of radical movements in different countries. Radical movements of Latvia are represented by supporters of both extreme right- and extreme left-wing ideology. They are part of various small groups, which are divided according to ethnic principles; the Latvian groups 'tend to direct their antipathy towards Russians and to invoke inter-war authoritarian models, but Russian groups tend to direct their antipathy against the Latvian state and the West, while glorifying the Soviet Union or contemporary Russia' (Muižnieks 2005, 95).

However, radical right groups in Latvia are more strongly represented than those of the radical left. The reasons for this must be seen in the historical context of Latvia where National Socialism, as a prototypical extreme right movement, has been considered less harmful than communist ideology. This is explained, first, by the relative longevity of communism as opposed to National Socialism in historical memory, handed down from one generation to the next. National Socialism reached Latvia during the Second World War and reigned there only for four years (1941–1945), but communists ruled in Latvia for almost 50 years. The USSR occupied the Republic of Latvia in 1940, and the Soviet regime returned to Latvia after the end of the Second World War. It dominated in the country until 1989 when the Awakening Period commenced, resulting in Latvia regaining its independence *de facto* in 1991. Second, national socialists arrived in Latvia shortly after the repression of civilians by the Soviet regime and played the role of liberators. On the night of 13–14 June 1941, more than 15,000 inhabitants of Latvia were deported to Soviet concentration camps located in remote regions. When national socialists invaded the USSR on 21 June 1941, they successfully used the trauma inflicted on Latvia's society by communist terror in their propaganda. It can be assumed that due to these reasons there is still better breeding ground for activity of the radical right rather than radical left in Latvia.

Currently the radical right in Latvia are represented by *Gustava Celmiņa centrs*,[2] *Latvietis*,[3] LNF, *Antiglobālisti*,[4] *Nacionālā Savienība 'Taisnīgums'*,[5] *Tēvijas sargi*[6] and *Latvijas Republikas Tautas tribunāls*.[7] In addition, the Security Police have found that individual supporters of radical right ideology are active participants of fan clubs (Latvian Security Police 2013) of various sports. However, annual Security Police reviews on the activities of radical and extremist organisations in Latvia reveal that the intensity of their activities is low (Latvian Security Police 2014) and that they are unlikely to orchestrate serious violent activities.

Latvian radical right organisations do not get involved in the processes of mobilisation of radical and extremist forces, which take place intensively nowadays outside Latvia, and, as a consequence, they do not take part in the global war between movements of the left and the right. They express ideological positions orientated towards the local political situation, meant for local consumption and in which ideas from the left and right are combined (Berdņikovs 2011). Even though contradictory combinations of the left- and right-wing ideology can be encountered in Western democratic countries, for example, the National-Anarchism movement (N-AM) in the UK and *Nouvelle Droite* (the New Right) in France, today they are found predominantly in Russia and elsewhere in the post-Soviet space. In Latvia, such a combination is found among the *Kreisie patrioti* (Left Patriots) founded in 2013, which attempts to combine moderate nationalism with leftist economic policies.

Radical right groups in Latvia do not enjoy broad public support. Numerically, their membership is small and they lack strong and charismatic leaders able to unite smaller groups and supporters of right-wing ideology or attract new supporters and financial resources for the implementation of important activities. As a result, activities by supporters of extreme right-wing ideology have been limited primarily to their activity on social networks and participation in public events organised by other organisations. However, the situation changed during the refugee crisis in 2015 when radical right organisations became more active, organising several anti-migrant events involving large numbers of participants, which was unusual for Latvia.

## Emergence of the LNF

Researchers tend to explain the creation of right-wing radicalism in the post-Soviet countries as rooted in 'the need for protection against the destabilising effects of the transition to competition and the market' (Tismaneau 2007, 37). This should not obscure, the socio-political dimension, however. With the fall of the Soviet system, Latvia was faced with the dilemma of how to relate to functionaries of the communist regime. Very different solutions to this problem were developed by two emergent political forces: *Latvijas Tautas fronte* (Latvian Popular Front) (1988) and *Latvijas Pilsoņu kongress* (Latvian Citizens' Congress) (1989). The attitude of the Latvian Popular Front towards Soviet functionaries was tolerant, but the Latvian Citizens' Congress emphasised 'restorationalism', that is, purging the country of its Soviet legacy and defending the principle of legal continuity with the first period of independence. This meant cleansing public institutions of the influence of former Communist Party members and 'decolonisation' – encouraging Soviet-era migrants, mainly Russians, to return 'home' (Auers and Kasekamp 2013, 237). In 1990, the Latvian Citizens' Congress promoted 'a boycott of elections to the Latvian Supreme Soviet, claiming that the electoral participation of the Soviet military and "civil occupants" rendered the exercise illegitimate' (Muižnieks 2005, 95). As the position of the Latvian Popular Front prevailed, the LSSR Supreme Soviet proclaimed the independence of the Republic of Latvia on 4 May 1990. Invitations to undertake the decolonisation of Latvia became marginalised, but found a stable position within the narrative of some small political groups. The LNF was founded in 1997, with the aim of achieving the deoccupation and de-colonisation of Latvia and restoring the Republic of Latvia, which was established in 1918, as the LSSR Supreme Soviet did not have the legal right to do so.

The LNF's development was influenced by Jean-Marie Le Pen's National Front, which at that time was trying to find an opportunity to gain a footing in Latvia. The founder of the LNF Viktors Mūrnieks (b. 1940) explained:

> In 1996, representatives of France's National Front visited Latvia. I became very fond of the organisation led by Le Pen at the time, and therefore we researched deeply into its operations and structure and concluded that this was a good tool for defending a nation's national interests. (Mūrnieks 2012)

Aivars Garda (b. 1955), a theosophist and publisher of esoteric literature, was elected Chairperson at the LNF Congress in 2001. LNF activism increased when its leadership was taken over by Garda and his closest compatriots – four female students, who had attended his lectures on Agni Yoga/Living Ethics at the Latvian Academy of Culture. At that time Garda was a frequent guest on the Latvian Radio, where he expounded on the esoteric teaching of the Roerichs, but he lost these opportunities as soon as he joined the radicals on the right and started to take a strong stance against LGBT publicly.

The LNF is not the only radical right-wing group involving women in its activity, but it is the only radical group in which women take hierarchically leading positions. The so-called Garda's girls are the most active mouthpieces of the group leader's theosophical and political views. These women also constitute the editorial staff of the LNF newspaper *DDD* (issued as of 2 May 2002; circulation 3000), which replaced the previously registered LNF newspaper *Akmens* (Stone). The political credo of *DDD* is revealed by the name of the publication: *Deokupācija. Dekolonizācija. Deboļševizācija* (Deoccupation. Decolonisation. Debolshevisation). The LNF became widely known in Latvia in 2001 and 2002 when it organised schoolchildren's essay competitions about anti-Russian themes. Collating the submitted essays, three collections entitled 'Nevienam mēs Latviju nedodam' (We Won't Give Latvia to Anyone), 'Par Latvijas dekolonizāciju' (For Decolonisation of Latvia) and 'Tautu tiesības' (The Rights of Nations) were published.

## Esoteric background of the LNF

In the LNF, esotericism and politics are intertwined. This is not a new phenomenon; it became particularly apparent in the nineteenth century when the early socialists expected the coming of the Age of Spirit. At that time, Barthélemy Prosper Enfantin (1796–1864) hoped to await the female Messiah and narratives about secret wisdom being kept in mysterious sacred places became increasingly more popular. In this way the idea of the Age of Enlightenment underwent transformation; the world would be saved not by ordinary knowledge but by some special secret wisdom.

Gender issues figure prominently in the interaction between esotericism and right-wing radicalism. In fact, esotericism stands out in terms of the number of females who played and still play a leading role from both the organisational and doctrinal point of view. In the case of theosophy, which was established by Helena Blavatsky (1831–1891), the key religious authority was assigned to a woman. The ideas of Helena Blavatsky were taken up by the next-generation theosophists, including the Russian painter Nicholas Roerich (1874–1947) and his spouse Helena Roerich (1879–1955), who developed a new form of Theosophy – Agni Yoga/Living Ethics. Esotericism, gender and political intertwinement, which expanded widely through the activities of Theosophical Society founder Helena Blavatsky (Goodrick-Clarke 2002) and her feminist co-member Annie Besant (1847–1933) (Besterman 2003, 112–128), is also a characteristic of the branch of Theosophy founded by the Roerichs which is represented by the leaders of the LNF.

The historical roots of the political activity of contemporary theosophists in Latvia stretch back to the political aspirations of Nicholas Roerich. He strived to found a New Country (*Novaia Strana*) that would stretch from Tibet to South Siberia comprising the territories governed by China, Mongolia, Tibet and the USSR. The New State was conceived as the kingdom of Shambhala[8] on the earth, and in order to form this state, Nicholas Roerich aspired to acquire the support of various political systems (Andreev 2003; Rosov 2002, 2004).

In the early twentieth century, esotericism and intertwinement in politics also manifested themselves among Latvian theosophists; the Soviet regime successfully made use of Roerich's adherents, propagating communist ideology in Latvia. In the 1920s and 1930s, the USSR Embassy in Riga maintained close contacts with Roerich's adherents in Latvia and placed strong pressure on the Latvian government not to ban the Roerich Museum's Friends Society, which actively promoted the success of Soviet culture and its economy (Niedre 2001, 133–134). On 17 June 1940, the Soviet army occupied Latvia, and Haralds Lūkins, a son of the founder of the Roerich Museum's Friends Society, was elected to the first government of Soviet Latvia. Nevertheless, after the official annexation of Latvia to the USSR on 5 August 1940, all societies, including the Roerich Museum's Friends Society, were closed. Since the members of the movement continued to meet regularly, Haralds Lūkins was arrested in 1949 for leading an illegal organisation.

After the Second World War, it was women who were the most active upholders of the theosophical 'tradition' in Latvia. They used typewriters to type the Roerichs' works unacceptable to Communist ideology and distributed them among dissident intellectuals. The books of Agni Yoga/Living Ethics were clandestinely translated into Latvian by Meta Veinberga; in this way was women who made the Roerichs' teaching available in Latvia also during the Communist regime.

With the collapse of the Soviet regime, activities of Roerich's followers recommenced throughout the former territory of the USSR. Latvia's followers of Roerich gained legal status in 1988 as the Latvian Roerich Society. In the first years of operation of the restored organisation, about 1000 members joined, but soon the movement shrank and split according to geopolitical orientation. This explains the existence currently of a number of groups of Roerich followers in Latvia: (1) the Latvian Roerich Society, which has a mainly Western orientation and collaborates with groups from the USA and Western Europe and those Eastern European groups that are not subject to Moscow's International Roerich Centre; (2) the International Roerich Centre's Latvian branch, which is firmly oriented in Moscow's direction; (3) Aivars Garda's group, which is quite an isolated group attracting radicals of the right.

Even though the members of these theosophist groups are critical of activities by other groups, there are no serious differences of opinion among Roerich followers in Latvia, as each group operates in its own field (Stasulane et al. 2009): culture is the centre of the value system of the members of the Latvian Roerich Society, the International Roerich Centre's Latvian branch focuses on the field of education and has been able to gain influence in Latvia's education system. Meanwhile, Garda's group is involved in the publication of esoteric literature through the 'Vieda' (Wisdom) Publishing House (1989).

Just like Nicholas Roerich, who attempted to use politicians in the implementation of his ideas, Garda too strives for political power in the new post-communist Latvian government. To create an opportunity to achieve his political goals, Garda, together with the female activists of his group (Līga Muzikante, Liene Apine, Ilze Liepa, Līga Krieviņa and Vita Ņikitina), stood for election in the 2002 Latvian Parliament elections as part of the 'Latvian parties' list, but was unable to garner sufficient votes to get into parliament. Just like Nicholas Roerich, Garda too suggests Agni Yoga/Living Ethics as the foundation of the structure of society:

> [ … ] the New Age Teaching, which is available to everyone, clearly points towards the further direction of evolution of all the people of the world, which has to be adopted without delay: the acquisition of psychic energy, a cooperative public system, a women's movement or the special role of women in public life. (Nevienam 2001, 3–4)

## Esoteric interpretation of the feminine

An important determining factor of the LNF's attitude towards gender issues is the idea of a woman's special mission explained through the lens of esotericism. According to theosophists, the order in the universe is determined by 'the great law of the Equilibrium of the Elements' (Roerich 1954, 457). Violation of this law produces all the negative things in the world, that is, imbalance prevails on the planet Earth since the Feminine Principle has been reduced. The Roerich were enthusiastic about Eastern religions and criticised Christianity; mankind, they stated, had degenerated due to the Christian Church, which 'has humiliated woman to the extent that during the marriage service the minister proclaims "the wife shall obey her husband"!' (Roerich 1954, 457).

Glorification of the feminine culminated, first, in the image of the Mother of the World, painted by Nicholas Roerich, which is of a religious character. The Roerichs understood the important role the female archetype played in every religious system. However, they concluded that the various deities worshipped in different religions were manifestations of the single Mother of the World, that is, the Roerichs reduced all religions to the cult of the Mother of the World. Obviously the artist was inspired by the tradition of paying homage to the Virgin Mary practised by the Orthodox Church, but he included elements of the Eastern culture and religion in the image of the Mother of the World (for details see

Stasulane 2013). The religious function of the image has been confirmed by a special prayer devoted by the Roerichs to the Mother of the World (see: Anon 1956, 44), which is considered the Highest Reality. During the interviews LNF female respondents acknowledged that they consider the Feminine as a cult element: 'The Roerichs already recognised the original Mother from whom all of the origins of the female came, they also wrote about her – the Mother of the World' (LNF1).

Second, the celebration of the feminine echoed also in the understanding of the world by the Roerichs. They taught that the development of the universe takes the form of a spiral, and that there is only one Teacher (*Mahātma*) who communicates all the crucially necessary knowledge for the development of mankind in each circle of the evolutionary spiral, that is, a new part of *philosophia perennis* is received in any epoch. Agni Yoga/ Living Ethics was put in the hands of mankind in the 20th century. Claiming that Helena Roerich received messages from Teacher Morya, the Roerichs published new sacred texts – the books of Agni Yoga. To highlight the great merits of Helena Roerich, she is named the Mother of Agni Yoga who has a redemptive function in the theosophical system of the Roerichs: 'The Mother of Agni Yoga brings the chalice of salvation to mankind' (Anon 1956, 186). In the twentieth century, spirituality of mankind had sunk to very low levels and, with the fire energy approaching the Earth, someone had to transform the highest space energies in such a way that mankind could receive them. It was done by Helena Roerich, who saved the world in this way.

The role Roerich assigned to his wife – the Mother of Agni Yoga – is closely linked to the idea of the special mission of a woman in the promotion of the evolution of mankind. In 1924, Nicholas Roerich published an article 'The Star of the Mother of the World' in a magazine 'The Theosophist' in which he announced the beginning of a new era – the Era of the Mother of the World – which would bring peace and balance (Roerich 1985, 154). The Roerichs pointed out that a special sign would herald the beginning of the new era; in 1924, Venus (Roerich 1954, 376), that is, the Star of the Mother of the World, would shortly approach the Earth.

The Roerichs called for the restoration of the lost balance between the masculine and feminine. To achieve this, the Roerichs encouraged women to carry out a two-fold mission: (1) the mission of a mother who gives life; (2) the mission of a man's inspirer and companion. They believed that the key driver of the evolution of mankind is a woman: 'The Banner of the great Equilibrium of the World must be raised by woman' (Roerich 1954, 276).

Becoming part of the social context of their epoch (for details see Dixon 2001) the Roerichs highlighted the problem of female equality and tried to address it by urging the establishment of female groups in the theosophists' movement, for example, the Sisters of the Golden Mountain (Altai Sisters) and the Unity of Women (Roerich 1931). The idea cherished by Helena Roerich for a long time was implemented in these groups;

> The idea of a mission for women was my dream from early youth; I called it 'The community of the Heroine Sisters' and I imagined them bringing light and joy into the hard conditions of the life of our country. (Roerich 1954, 291)

Roerich supported his wife in her endeavours to achieve female equality. They highlighted the leading role of women (Roerich 1924) by declaring that 'woman stands high as a mother, not only as mother in the family, but as Mother and Great Teacher of the consciousness of nations!' (Roerich 1954, 461).

## Woman's mission in the LNF

On the basis of the theosophical system created by the Roerichs, female members of the LNF understand that their task is to play a pioneering role and to be leaders. According to a female respondent, a woman is spiritually superior to a man: 'Well, males are generally more grounded. We females proceed more quickly along this theoretical [Agni Yoga/ Living Ethics] path' (LNF2). Another female respondent mentioned the psychological advantages of women;

> [ … ] to me, a female generally seems a much more interesting creation than a male, as she is more flexible, she has much greater emotionality with her mind, which is necessary in life, that's why I'd like it if females would express themselves much more nowadays as well. (LNF1)

The women involved in LNF activity have a strong awareness of their mission and they feel invited to be the 'daughters of the Great Mother of the World' (Roerich 1933) and implement their mission via perfecting themselves spiritually, ethically and intellectually and above all – 'to uplift her eternal companion, man' (Roerich 1954, 279).

Regarding their moral stance, female theosophists perceive themselves to be elite since they consider other females to be creatures of a lower evolutionary stage:

> Women have now totally degraded themselves. They are like crazy if they don't have a man. She has divorced, now for her it's any man, as long as she gets a man. She can forget everything. There's only sex in her head. (LNF2)

Although 44.6% of top positions in Latvia are occupied by women (International Labour Organization 2015), LNF female members believe that a woman is still subordinate to a man in politics and business:

> Even though recently the female has become more decisive within the family, in the business of the state and in business too, the female submits to the male, and doesn't express herself in the way she should – to be more decisive in the way she views her life. (LNF1)

They believe that 'politics would be more honest and the nation too would possibly be more successful and thriving if a female had a greater say' (LNF1).

## Women's participation in the LNF

The LNF is publicly presented as a monolithic and strongly structured group. The fieldwork revealed, in contrast, that it has two distinct wings; one section of its members has come to the LNF through an interest in esotericism, while another has joined due to their political leanings. Some women indicated that they got involved in the group through their interest in esotericism:

> He [Garda] was giving lectures on 'A New Age view of the world' [at the Latvian Academy of Culture]. And at the end of [19]99, he wrote an article 'Latvia on the threshold of a new century', in which he wrote about the great hurt of the Latvian people in a very concentrated way, about the deoccupation, which didn't take place, decolonization, about the degradation

of awareness and everything. And then we understood, in principle, that this was the moment when one had to start doing something. (LNF23B)

Although the most active LNF women joined the group through the esoteric route and esotericism plays the key role in the ideology developed by the group leaders, it cannot be stated unequivocally that esotericism is the decisive factor for women's involvement in the group. Interview data suggest that female members also have become part of the group through the political route, usually in order to defend their rights to use the Latvian language in Latvia. The involvement of respondent LNF19, for example, was motivated by her experience gained from working in the service sector where she received verbal attacks from a client for failing to communicate in Russian.

In the case of both the esoteric and the political streams, the LNF members have been captivated by the leader's personality:

I felt that they [Roerich's teachings] gave him such strength and his eyes such a sparkle that he was coming awake like a child, happy and with a half-running gait, and then I just wanted to understand what it was. (LNF11)

In the leader they see 'a very bright and pure person' (LNF9), 'an energetic and charismatic person, who knew very well how to justify his idea' (LNF 27), who 'was best able to justify his tactical solution about how a nationalist should operate in Latvia' (LNF 18). Enthusiasm about the leader's personality seems to be the determining factor;

And then I met a person who lived according to these ideals. He simply ignored the world around him, he was honest, open, jovial, inquisitive, full of the idea of culture and all the world came in contact with him and thrived. I understood that I wanted to live like that as well. It was my greatest revelation that I could be like I am. That's why I also got involved in this movement. (LNF 9)

The 'Garda's girls' admitted that they themselves had not even analysed 'why and how, through what motivation' (LNF 27) they had joined the group. However, in interviews they talked about being suddenly enlightened;

When I read the book [Agni Yoga/Living Ethics], it seemed to me [ ... ] that it was the only book in the world in which there was something I could read with real joy, as up till then books didn't really attract me [ ... ], I began to see a deeper meaning. (LNF 13)

The respondents explained that they had experienced a radical revolution in their consciousness:

It is the teaching in which I can find answers to all of my questions, [ ... ] a new system of thinking is provided there. And another thing – in this teaching, the scientific world model of understanding, as well as a kind of metascientific model merge together into a whole. [ ... ] Some sort of cognition of the world with the senses. That's also the most valuable thing which attracts one to this teaching. (LNF 10)

Moreover, it was not only the esoteric stream respondents who talked about their experience of a sudden revelation, but also those who were attracted to the group because of its political aspects:

Well, that entire national thing, well, that was pretty new to me! And those ideas were something I hadn't, up till then, been able to formulate in words, about how I feel in Latvia and about how things should really be. (LNF 27)

## The prominent position of females in the LNF

In terms of gender, the LNF is entirely different from other groups of the radical right in Latvia whose members are mainly male. Although there is no women's division in the LNF, the striking feature of the group is the pronounced presence of women who are given prominent roles. In the public domain, the LNF is most frequently represented by the group leader's former female students. Therefore, it seems that the majority of the group members are female. However, the fieldwork data suggest that the gender distribution in the group is equal. It is difficult to determine the number of women in the LNF, since the group does not register its members. The interview data show that the group is small in number. The followers of Roerich have the belief that esoteric teaching can be understood only by those who have reached a sufficiently high level of spiritual evolution. This is why Garda's group is characterised by a sense of elitism, and they do not try to develop a group with large numbers of members. The criterion of ethnic belonging is not among the group's organisational elements, as other nationalities, including Russians, are connected with the LNF. Neither the founder of the LNF nor its current leaders were able to give an accurate count of the group's numbers, and only an approximate total number was mentioned: 400–500 members and supporters (LNF28), a half of which might be women.

The involvement of women in the LNF has had a substantial impact on its activity. The LNF became more dynamic when its leadership was taken over by Garda and the so-called Garda's girls became the backbone of the LNF. As a result of the visible presence of women in the group, there was an opportunity to create a new LNF image – smiling young girls in Latvian national costumes, and the organisation gained a reputation as a group for young people, which the LNF tried to maintain, placing photographs of young people on the covers of its publications. LNF leader Aivars Garda was not included in the visual image of the group. Women – actually, young girls – are still part of the LNF visual image, which lately serves also for commercial purposes, for example, girls reading *DDD* is the commercial for the newspaper (*DDD* 2015).

Latvia is not a country in which women dominate in politics: 'Women in Latvia are not prohibited from assuming governance functions and responsibility; however, widespread representation of women in the most important decision-making bodies is regarded as undesirable' (Ijabs 2015). Women are still under-represented in political parties;[9] therefore, female activity in the LNF is easily noticed by the public. The presence of these women has made the far right more acceptable to women, for example, the newspaper *DDD* regularly publishes interviews with publicly well-known women who take the same view as the LNF in relation to relevant political issues. Comments on the articles published in *DDD* lead to a conclusion that the activity of 'Garda's girls' brings new female supporters to the LNF, as women are active in offering their reflections on the internet.

Since both genders are represented in the LNF, the question arises as to how power is distributed and shared within the group between the two genders. There is a view that, unlike men, women are not inclined to create hierarchies, that is, male groups are vertically structured, but female groups are organised in a more democratic way. This assumption is based on research in 'social dominance orientation' (Pratto et al. 1994): in contrast to men, women score lower in social dominance orientation and therefore favour intergroup relations to be equal rather than hierarchical (Pratto, Stallworth, and Sidanius 1997).

The 'social dominance orientation' research suggests that females are not inclined to formation of hierarchical organisations. However, this study found that the LNF has a *pyramidal* power *structure with a male leader and female corner-stones*. Although *during the project* gender differences were not directly investigated in the group, and there is a lack of empirical evidence pertaining to the description of the hierarchical structure of the LNF, the research evidence indicates *that, on the one hand, the so-called Garda's girls are submissive to the leader, but, on the other hand,* informal dominance of women prevails in the radical right group.

Female members of the LNF have accepted their role in the group and follow the conservative model of gender relations. Therefore, the LNF discourse does not include the gender equality issue, which is not perceived as a problem in Latvia.[10] Even though it would be wrong to consider Latvian society highly patriarchal, the view of strictly separated social roles for women and men is clearly perceptible. The LNF leader has succeeded in mobilising women into fulfilling the most important responsibilities and they collaborate successfully not only with the male leader but also with male subordinates. Women help to optimise group activities and even inspire the leader.

Regarding gender responsibilities in the LNF, it should be emphasised that the leader of the group is also the owner of the publishing house 'Vieda'. Therefore, publishing dominates in the spectrum of LNF activities. A wide range of esoteric literature and historical political literature is published, but the most important carrier of the LNF's ideas is the newspaper *DDD*. When explaining the idea of issuing the newspaper, the LNF leader mentioned the analogy with the newspaper *Iskra* (Spark) published by Lenin, and expressed the hope that *DDD* too will be able to gather like-minded people and mobilise society (LNF28). 'Garda's girls' perform all the duties related to the publication of the newspaper *DDD*, and they perceive this as fulfilment of their mission:

> In these times to maintain even this newspaper, which costs money, and to publish it twice a month regularly, without interruption – that's heroic in itself, and, in addition, maintaining in full this national idea and these goals which are published in this newspaper. (LNF28)

## The discourse of LNF promoted by women

Since 'Garda's girls' are members of the editorial board, they also determine the LNF discourse. It is women who provide the content of the newspaper. They interview publicly well-known people, as well as select material sent by 'freelance correspondents' for publication. Even though it is a political newspaper in terms of its published content, the introductory article is often written by the LNF leader, who writes about the teachings of Agni Yoga/Living Ethics.

Participation of women in the group also determines the character of the discourse, that is, the LNF does not organise protests, but it wages 'cultural war' against its enemies: (1) the Soviet-era migrants who are badly integrated into Latvian society; (2) politicians who do not accept the political course offered by the LNF. The LNF defines its activities as the 'fight between the forces of light and the darkness, the [fight] for people's minds, and people's awareness is the arena for this battle' (LNF8). Thus, the dualism characteristic of the system of theosophical thinking gets interpreted in its political aspect: the LNF, as the good, fights with evil in the form of 'immigrants from other countries' (LNF3); and 'with state power, so that it does what it really should be doing' (LNF8).

According to general radical right narratives, there are always one or more enemies demographically dangerous for the nation. The LNF falls within the general narrative of the radical right and it distinguishes between 'Us' and 'Them' (cf. Nagel 1998). The Russian-speaking immigrants of the Soviet era are considered a threat to the indigenous nation of Latvia, as 'They' will outnumber the Latvians, 'Us', who will, in turn, lose their majority in the country, and may eventually even disappear.[11] The respondents' answers provided evidence of the role of historical memory in relation to Soviet immigrants, as Latvians hoped that, with the renewal of Latvia's independence, the consequences of the Soviet Union's migration policy aimed at Russification would be resolved. In addition, they expected that the indigenous nation would again dominate the ethnic make-up of Latvia's residents, just like it did in 1935 when there were 75% Latvians in Latvia. The LNF announced itself loudly by demanding the repatriation of Soviet-era immigrants following the group leader's announcement that the 700,000 Russian-speaking people had to leave Latvia (Nievienam 2001, 378). New geopolitical tensions between Western powers and Russia provide an opportunity to place further emphasis on the image of the country's internal enemy.

In order to keep the nation both quantitatively and qualitatively pure, far-right movements seek to mobilise 'proper' women to bear children, mainly in the frame of eugenic discourses (Yuval-Davis 1997). Although the LNF falls within the scope of the general radical right discourse about 'the death of the nation', interpretation of the demographic issue in the light of the nation's biological reproduction is not inherent to the LNF. As in other radical right groups, LNF women also sometimes articulate quasi-feminist statements in a strong anti-feminist discourse (Dauber 2014).

An essential element of the LNF discourse is opposition to the politicians who do not implement the political programme of *DDD*:

> So, we very quickly understood that these policies, the state's internal and external policies began to be created by the so-called second echelon, which came after the first who were on the Barricades, who fought for freedom, a truly independent Latvia. Free of occupants and, as it often happens in history, the revolution is carried out by one group and the subsequent events are taken over by a completely different one. (LNF28)

Since its establishment, the LNF has been trying to secure the consistent implementation of its goal, that is, deoccupation and decolonisation of Latvia and the renewal of the Republic of Latvia established in 1918, as the Supreme Soviet of LSSR was not entitled to do so. In this respect, the opinion of Garda's group is consistent with the views expressed by the current political elite of Russia.

The LNF is still raising the question of how to treat functionaries of the communist regime:

> And all of them were mainly people who were in the Communist Youth organisation or Cheka during the Soviet period, who were connected with the old system. They just, quite simply, changed their direction very successfully, they had connections with the old system, there was an economic basis for them to best reorient themselves to the new conditions. (LNF18)

The so-called case of the sacks of Cheka is an ideal precondition for keeping the problem alive. The names of KGB employees and informants are still not available to Latvian society.

Since 'antisemitism remains a core element of radical right ideology, old and new' (Rensmann 228), it is not surprising that it has become part of the LNF discourse. 'The Protocols of the Elders of Zion' were published in parts in several issues of the newspaper *DDD* in 2003. Before the Second World War antisemitism in democratic Latvia and even during the authoritarian regime of Ulmanis (1934–1940) was 'more moderate than in other countries of Central and Eastern Europe of that time' (*Antisemītisms 2015*, 4), but the crimes committed and deportation of the population carried out at the time of the first Soviet occupation (1940–1941) had a significant impact on ethnic relations in Latvia and provided an opportunity for those exercising Nazi power to position themselves as liberators and interpret the crimes committed by the Soviet regime as crimes of 'Yiddish Communism'. The idea of Jews as founders and implementers of Communist ideology has always played an important role in the antibolshevist environment and at the end of the 1980s talk about the high proportion of Jews among Soviet functionaries became louder.

The LNF continues this anti-semitic discourse by calling for debolshevisation. In 2006, the editor-in-chief of the newspaper *DDD* Līga Muzikante, its journalist Ilze Liepa and the head of the LNF Aivars Garda were brought to justice for incitement to ethnic hatred and intolerance. The Prosecutor's Office indicted: the editor-in-chief of the newspaper *DDD* Līga Muzikante for publishing articles facilitating discord and hostility in relation to Jews and other nationalities; Ilze Liepa for a hostile attitude repeatedly expressed towards non-Latvians living in Latvia in her article 'Latvians Must Be Masters in Their Country'; and Aivars Garda for unequivocal statements against Russian-speaking people who arrived in Latvia in 1940–1991 expressed in his article. The accused were acquitted due to the lack of *corpus delicti*. Although the LNF management is more reserved with regard to the use of ethnically offensive statements after the litigation, antisemitism is still present in LNF rhetoric.

Since 2002, anti-LGBT rhetoric has a particularly strong place in LNF discourse. The LNF has expressed its position against the LGBT community openly and loudly by organising an essay competition for students and publishing a book '*Homoseksuālisms – cilvēces negods un posts*' (Homosexuality – the Disgrace and Ruin of Mankind). LNF members believe that homosexuality is a sign of humanity's degradation. Such views were held not only among LNF respondents, who are Roerich's followers (homosexuality is strongly condemned in Agni Yoga/Living Ethics) but also among those respondents connected to the LNF only for political reasons. In the interviews, homosexuality was described as degeneration of consciousness (LNF13), illness (LNF2), lechery (LNF30) and perversion (LNF8). When clarifying their attitudes towards LGBT, respondents referred to the examples of the perished ancient civilisations of Ancient Greece and the Roman Empire, the degradation of which was attested to by the practice of homosexuality. As theosophists believe that a person's consciousness either spiritually develops or degrades during one's life, homosexuals were ranked in the lowest-animal consciousness level. The LNF leader's position shows that the critical position towards the LGBT community is used as a unifying factor of the group, that is, taking a stance against official policies and receiving criticism from various government institutions to promote the unity of group members. LNF members severely criticise the position of media representatives on the LGBT issue calling it homosexual propaganda (LNF23A), which threatens the morality of the younger generation. Respondents expressed their deep regret and chagrin, pointing out that politicians support the LGBT community.

## Conclusion

Activisation of radical right forces is directly proportional to action of the parties in power: it becomes activated when the ruling parties do not give enough attention to the issues important for the nation, including corruption, integration of society and immigration (Langenbacker and Schellenberg 2011). Ideas of radical right-wingers usually find fertile soil in ethnic prejudice and anti-immigration sentiment (Mudde 2012) that manifests itself in the Latvian context as ethnic prejudices against the Soviet immigrants. Unlike Western Europe, in Latvia, the radical right-wing groups emerged as a post-Communist phenomenon, largely addressing post-Communist issues, mainly such as corruption, ethnic minorities and EU enlargement (Mudde 2005).

The refugee crisis of 2015 in Europe enables the LNF to put further emphasis on the opposition to multiculturalism and immigration:

> And together we must fight against that cosmopolitanism, against all the wanderings of nations, against all of those perversions and the denial of everything national, we must fight together, as Latvians can't do it alone, Latvians can be in the avant-garde. As we were in the avant-garde when we dismantled the tsar's empire, but now we wouldn't be able to do it by ourselves. (LNF4)

LNF members are not in favour of immigrants, as they believe that each nation should live in its own homeland, and see people looking for a better life elsewhere in the world negatively. Respondents expressed concerns about the existence of Latvian identity in the future, pointing to globalisation processes as the greatest threat. In the ranks of the LNF, being a Latvian is understood as ethnic belonging, which should be maintained without mixing with other nationalities. However, LNF members did not express racist ideas and they are not followers of the 'pure blood' idea, as the main requirement for immigrants is knowledge and the use of the Latvian language.

Islamophobia is a new feature in the LNF discourse. The newspaper *DDD* targeted Soviet immigrants before the refugee crisis, but currently it is targeting Muslim immigrants who are considered more dangerous than Soviet colonists (Liekmanis 2015, 3). In 2015, the newspaper *DDD* published Islamophobic poetry (Rīts 2015, 4) and an article in which migration processes are treated as organised international conspiracy – the arrival of refugees in Europe is compared to the Trojan horse, meaning that 'infantry trained at reconnaissance schools will be among refugees. It will have to open the eastern border, organise unrest and capture strategically important facilities at the right time' (Čangaleišys 2015, 5).

The new geopolitical tension provides an opportunity for the radical right to define their objectives more clearly and strengthen their identity among Latvia's political forces. Since the refugee crisis has contributed to an increase in anti-Muslim sentiment and highlighted the issue of women's equality, the radical right has an opportunity to mobilise women. Observations made during the events organised by the radical right in 2015 against the reception of refugees have led to the conclusion that women's activity in these groups has significantly augmented. It can be projected that mobilisation of women in right-wing groups in Europe will also continue in the near future, as the 2016 New Year's Eve events in Cologne provide an opportunity to present women as victims of 'massive immigration' and 'anti-white racism', as well as treat immigration from Muslim countries as a threat to women's rights.

## Notes

1. Grant agreement no. 266831.
2. *Gustavs Celmiņš Centre* (2007) is the new name of a violent conspiratorial and anti-Semitic group *Pērkonkrusts* (Thundercross), which tried to blow up the Soviet Victory Monument in Riga. It is led by Igors Šiškins (b. 1959), who was released from prison in 2001.
3. *Latvian* (1998) with the motto for a 'Latvian Latvia', published a newspaper 'Latvietis Latvijā' (Latvian in Latvia) until 2005, but currently operates as radio *Merkurs*.
4. *Anti-globalists* (2009) call for the re-establishment of its national currency the lats, a review of Latvia's membership of the EU, protection of the local market, prevention of immigration and restriction of LGBT public activities.
5. *National Union* 'Justice' (2008) explains its ideology as opposition to multiculturalism, internationalism and cosmopolitism, to enforced immigration, diktat of Moscow, Brussels and Washington and to the Euro.
6. *Guards of Fatherland* (2006) is an association whose objective is to teach the skills of military hand-to-hand fighting, stimulate interest in militarisation and the military history of Latvia.
7. *People's Tribunal of the Republic of Latvia* (2009) has divided the population of Latvia into three categories: (1) 'communists and chekists [reference to the first Soviet secret police service or Cheka]' – everyone who was well-known and publicly active during the Soviet era; (2) 'Yids, Yiddish Russians, Zionists' – those who are active today; (3) Grantiņš, a group leader, and his co-thinkers, who criticise the country's political and economic system governed by the 'mafia of Yiddish communists' and law enforcement institutions managed by 'chekists-killers'.
8. Shambhala is a mystical kingdom, which, according to the beliefs of the Tibetan Buddhists, is located somewhere in the North of Tibet where the true version of the tantric text 'Kalachakra' can be found. After the consolidation of Islam in India, the Buddhists believe that Shambhala had become invisible, and hope that it will become visible when the leader who conquers the Muslims arrives (Keown 2003, 257).
9. The index of female political influence in Latvia is considerably lower than the EU average: 42.6 and 49.8 respectively (European Institute for Gender Equality 2012).
10. The majority of respondents from Latvia (54%) consider that gender inequality is rare in their country. (TNS Opinion & Social 2015).
11. The data of the last Population Census show that the Russian population constituted 26.9% of the total population of Latvia in 2011 (The Central Statistical Bureau 2011).

## Disclosure statement

No potential conflict of interest was reported by the author.

# References

Anon. 1956. *Infinity*. I vol. New York: Agni Yoga Society.

Andreev, A. 2003. *Soviet Russia and Tibet: The Debacle of Secret Diplomacy, 1918–1930s*. Leiden: Brill.

Auers, D., and A. Kasekamp. 2013. "Comparing Radical-right Populism in Estonia and Latvia." In *Right-wing Populism in Europe: Politics and Discourse*, edited by R. Wodak, M. Khorasvinik, and B. Mral, 235–248. New York: Bloomsbury Academic.

Berdņikovs, A. 2011. "Aiz Breivīka Frontes Robežas." In *Politika.lv*. http://politika.lv/article/aiz-breivika-frontes-robezas.

Besterman, T. 2003. *Annie Besant: A Modern Prophet*. Whitefish: Kessinger.

Čangaleišys, J. 2015. "Trojas Zirgs." *DDD*, September 11–24.

Dauber, S. A. 2014. "Not All Nazis Are Men: Women's Underestimated Potential for Violence in German Neo-Nazism. Continuation of the Past or Novel Phenomenon?" In *Gendered Perspectives on Conflict and Violence: Part B*, edited by M.T. Segal and V. Demos, 171–194. Bingley: Emerald.

*DDD*. 2015. "Abonē." October 9–22.

Dixon, Joy. 2001. *Divine Feminine: Theosophy and Feminism in England*. Baltimore: The Johns Hopkins University Press.

European Institute for Gender Equality. 2012. "Gender Equality Index." http://eige.europa.eu/gender-statistics/gender-equality-index/2012/country/LV.

Félix, A. 2015. "Old Missions in New Clothes: The Reproduction of the Nation as Women's Main Role Perceived by Female Supporters of Golden Dawn and Jobbik." *Intersections: East European Journal of Society and Politics* 1 (1): 166–182.

Fontana, M. C., A. Sidler, and S. Hardmeier. 2006. "The 'New Right' Vote: An Analysis of the Gender Gap in the Vote Choice for the SVP." *Swiss Political Science Review* 12 (4): 243–271.

Givens, Terri E. 2005. *Voting Radical Right in Western Europe*. Cambridge: Cambridge University Press.

Goodrick-Clarke, N. 2002. *The Occult Roots of Nazism: Secret Aryan Cults and Their Influence on Nazi Ideology*. New York: New York University Press.

Ijabs, Ivars. 2015. "Political Participation." http://www.szf.lu.lv/fileadmin/user_upload/szf_faili/Petnieciba/sppi/demokratija/ENG_Audit_of_Democracy_2015.pdf.

International Labour Organization. 2015. "Women in Business and Management." http://www.ilo.org/wcmsp5/groups/public/---dgreports/---dcomm/---publ/documents/publication/wcms_334882.pdf.

Keown, D. 2003. *A Dictionary of Buddhism*. Oxford: Oxford University Press.

Langenbacker, N., and B. Schellenberg. 2011. "Introduction: An Anthology about the Manifestation and Development of the Radical Right in Europe." In *Is Europe on the 'Right' Pass? Right-Wing Extremism and Right-Wing Populism in Europe*, edited by N. Langenbacker and B. Schellenberg, 11–25. Berlin: Friedrich Ebert Foundation.

Latvian Security Police. 2013. *Drošības Policijas 2013. gada pārskats* [2013 Security Police Review of Activities]. http://www.dp.gov.lv/lv/.

Latvian Security Police. 2014. *Drošības Policijas 2014. gada pārskats* [2014 Security Police Review of Activities]. http://www.dp.gov.lv/lv/.

Liekmanis, J. 2015. "Bēgļu Jautājums." *DDD*, August 28–September 10.

Mayer, N. 2013. "From Jean-Marie to Marine Le Pen: Electoral Change on the Far Right." *Parliamentary Affairs* 66 (1): 160–178.

Mudde, C. 2005. "Racist Extremism in Central and Eastern Europe." *East European Politics and Societies* 19 (2): 161–184.

Mudde, C. 2012. *The Relationship between Immigration and Nativism in Europe and North America*. Washington: Migration Policy Institute.

Muižnieks, N. 2005. "Latvia." In *Racist Extremism in Central and Eastern Europe*, edited by C. Mudde, 93–119. London: Routledge.

Mūrnieks, Viktors. 2012. *Mērķis – patiesi brīva Latvija. Saruna ar Latvijas Nacionālās frontes dibinātāju un tās bijušo priekšsēdētāju Viktoru Mūrnieku* [The Aim – A Truly Independent Latvia. Conversation with a Founder of the Latvijas Nacionālās fronte and its Former Chairperson]. http://fronte.lv/2012/12/merkis-patiesi-briva-latvija.

Nagel, J. 1998. "Masculinity and Nationalism: Gender and Sexuality in the Making of Nations." *Ethnic and Racial Studies* 21 (2): 242–269.

Nevienam. 2001. *Nevienam mēs Latviju nedodam.* Rīga: Vieda.

Niedre, O. 2001. "Pasākumi pret LKP un tās satelītorganisāciju nelegālo un legālo darbību." In *Latvijas izlūkdienesti 1919–1940: 664 likteņi*, edited by V. Kaņepe, 139–155. Rīga: LU 'Latvijas Vēsture' fonds.

Pratto, F., J. Sidanius, L. M. Stallworth, and B. F. Malle. 1994. "Social Dominance Orientation: A Personality Variable Predicting Social and Political Attitudes." *Journal of Personality and Social Psychology* 67 (4): 741–763.

Pratto, F., L. M. Stallworth, and J. Sidanius. 1997. "The Gender Gap: Differences in Political Attitudes and Social Dominance Orientation." *British Journal of Social Psychology* 36 (1): 49–68.

Rīts, J. 2015. "Imigranti." *DDD*, September 11–24.

Roerich, Nicholas. 1924. "She Who Leads." http://www.amazon.co.uk/Print-She-Leads-1924-Artist/dp/B00G6M94P8.

Roerich, Nicholas. 1931. *Realm of Light.* New York: Roerich Museum Press.

Roerich, Nicholas. 1933. *Fiery Stronghold.* Boston: The Stratford Company.

Roerich, Helena. 1954. *Letters of Helena Roerich: 1929–1938.* I vol. New York: Agni Yoga Society.

Roerich, Nicholas. 1985. *Shambhala.* New York: Nicholas Roerich Museum.

Rosov, A. V. 2002. *Nikolai Rerikh: Vestnik Zvenigoroda. Ekspeditsii N.K.Rerikha po okarainam pustyni Gobi. Kniga pervaia. Velikii plan.* St Petersburg: Ariavarta- Press.

Rosov, A. V. 2004. *Nikolai Rerikh: Vestnik Zvenigoroda. Ekspeditsii N.K.Rerikha po okarainam pustyni Gobi. Kniga vtoraia. Novaia strana.* St Petersburg: Ariavarta- Press.

Stasulane, A. 2013. "Theosophy of the Roerichs: Agni Yoga or Living Ethics." In *Handbook of the Theosophical Current*, edited by O. Hammer, and M. Rothstein, 203–206. Leiden: Brill.

Stasulane, A., and J. Priede. 2009. "The Reconfiguration of Values and Beliefs: A Study of Contemporary Theosophy in Latvia." In *Cultural Identity Studies: Subcultures and New Religious Movements in Russia and East-Central Europe, Vol. 15*, edited by G. McKay, C. Williams, M. Goddard, N. Foxlee, and E. Ramanauskaite, 365–391. Oxford: Peter Lang.

Stratigaki, M. 2013. "Gender in Economic Crisis and Political Change: The Case of Greece." In *'Woman Up!' Political, Business and Academic Perspectives on Women's Representation. A Transatlantic Gender Dialogue*, edited by J. Tánczos, 41–50. Brussels: Foundation for European Progressive Studies.

The Central Statistical Bureau. 2011. "2011 gada tautas skaitīšanas dati īsumā [Results of Population and Housing Census 2011 in Brief]." http://www.csb.gov.lv/sites/default/files/publikacijas/nr_13_2011gada_tautas_skaitisanas_rezultati_isuma_12_00_lv.pdf.

TNS Opinion & Social. 2015. "Gender Equality Report." http://ec.europa.eu/justice/genderequality/files/documents/eurobarometer_report_2015_en.pdf.

Tismaneau, V. 2007. "Leninist Legacies, Pluralist Dilemmas." *Journal of Democracy* 18 (4): 34–39.

Yuval-Davis, N. 1997. *Gender and Nation.* London: Sage.

# Soldier, sailor, rebel, rule-breaker: masculinity and the body in the German far right

Cynthia Miller-Idriss

**ABSTRACT**

Drawing on a unique digital archive of thousands of images of far right symbols and commercial products in Germany, combined with 62 interviews conducted with German youth and their teachers in 2013–2014, this article examines young Germans' sense of style and their interpretation of far right-wing symbols and codes in commercial products, clothing, and tattoos. The article focuses on the role that perceptions of masculinity and body image play in the appeal of clothing brands and styles popular with the far right. The analytical focus is on two iconographical tropes – the soldier/sailor and the rebel/rule-breaker – as devices that help articulate how a hegemonic far right version of masculinity is inscribed through male bodies. The article thus identifies subcultural style as a key mechanism through which masculinity and nationalism are linked and mutually reinforced.

## Introduction

Far right German youth subculture has undergone a radical transformation, as youth have gravitated away from the singular, hard-edged skinhead style in favor of sophisticated and fashionable commercial brands which deploy coded far right, extremist symbols. While the style of each of the brands varies, what they have in common – compared with the traditional skinhead scene's black bomber jacket, camouflage fatigues and high black combat boots – is their similarity to mainstream youth clothing styles. In other words, the new brands in the far right scene are virtually indistinguishable in style from other clothing popular with youth.

Many of the symbols deployed in the new brands directly or indirectly reference far right ideologies, heroes, legends, or histories. For example, the brand Thor Steinar has sold a t-shirt with an image of a fox and the words 'Desert Fox: *Afrikakorps*' – codes which refer to the nickname of Erwin Rommel, who commanded German troops in North Africa during World War II. Other codes are more straightforward, like the t-shirt with the word 'Aryan' sold by Ansgar Aryan. The largest German brand, Thor Steinar, is widely recognized as a brand embedded in far right extremist scenes; it is banned in German Parliament as well as in some schools, stadiums and at least one university. The Office for the Protection of the Constitution (*Verfassungsschutz*) in Brandenburg contends that the Thor Steinar brand serves as a 'scene-typical badge of recognition and demarcation.'[1]

In this article, I examine iconographical images and symbols depicted in far right subcultural style, focusing on two ways in which the emotional appeal of the styles leads to the articulation of a hegemonic masculinity associated with the far right. I argue that far right style links masculinity and nationalism by articulating shared aspirations for ideal traits bound to masculinity and nationalism, clearly identifying what it means to be a 'real man' within the nation.[2] It does so by playing on two emotional impulses that appeal to marginalized men in particular: the desire for male comradeship and belonging, and the urge to express anger and frustration at mainstream society. The first articulation relies on iconographic and textual tropes of the male soldier/sailor/warrior to valorize traits like conformity, belonging, trust, loyalty, solidarity, comradeship, courage, and heroism, while the second articulation draws on the rebel/rule-breaker trope to valorize traits like transgression, challenge, rebellion, hatred, anger and violence. Several additional traits – such as strength, power and bravado – are shared across both articulations. Each articulation enables the far right to mobilize young men around a core set of values that are framed as what good nationalists believe and do. Together, these articulations of a hegemonic far right masculinity reveal that the male body is a key site for inscribing, articulating and performing far right-wing ideology. The emotional appeal of subcultural style as a place to reinforce a sense of identity and group belonging and as expressions of resistance against mainstream society[3] can thus be understood as a key mechanism through which nationalism and masculinity become mutually self-reinforcing. This mechanism represents a key contribution to a burgeoning literature on nationalism which has clearly identified masculinity's link to the nation, but has not adequately explained *how* masculinity and nationalism work together.

## Data and methods

This article draws on two sets of primary source material: a digital archive of thousands of images, and 62 interviews with students ($N = 51$) and teachers/administrators ($N = 11$) at two Berlin vocational schools. The images in the digital archive are drawn from five main sources. First, historical images from the 1930s to 1940s are drawn from the special collections of confiscated prints, photographs, and Nazi propaganda at the John W. Kluge Center at the U.S. Library of Congress. Second, historical images from the 1930s to 1940s are drawn from the digitized collections housed at the U.S. Holocaust Memorial Museum, which includes photographs of insignia of various Nazi groups, digitized slides from Hitler Youth propaganda films, and images of a wide variety of Nazi symbols on display at various events. Third, more recent historical images from the 1980s and 1990s, as well as contemporary images from the past decade, are drawn from the collections at the Anti-Fascist Press Archive and Educational Center in Berlin, which has an extensive historical archive and repository of far right extremist artifacts, including product catalogs, flyers, stationary, political brochures, and other material objects on which logos and symbols are visible.

Fourth, the digital archive includes thousands of contemporary images from the digitized collections of three professional German photographers who specialize in photographing far right extremist and neo-Nazi groups. The German photographers track the extreme far right throughout Germany, at neo-Nazi rallies and protest marches as well as in everyday life settings (such as on license plates, at soccer games and on storefronts) and generously gave me access to their archives for research purposes. Finally, the digital archive also includes screen shots of the websites of several commercial brands that sell clothing and products popular with the far right, and a limited number of digital images I captured on the street in Berlin and other German cities, including, for example, images, stickers, posters, graffiti, buttons, patches, banners, flags, and clothing. Images were selected for inclusion in the archive based on their use of symbols, coded messages, or iconography which in some way referenced far right ideology.

Taken together, my research assistant and I initially assembled 4221 images, and then deleted 1297 duplicate or irrelevant images (e.g. where a photographer had taken multiple images of the same scene or symbol from different angles). Many of the images then had to be 'cleaned' and resized before they could be analyzed. The final, original digital archive was comprised of 2924 images. However, over the years, I continued to take additional screenshots and photographs as new brands, product lines, symbols and coded references appeared. Moreover, at least a few dozen of the original 2924 images were essentially duplicate images that were retained – for example, images of a t-shirt photographed from two angles in order to make text legible or parts of a symbol more visible. For this reason, quantitative descriptors for the archive turn out not to be very useful except to illustrate its scale and scope, and for some measure of frequencies (see Figure 1).

The images were coded both inductively and deductively, using a predetermined code-book but adding new codes as they emerged. Figure 1 offers a list of sample codes and their frequencies to illustrate the scope of the digital image coding. The analysis of the image archive took place in several phases. First, all images in the initial archive were coded in Atlas.ti, a computer-assisted qualitative data analysis software program, which essentially entailed assigning a 'tag' to a portion of an image to enable them to be sorted and analyzed at a later date. Images were kept whole unless they had been digi-tized in parts (e.g. to zoom in on a sleeve, or a logo), in which case there were multiple images for one clothing item, for example. Any given image might thus have multiple 'tags' or codes associated with it, depending on the complexity of the references within the image. The utility of this first round of coding was primarily in helping to break the digital archive down into manageable, sortable categories. This helped to reveal patterns in the use of particular kind of images – such as Nordic references.

Following this initial coding in Atlas.ti, I analyzed selected images and groups of images within the coded categories. Here, I spent much more time with individual images, focus-ing on how the symbols were being used, what the codes meant, and what groups of codes as a unit – such as 'Nordic symbols' – might mean for our understanding of the appeal of far right symbols more generally. This was a slow process that focused on con-sidering individual symbols in context, including the setting in which the symbol was present – such as a protest march – as well as the position, facial expressions, and activities of other youth, counter-protesters, and police around the individual wearing the clothing. For catalog and website products, I paid increasing attention to the model's musculature and tattoos, their haircuts and facial expressions, the background imagery, the colors and form of the script, and the framing. This same point – that context mattered – would later be echoed in interviews with youth as they often insisted that the meaning of a symbol could not be understood outside of a particular context.

| CODE | FREQUENCY | DEFINITION |
|---|---|---|
| USEDBYNAZIS | 429 | symbols used by Nazi party directly, e.g., runic symbols, swastika, flag colors, etc. |
| NAZIERAREF | 534 | reference to the Nazi era more generally, like fox/desert fox, images of Nazi soldiers, alphanumeric codes that refer to Hitler (88, 18, 28) etc. May overlap with USEDBYNAZIS |
| GERMANIC | 234 | references to Germanic myths, script, etc. May be double-coded with OTHERHISTORICAL |
| COLONIALREF | 51 | references to the Colonial era, to German colonialism, to countries that used to be German colonies, to a "bigger Germany," etc. |
| OTHERHISTORICAL | 203 | referring to other historical issues or eras in German history that are not reflected in other codes, such as pre-Third Reich flag color, use of Germanic script or pre-WWII history |
| TOTENKOPF | 53 | use of the 'death's head' skull and crossbones |
| NORDICMYTH | 75 | Nordic/Norse mythology references, such as Nordic gods (THOR), mythological places (VALHALLA), etc. |
| NORDICVIKING | 78 | Viking references |
| NORDICIMAGERY | 70 | images that evoke the 'Nordic': sailboats, boatyards, icebergs, snowy ski slopes, Scandinavian flags and town names, runic letters/symbols, Vikings |
| OTHERNORDIC | 125 | Nordic symbols that don't seem to fit in other categories |
| ALPHANUMERIC | 62 | codes that are sequences of letters or numbers. Explanatory memo attached to code if meaning is not obvious. |
| NATIONALPRIDE | 295 | refer to or aim to evoke pride; including national flags, national colors, the word 'Stolz,' etc. |
| ANTIIMMIGRANT | 49 | symbols which are anti-immigrant, Islamophobic, xenophobic, etc. |
| USEOFENGLISH | 238 | codes and symbols, slogans in English |
| COOPTEDBRANDS | 234 | brands coopted (New Balance, Lonsdale, etc.); also include here brands that are modeled off those logos (like Masterrace etc.) |
| OTHERNATIONS | 189 | reference to other nations' extremist movements or draw on those legacies; also symbols that reference other (real or perceived) liberation movements; gang culture from overseas; etc. |
| PANARYAN | 95 | draw on the global pan-Aryan movement, white power, etc. |
| BRICOLAGE | 21 | when two or more cultural references or symbols are combined; stitching together of disparate elements into a new symbols; layering of symbols (i.e., two runes combined into a new symbol signifying Christian neo-Nazis) |
| MILITARYREF | 194 | direct or indirect military reference; imitate current or historical military uniforms, colors, patterns (camouflage etc.) |
| MASCULINITY | 60 | instances where idealized images of males or females might play a role (i.e., inflated biceps of Vikings, broad-shouldered sailors, references to manliness or femininity in catalogs, 'toughness' etc.) |
| OLDSKINHEAD | 143 | old skinhead style of black boots, shaved heads, etc. |
| BRANDS | 695 | brands of clothing |
| AUTON-NATIONALIST | 306 | right-wing extremist style imitating radical left-style (all black etc.) |
| ANTISEMITIC | 25 | anti-Semitic references |
| RESISTANCE | 317 | specific references to resistance to society/societal norms |

**Figure 1** . Sample codebook, digital image coding.

The decoding process was also slow and deliberate. I already knew the meaning of some symbols, but had to spend considerable time disentangling the meanings of others. I spent significant time consulting historical sources and speaking with anti-fascist experts and scholars in the field. My native German research assistants were also very helpful throughout the decoding process. Despite these efforts, there are no guarantees as to the 'correctness' of my interpretations. Symbols are multi-vocal, and the coded products deliberately convey multiple meanings in order to avoid legal problems and social stigma. I opted to steer a very conservative path in terms of image selection, using only symbols where I felt confident that multiple contextual clues indicate a clear link to far right ideology.

Following the image collection and analysis, I and a research assistant conducted interviews in 2013–2014[4] at two vocational schools for construction trades in Berlin, focusing on how young people interpret the brands and symbols and the effect of school bans on the game-playing nature of coded extremist symbols. One of the two schools bans all symbols, brands, and representations that convey ideological positions, while the other does not. The interviews aimed to understand whether young people – who were aged 16–39 at the time of their interview, with an average age of 21 – own or wear any of the banned clothing, how they define their own sense of style and its meaning to them, how they feel about school bans of symbols or clothing brands, and how they interpret a series of images depicting far right symbols in clothing. Using a semi-structured interview instrument, in interviews which averaged 50 minutes with a range of about 30–90 minutes, we asked youth to describe their own personal style and its evolution over time, and to talk about how important their style was to them. We asked what brands of clothing they like, how similar or different their own personal style is to that of their closest friends, and whether their style changes depending on where they are (school, work, home, parties, etc.). We asked their opinions about school bans of clothing, why they think such bans exist, how they became aware of the bans and whether they had seen them enforced. In the second half of the interview, we asked specifically about brands of clothing known within the far right scene. We talked about whether they or people they knew owned any of the brands, how they acquired it and why they own it. They talked about how the clothing makes them feel and what kind of message they think it sends to people who see them wearing it.

Finally, perhaps the most important data to emerge from the interviews came from the portion of the interview when we had the participants review a binder with 34 images of clothing, tattoos, and other subcultural styles and tell us what they saw in the images and how they understood them – the symbols, iconography, and styles. We asked what they thought about the clothing and what kind of message, if any, they think the clothing, symbols, or styles might be trying to send. Following the image-analysis, we asked directly about the far right youth scene for the first time in the interview, specifically asking youth to talk about their knowledge of the scene and whether they had observed any stylistic changes in recent years.

Two of the 51 youth were female, which is consistent with male-dominated fields in construction. Although some of the brands have limited women's product lines, there are far fewer options and the iconography tends to contain fewer coded symbols, compared with the men's clothing, and so the study intentionally focused on young men as the primary target group. Although we did not officially restrict the sample to men, we knew we were likely to have primarily male volunteers in construction trades, since many of the classrooms do not have any women in the cohort. The two young women in the study happened to be in classrooms where we recruited volunteers, and each volunteered to participate in an interview.

The two tropes which I articulate here emerged over years of data collection and analysis, across the interviews and the image-analysis, as reflective of the most consistent reasons why young people were drawn to far right subcultural groups or its style. Across a number of thematic areas that I explore in greater depth in a book manuscript (Miller-Idriss, forthcoming), such as the role of sacred origins and myths, death symbols, or masculinity, I consistently found that these two themes – wanting to belong and wanting to rebel – emerged again and again. In this article, I explore how these two emotional impulses are articulated through expressions of masculinities. Because analysis of the interviews was ongoing at the time of this writing, this article relies primarily on the image archive, but draws in supplemental ways on the interview data.

## Masculinity and the embodiment of nationalism

Much of the scholarship on the intersections among masculinity, youth and violence can be traced to Connell's (1995) seminal conceptualization of hegemonic masculinity and its many subsequent elaborations. Connell's framing argues that specific constructions of masculinity become culturally ideal, or 'hegemonic,' during particular historical eras, while subsequent scholars have extended this work to show that multiple hegemonic and marginalized masculinities can coexist and interact across various social settings and milieus (Meuser 1998; Virchow 2008). Thus, we can speak of the hegemonic masculinity of the German far right, for example, while recognizing that youths' lives are likely to also be embedded in competing, subordinated, marginalized, or oppositional masculinities within the broader social contexts of their lives – such as school, work, home, and broader peer group.

In the German case, early nationalist expressions clearly identified masculinity as a key part of national dominance, alongside the emerging ideal of a masculine master Aryan race (Bernal 1995, 1008). By the end of the eighteenth century, the physically and mentally strong German man had become the bourgeois ideal, identifying a physically fit body as reflective of traits like 'strength, willpower, determination, bravery and a readiness to resort to violence' (Caplan 2003, 177; Mosse 1985). The Nazi party had a well-documented cult of the body – expressed through physical fitness regimes as well as eugenics and an obsession with white skin and the purity of German blood (Linke 1999); for the Nazis, the perfect, sculpted male body symbolized the nation's strength, virility, and manliness (Mosse 1985). In fascist Germany, this hegemonic masculinity was reinforced through both everyday cultural practices and military violence (Linke 1997, 564).

The Nazi cult of the body illustrates how important physical bodies are for the expression and articulation of identities (Richardson and Locks 2014, ix); bodies are 'means through which we think' (Patterson 2014, 10). But bodies are also subject to a broad cluster of forces and cues which help define what is normal, what is appropriate, what is expected, and what is idealized for bodies at any given place and time (Ghannam 2013, 5; Richardson and Locks 2014, 23). This regulation and its power is part of what explains why the body is so often the site for resistance against mainstream norms, as Richardson and Locks (2014, 24) argue, noting that adolescents' initial acts 'of rebellion, against parental or school authority, will nearly always be manifested via the body.' In this way, hair dye, piercings, or tattoos thus might be regarded as transgressive acts through which young people challenge the establishment's social rules or 'boundaries of propriety' (24). Personal style is part of these expressions and rebellions. How youth dress and stylize their bodies, hair, clothing, and their views on appropriate style for various contexts (e.g. work, sports, school, social events, etc.), as well as how we perceive and judge others' styles or their reactions to their own style, are negotiated in the context of what their parents, teachers, employers, and others mandate and how they react to those conditions. Youth style and bodies are not only reactive and regulated, of course; they are also constituted and enacted by their own and their peer groups' beliefs and practices. Youth style thus serves both as a means of group cohesion and identity and as a reactive expression against mainstream society (see also Pilkington 2010).

More centrally for this article, through the use of clothing and style, youth bodies are also sites through which nations and national identities are constructed and reinforced. Bodily practices – from wearing national costumes to participating in a protest march or performing traditional dances or ceremonies – can be physical and emotional embodiments of nationhood, using the corpus to enact and literally in-corporate the nation (Surak 2013, 5–6), to embody political action, and to express individual affect and subjectivity (Adelman and Ruggi 2015). In some cases, understandings of national membership even become intertwined with biological markers like blood (Miller-Idriss 2009). This understanding of the importance of bodily practices to the nation also helps to explain why bodies are so often the primary targets for judgement and disdain of practices deemed non-national (such as wearing headscarves in France) and why bodies are the sites of much violence directed against those deemed not to belong to the nation.

Kristin Surak (2013) argues that physical embodiments of nationhood are not only performative but also have a pedagogical quality – cultivation – which 'works to transform people into better or idealized members of the nation … ' (5). After formal schooling, Surak argues, the bodily practices through 'which nationhood is in-corporated and enacted' (6) represent some of the most powerful means through which the nation is constituted and reconstituted. Clothing, fashion, and style are part of this – not only in the most obvious ways (i.e. traditional national costumes, colors, or distinctly national styles of dress) – but also in symbols woven into clothing. This chapter extends Surak's work by showing how the bodily incorporation of nationhood is inextricably linked to gender and ideas about masculinity and femininity. The nation is indeed embodied and enacted through physical form – but this happens in gendered ways (see, e.g. Enloe 2001; Kanaaneh 2002; Kimmel 2013; Linke 1999; Nagel 1998; Yuval-Davis and Anthias 1989).

As the following sections argue, masculinity is no less important to the far right-wing scene in Germany than it was in the past, but its expressive form has shifted. During the 1980s and 1990s, traditional skinhead style – in Germany as well as elsewhere in Europe, the UK, and North America used 'heavy industrial boots' along with work clothes like jeans and suspenders [braces] and shaved heads to project 'a tough masculinism, chauvinism (anti-gay and anti-black), puritanism, and working-class communalism' Pilkington (2010, 144). Anoop Nayak explains that skinhead style articulates 'multiple masculine fantasies of existence related to manual labor, militarism, prison identity and "hardness"' (Nayak 2005, 150; cited in Pilkington 2010, 156). Today, scholars have consistently shown that the hyper-masculine nature of much of the far right (Ferber 1998; Simi, Bubolz, and Hardman 2013; Virchow 2008) and its idealized notions of manhood and of what a 'real man' does for the nation remain key to far right and right-wing extremist scenes and groups (Kimmel 2004).[5] The stylistic shift away from skinhead style since the early part of the twenty-first century, however, means that these idealized notions of manhood are being performed and enacted in new ways.

## Embodying extremism

Although some women's lines exist in the clothing I studied, they are smaller, with a more limited range of products. By and large, this is clothing designed for and worn by men, with messages inscribed in codes and iconography draped across the broad chests and backs of t-shirts and hoodies. Idealized images of male bodies abound: catalog and website shots feature broad-shouldered, young men with bulging biceps and six pack, washboard abs, positioned in catalogs to maximize images of strength and manliness: lifting something in a boatyard, crossing arms across a hyper-masculine chest, or hunched over an open fire. The clothing does more than promote physical ideals of manliness or masculinity, however; it also markets traditional masculine ideals around belonging and resistance, as I discuss below.

Previous scholarship has convincingly shown that consumption can be a 'constitutive act,' (Comaroff and Comaroff 2009; Lee and LiPuma 2002, 192; Lamont and Molnár 2001; Todd 2004), meaning that consumer products and brands marketed to far right youth have a capacity to create community (MacInnis, Park, and Priester 2009) and forge identities, rather than merely reflect them. Young people's clothing choices, fashion and style are deeply linked to their broader peer groups (Hebdige 1979). When those peer groups are part of extremist scenes, clothing choice becomes part of the embodiment of extremist ideology (Miller-Idriss, forthcoming; Pilkington 2010). In the following sections, I explore how these extremist and nationalist ideologies become articulated with the hegemonic masculinity of the far right through the use of the tropes of the soldier/warrior and the rebel/rule-breaker.

## Soldier, warrior, Viking sailor: Male comradeship and belonging

Virchow (2008) identifies a cluster of factors which are repeatedly manifested in the hegemonic masculinity of the German far right: idealized images of soldiers, a sense of service to the nation and its people, valorization of heterosexuality and national reproduction through fatherhood and childrearing, and a set of characteristics including strength, self-sacrifice, heroism, comradeship, loyalty, discipline, order, bravery, toughness, and courage in the face of death. The constant portrayal of soldiers in the organized far right's printed materials helps to construct a hegemonic far right masculinity, Virchow argues, by strengthening the impression that a 'strong German nation' only exists with a strong military and brave, male soldiers who engage in the face of 'real or imaginary danger' (vi; also see Hopton 2003). Thus, conceptions of nation are semantically linked to ideals about manliness, power, aggression, and violence. Similar formulations of this hegemonic masculinity appear in far right and neo-Nazi music lyrics as well (Virchow 2008, p. v).

The militarized man as warrior-hero is not unique to Germany, of course; it is a common trope cross-nationally within far right cultural scenes. Right-wing militias and white supremacist groups in the United States, for example, consistently promote a fantasy about the 'real' American manhood which will be violently restored to its former glory (Kimmel 2004, 422). Simi, Bubolz, and Hardman (2013) note that the hypermasculinity and authoritarian attitudes so central to far right extremist groups are also traditional characteristics of the military. In Germany, military iconography is peppered throughout the commercial clothing of the new German far right youth subcultural scene. Military motifs like camouflage are common, along with references to German colonialism and Nazi military expeditions, or to commanders and leaders like Rudolf Hesse and Erwin Rommel. The 'heroes' of the U-Boot fleet are valorized in a t-shirt by Ansgar Aryan, while the Nazi expedition to Tibet led by professor and SS-*Hauptsturmführer* Ernst Schäfer is celebrated in a Thor Steinar t-shirt.

The trope of the soldier/warrior articulates an ideal male body image which includes physical traits like muscular strength and stamina. But it also conveys a set of non-physical traits common to the soldier/warrior trope, such as loyalty, integrity, belonging, and male comradeship. Such traits have already been shown to appear with regularity in the printed materials of the far right across national cases; in a comprehensive analysis of right-wing extremist group statements in Italy, Germany and the U.S., Caiani et al. show that the far right presents itself to members as 'omnipotent, able to solve every problem,' and as an 'active and hard-working part of society' reflecting virtues like 'honour, nation, and comradeship' (Caiani, della Porta, and Wageman 2012, 122). This article extends Caiani et al. and Virchow's work by showing how such traits are evidenced not only in the printed material of formal and organized far right groups but also in the iconography of far right subcultural style, as depicted in commercial far right products.

Traits like male comradeship, loyalty and belonging were clearly evident in the far right symbols and commercial products I analyzed. For example, Ansgar Aryan sells a t-shirt which notes 'Volksgemeinschaft statt New World Order' on the front ('The people's community instead of new world order') and on the arm, in smaller print, the words 'Loyalty, Respect, Togetherness.' Other products also evoke or directly reference trust, togetherness, or belonging, such as a t-shirt from Erik & Sons, named 'Trust' or a Thor Steinar t-shirt which proclaims in bold text across the back, 'You'll Never Walk Alone!'[6] Another strategy is the use of the pronouns 'we' and 'our' to clearly demarcate belonging to the group. An Ansgar Aryan t-shirt uses the words 'Hate Crew' in large print on the front, over an image of a masked face and two bloody cleavers; underneath that image are the words 'our day will come.' Bold lettering on the back of the t-shirt more clearly identifies the 'us' and 'them,' noting 'We know where you work; we know where you live; you're not that hard to find.' In another example, an Erik & Sons t-shirt depicts a group of figures clad in Ku Klux Klan white hooded gowns, with the phrase 'team player' in the middle.

In some cases, national solidarity is directly invoked, as in an early mail-order catalog sweater with the words 'I am proud to be a German' in large stitching; the catalog text suggests the sweater is a 'wonderful Christmas gift' for anyone who wants to 'express their patriotism.'[7] In other cases, belonging to a group defined by racial purity is implied or directly referenced, as in the Thor Steinar t-shirt with giant letters proclaiming '100% Pure Viking Blood.' As I explain in greater detail elsewhere (Miller-Idriss, forthcoming), Nordic symbols and imagery are closely connected to far right ideology in Germany, because the far right posits a genetic linkage between Nordic tribes or Vikings and Germanic tribes, arguing that contemporary Germans are the direct descendants of Nordic tribes whose origins were in turn Aryan. Nordic references thus directly link or evoke a sense of belonging to a white community. Viking warriors or weaponry are often depicted on t-shirts or tattoos; one t-shirt shows a raised hand wielding a Nordic hammer over the words (in old Germanic script) 'Help us Thor!!!' In addition to evoking the warrior/soldier trope, Viking sailors 'represent an untrammeled masculinity, an "armed brotherhood" of heroes and martyrs' (Kimmel 2004, 424, citing Bjorgo 1997, 136). Klaus, a 21-year-old first-year roofing apprentice, looked at a photo of a man wearing this t-shirt and remarked, 'that's sort of a Viking-type … what is that trying to symbolize? To be a real guy, or something … he looks pretty brawny, y'know?' Catalog and website models also often reflect hyper-masculine features like bulging biceps and are positioned in ways to showcase strength, muscularity, and power.

Such products do much more than market male comradeship and strengthen group belonging, of course. They convey clear xenophobic, racist, nationalistic, and extremist content. But that content is couched in iconographic tropes and images which explicitly aim to forge solidarity, togetherness, unity, trust, and a sense of belonging to a group, packaged within clothing that is marketed explicitly to men. Such performances of masculinity not only reflect the normative practices and beliefs of the far right scene, but also help constitute and strengthen individuals' identities and sense of self – including their sense of manhood and masculinity more generally (Pilkington 2010).

The soldier/warrior trope, and all that it evokes in terms of male comradeship and belonging, is only one of the two dominant tropes I identified that reflect the hegemonic masculinity of the German far right. The rebel/rule-breaker trope, which reflects a desire for resistance and cultural subversion, is equally powerful and is discussed in greater detail below.

## Rebels and rule-breakers: resistance, power, and machismo

The 2015 winter collection on the Ansgar Aryan website featured a male model staring into the camera, defiantly raising a black-gloved, middle finger. Elsewhere among the brand's products are t-shirts that prominently state 'Aryan Resistance,' a pair of sweatpants with 'my life my rules' printed across the seat of the pants and in large print down the outside right pant leg, and another pair of pants with 'Fuck your Society' printed along the back of the left leg. The product line's name is H8CORE – shorthand for 'hate core'. Other brands also play directly on the appeal of resistance and anger toward mainstream society. One Thor Steinar t-shirt features a large gun at the end of an outstretched hand over the words 'straight answer,' while another shows an image of a Viking yelling and wielding an ax, over the word 'Reaction' printed in old Germanic script.

Products like these illustrate the extent to which commercial products that are marketed to far right youth do not only forge community and a sense of belonging for male consumers. They also deploy the body as a place to express and perform anger and resistance against mainstream society in direct and indirect ways, all while clearly identifying these activities as part of masculine nationalists' landscape. Both iconography and text in the far right brands repeatedly emphasize resistance and rebellion. One of the most subtle and complex extremist brands, Reconquista, had a series of tag-lines flashing across the top of their commercial website, including the phrase 'Widerstand ist anziehend,' which carries a double meaning, because 'anziehend' means 'attractive' but also means 'wearable,' from the verb anziehen, which means 'to put on.' Reconquista is thus selling 'wearable' resistance which makes one attractive. Reconquista thus used the notion of resistance to market coded extremist clothing. In this light, resistance itself becomes commodified.

Work on oppositional subcultures has shown that boys' rebellion – through things like pranks and vandalism – can be a means to express and validate hegemonic masculine ideals that conflict with the obedience and restraint required of boys by their teachers and other authority figures (Messerschmidt 1993, 94–95). Previous research also has demonstrated that right-wing extremist radicalization is closely tied to a sense of injustice, being disgruntled and angry at societal institutions that are deemed to have let one down (Simi, Bubolz, and Hardman 2013). Subcultural style can be a part of such resentment and rebellion, particularly in light of research showing that style does not only strengthen internal group values and belonging but also acts to deliberately engage the outside world (Pilkington 2010). In the following discussion, I explain how the rebel/rule-breaker trope valorizes key traits like transgression, challenge, rebellion, hatred, anger, and violence in ways that mutually reinforce masculinity and nationalism.

In interviews, young Germans repeatedly identified far right clothing brands, symbols and iconography as 'provokant,' meaning that they are intended to provoke a reaction in observers. In some cases, the intended reaction is clearly fear. Martin, who at age 16 is training to be a mason and self-identifies as a right-wing nationalist, explained that he was initially attracted to the style of right-wing extremists because it evokes fear in others:

> I always found it … somehow fascinating, because in my view there is an embodiment (Ver-körperung), when you appear dangerous and that's how others view you, then other people receive you with a sort of respect or fear … if one sees three people standing there dressed like [a right-wing extremist], then one normally doesn't get closer.

Georg, a first-year scaffold-builder trainee, now aged 21, deliberately wears clothes that are provocative, primarily from the brand Yakuza, which sells high-quality clothing laced with a variety of racist, misogynistic and other taboo-breaking iconography. He describes his own style as extremely important, in terms of both distinguishing himself from his friends and provoking mainstream society.

> Of course, one draws a kind of provocative attention to oneself, when you see the crass motifs from Yakuza, they provoke in a certain way … I like the crass expressions … I have almost only Yakuza things in my closet. … [it] gets the attention of people, and that's exactly why people want to wear it, because they want to show, 'whoa, look at that motif, totally crass.. when they see that on the street. That's why it's been my style for years. … It's also in the USA, there are even crasser motifs there, which would of course be banned in Germany.

> Interviewer: When you say 'crass motifs,' can you describe a little, because I don't know [the brand Yakuza]

> Georg: Well there was, for example a motif in Germany, in the early days [of the brand] they used the slogan, 'The Yakuza Deathfinisher,' or they had a girl kneeling near somebody in Ku Klux Klan robes holding a shotgun to her head and so, that was the beginning, y'know?

Rios and Sarabia (2016) suggest that marginalized men – who are economically or socially vulnerable – enact 'compensatory masculinities' (citing Pyke 1996) through deviant behavior (168). Such behavior helps men to 'illustrate resistance toward, and independence from, institutions and existing power structures' (168). In particular, they found that young men often responded to the emasculation brought on through interactions with police or 'institutions of control' by 'symbolically remasculinizing themselves by subjecting young women to physical and symbolic violence' (p. 175). For Georg – who was once 'taken away' by police for wearing a Thor Steinar jacket in public and allowed to leave with the jacket only after the police, as he describes it, 'ripped out the logo before my eyes' – misogynistic iconography is clearly part of Yakuza's appeal, as are textual references which threaten violence toward immigrants or those not given legitimacy in the nation. Such iconography thus simultaneously remasculinizes and asserts racial and ethnic dominance, clearly identifying what it means to be a 'real' man in the German nation.

Although further research is needed to explore the question of economic marginalization in greater depth, it is worth pointing out that the young men I interviewed – future masons, roofers, scaffold-builders, concrete-layers, and related occupations – are not a part of what Kimmel (2004, 415) refers to as 'global hegemonic masculinity' (also see Messerschmidt 2000, 10). Indeed, the working-class young men I interviewed are increasingly marginalized from traditional notions of male success. Construction is a declining industry in Berlin; employment in the construction trades has dropped 300% in the past two decades, from nearly 61,000 employees in 1995 to under 20,000 in 2011, although the numbers have more or less stabilized since 2004. Employment numbers in construction in Brandenburg (the state surrounding Berlin) have experienced similar decline, dropping by more than half between 1995 and 2011, from 72,607 to 34,333.[8] More generally, the German vocational system has declined somewhat in status and relevance in the face of a labor market that increasingly values knowledge-based skills and flexibility over more predictable and physical manufacturing and craft trades. Once the global standard for non-university bound careers, the German apprenticeship model has struggled in several ways in recent years (Deissinger 2015). In this context, perhaps it is not so surprising that young German construction trainees would feel angry.

Scholars have demonstrated that frustration and anger play a key role in extremist group recruitment and radicalization. In research with US right-wing extremists, Simi, Bubolz, and Hardman (2013) found that radicalization was most likely to occur when anger about personal experiences – such as involuntary exit from the military – created a sense of personal failure in the face of an uncertain future. Importantly, 'anger finds greater focus after the person begins affiliating with similarly situated individuals' or meets people who are already extremists (2013, 662) – starting a process that ultimately redirects anger at a sense of personal failure toward the government and other groups (also see Cohen 1955). Former white supremacist Arno Michaelis recently described his own socialization into a hate group in the USA, explaining how the strong hatred he developed as a teenager – of his family, his teachers, his school, his town, and other kids – found its key expression when he encountered racist skinhead music. He discovered that the swastika 'is an effective way of angering others,' and that the hatred and anger he 'radiated' was in turn reflected back from others, which then 'validat[ed] the paranoid ideology that had become my identity' (Michaelis 2015). Related research with urban gang members (Rios and Sarabia 2016) has produced similar findings, arguing that boys who are frustrated with few viable employment opportunities or guidance from the adult world easily fall into 'the seductive arms of hypermasculinity' (p. 174), in which exaggerated displays of aggression and strength both express resistance and serve as a 'resource for self-affirmation' (Rios and Sarabia 175; also 173, citing Harris 2000).

Finally, it is important to note that far right-wing products do not only aim to provoke outsiders; they also valorize violence more generally, and they do so in clearly gendered ways. The phrase 'Kontaktfreudig und Erlebnisorientiert' – which loosely translates as 'eager/happy to be in contact and looking for adventure' – is used by Thor Steinar in both its men's and women's lines, for example, but is paired with very different iconographical images. In men's t-shirts and sport jackets, the phrase is written over an image of red, spattered blood; in the women's t-shirt, the phrase is written over an image of red, puckered, lipstick-covered lips. Men are thus depicted as seekers of violent adventure, whose contact with others will lead to their own or other's blood to splatter. 'Contact' for women, on the other hand, is sexualized, reflected in puckered lips ready to be kissed.

The clothing lines also valorize taboo-breaking, both through the use of iconography and text that offends social norms as well as by carefully toeing the line between legal and illegal symbol usage. The brands' symbols and iconography – including use of colors, text scripts, phrases, historic references, and more – break cultural taboos while toeing the line of legality – a line which in turn is used directly to market the products to consumers. Part of the attractiveness of these clothing brands to youth in and around the scene is that they carefully tread along the line of legality, enabling youth to resist mainstream norms and cultural rules while not getting into official legal trouble. Martin, who self-identifies as a right-wing nationalist, for example, explained that his parents do not approve of what he is doing but know that he will not do anything illegal.

## Dual articulations

While many of the traits associated with the hegemonic articulation of far right masculinity I have analyzed here fall into either the soldier/sailor or the rebel/rule-breaker categories, the division between the two categories is not a completely clear one. Masculine ideals like strength, power, and bravado are celebrated both in the valorization of military soldiers and sailing explorers as well as in rebels who provoke fear in mainstream society. Indeed, the Viking warrior may be so ubiquitous across the brands precisely because it epitomizes many of the ideals in both articulations. For youth in and on the periphery of the far right scene, hyper-masculine symbols like the inflated biceps of Viking gods depicted in right-wing tattoos may reflect youth fantasies of a romantic, pure, and untroubled past (also see Claus, Lehnert, and Müller 2010; Virchow 2010) in ways that help them navigate uncertain labor markets and transitions to their adult lives.

More generally, it is important to note that the desire to belong to a group and expressions of anger toward outsiders are likely mutually reinforcing emotional expressions. Enacting violence against others as part of a group may make an individual simultaneously feel more powerful and more closely bonded to his fellow aggressors. Articulations of masculinity are also deeply embedded in social contexts that are much broader than what I have been able to detail here. Young people position themselves against police actions, aggression from left-wing groups, or changing state policies on immigration, for example, in ways that link themselves more strongly to others within their group even as they are expressing anger or frustration against others. [9]

## Conclusion

I have sought to identify key mechanisms through which the appeal of a hegemonic articulation of masculinity intersects with nationalistic ideals in ways that mutually reinforce masculinity and nationalism. I argue that far right youth subcultural style in Germany valorizes hegemonic far right masculinity and appeals to young men's simul-taneous desire to belong to a group and to resist mainstream authorities. During stressful economic, political, or social periods in the nation's history, scholars have suggested that images of males and females may become increasingly idealized and romanticized

(Kimmel 2004; also see Nagel 2005). I would suggest that this is also the case for marginalized youth who are detached from mainstream notions of success and for whom traditional ideas about male and female roles, or masculinity and femininity, may have particular appeal.

I focused here on two primary ways in which the emotional appeal of the styles is particularly important in linking masculinity with nationalism through the expression of shared ideal traits. First, I showed how the desire for male comradeship and belonging is illustrated in iconographic and textual references to the male soldier/Viking sailor/warrior in ways that emphasize conformity, trust, comradeship, courage, heroism, loyalty, and belonging. Second, I showed how the appeal of expressing anger and frustration at mainstream society is expressed through the rebel/rule-breaker trope and its valorization of traits like rebellion, violence, transgression, hatred, and anger. By linking these traits to nationalistic, xenophobic, and racist content, the male body becomes a site for inscribing and performing far right-wing ideology and helps to articulate what it means to be a 'good nationalist man.' Subcultural style thus acts not only as a key site for reinforcing identity and belonging to a group and for expressing resistance against mainstream society, but also as a mechanism through which nationalism and masculinity are jointly articulated and reinforced.

These findings clearly demonstrate that clothing and subcultural style have the potential not only to reflect but also to create, cultivate, and strengthen identities, including masculinity and femininity and their intersections with nationalism. Far from being mere 'subcultural style,' I argue that commercialized extremist products can be a gateway to radicalization and violence by both helping to strengthen racist and nationalist identification and by acting as conduits of resistance to mainstream society. Future work on masculinity and nationalism could extend this finding by focusing on additional mechanisms that help explain *how* masculinity and nationalism work together in ways that might contribute to the appeal of extremist groups.

## Notes

1. http://www.verfassungsschutz.brandenburg.de/cms/detail.php/bb2.c.423435.de, accessed September 23, 2011. See Miller-Idriss 2012 and Miller-Idriss, forthcoming for a more in-depth discussion of the brands and the commercialization of the far right scene.
2. The peculiarities of the German context and the historical intertwining of nationalism, patriotism and racism means that all three concepts are linked with the broad spectrum of far right ideology, particularly as applied to subcultural style and groups as opposed to formal political movements. Nationalism is thus – at times – evidenced in this case through instances including calls to Nordic origins or to being proud of being German (see Miller-Idriss 2009). I thank Hilary Pilkington and an anonymous reviewer for helping me articulate this point.
3. As I explore elsewhere (Miller-Idriss, forthcoming), the new subcultural style not only resists mainstream society but is also reflective of conformity to mainstream fashions and style.
4. One interview was conducted in spring 2012, prior to the full data collection, due to an impending retirement.
5. Gender differences in right-wing extremist engagement have been well documented cross-culturally (Rippl and Seipel 1999; Gigengil et al. 2005), particularly in voting patterns and in acts of violence.
6. Importantly, this phrase is associated with a football team in Liverpool, UK.

7. See Miller-Idriss (2009) for a lengthier discussion of why this phrase itself is often a conscious expression of resistance in Germany.
8. Statistischer Bericht – Baugewerbe in Berlin 2011, SB E II 2/E III 2–j/11 – Berlin and Statistischer Bericht-Baugewerbe im Brandenburg 2011, E II 2/E III 2 – j/11, both published by the Amt für Statistik Berlin-Brandenburg in December 2011.
9. I am grateful to Will Baldet for pointing this out in his presentation, "The Hate Equation," from the ESRC Seminar "Right Wing Extremism in contemporary Europe: issues of policy and practice," *The Wiener Library for the Study of the Holocaust and Genocide,* November 13, 2015.

## Acknowledgment

I am grateful to Katharina Börner, Annett Graefe and Alessandra Hodulik for research assistance.

## Disclosure statement

No potential conflict of interest was reported by the authors.

## Funding

The larger project from which this research draws was funded by grants and fellowships from the Alexander von Humboldt Foundation, the German Academic Exchange Service/Deutscher Akademischer Austausch Dienst (DAAD), the Goethe Institute, New York University, the Spencer Foundation, and the University of Cologne's Morphomata Center for Advanced Studies.

## References

Adelman, Miriam, and Linnita Ruggi. 2015. "The Sociology of the Body." *Current Sociology Review* 64 (6): 1–2.
Bernal, Martin. 1995. "Race, Class, and Gender in the Formation of the Aryan Model of Greek Origins." Pp. 987–1008 in Mudimbe, V.Y. *Nations, Identities, Cultures. The South Atlantic Quarterly, Special Issue.* Vol 94, No 4, Fall.
Bjorgo, T. 1997. *Racist and Right-Wing Violence in Scandanavia: Patterns, Perpetrators, and Responses.* Leiden, The Netherlands: University of Leiden.
Caiani, Manuela, Donatella della Porta, and Claudius Wageman. 2012. *Mobilizing on the Extreme Right: Germany, Italy and the United States.* Oxford: Oxford University Press.
Caplan, Gregory A. 2003. "Militarism and Masculinity as Keys to the "Jewish Question" in Germany." In .*Military Masculinities: Identity and the State,* edited by Paul R. Higate, 175–190. Westport, CT: Praeger.
Claus, R., Lehnert, E., and Müller, Y. 2010. *Was ein rechter Mann ist…':  Männlichkeiten im Rechtsextremismus.* Berlin: Karl Dietz Verlag.

Cohen, A. K. 1955. *Delinquent Boys: The Culture of the Gang*. New York: The Free Press.

Comaroff, John, and Jean Comaroff. 2009. *Ethnicity, Inc.* Chicago, IL: University of Chicago Press.

Connell, R. W. 1995. *Masculinities*. Berkeley: University of California Press.

Deissinger, Thomas. 2015. "The German Dual Vocational Education and Training System as "Good Practice'?" *Local Economy* 30 (5): 557–567.

Enloe, Cynthia. 2001. *Bananas, Beaches and Bases: Making Sense of International Politics*. Berkeley: University of California Press.

Ferber, Abby. 1998. *White Man Falling: Race, Gender and White Supremacy*. Lanham, MD: Rowman & Littlefield.

Ghannam, Farha. 2013. *Live and Die Like a Man: Gender Dynamics in Urban Egypt*. Stanford, CA: Stanford University Press.

Gigengil, Elisabeth, Matthew Hennigar, André Blais, and Neil Nevitte. 2005. "Explaining the Gender Gap in Support for the New Right: The Case of Canada." *Comparative Political Studies* 38 (10): 1171–1195.

Harris, A. P. 2000. "Gender, Violence, Race and Criminal Justice." Stanford Law Review 52 (4): 777–807.

Hebdige, Dick. 1979. *Subculture: The Meaning of Style*. New York: Methuen.

Hopton, John 2003. "The State and Military Masculinity." In *Military Masculinities: Identity and the State*, edited by Paul R. Higate, 111–124. Westport, CT: Praeger.

Kanaaneh, Rhoda Ann. 2002. *Birthing the Nation: Strategies of Palestinian Women in Israel*. Berkeley: University of California Press.

Kimmel, Michael. 2004. "Globalization and its Mal(e)Contents: the Gendered Moral and Political Economy of Terrorism." In *Handbook of Studies on Men and Masculinities*, edited by Michael Kimmel, Jeff Hearn, and R. W. Connell, 414–431. Thousand Oaks, CA: Sage Publications.

Kimmel, Michael. 2013. *Angry White Men: American Masculinity at the End of an Era*. New York: Nation Books.

Lamont, Michèle, and Virág Molnár. 2001. "How Blacks use Consumption to Shape Their Collective Identity." *Journal of Consumer Culture* 1 (1): 31–45.

Lee, Benjamin, and Edward LiPuma. 2002. "Cultures of Circulation: The Imaginations of Modernity." *Public Culture* 14 (1): 191–213.

Linke, Uli. 1997. "Gendered Difference, Violent Imagination: Blood, Race, Nation." *American Anthropologist* 99 (3): 559–573.

Linke, Uli. 1999. *German Bodies: Race and Representation after Hitler*. New York: Routledge.

MacInnis, Deborah, C. W. Park, and Joseph Priester, ed. 2009. *Handbook of Brand Relationships*. New York: M.E. Sharpe.

Messerschmidt, James W. 1993. *Masculinities and Crime: Critique and Reconceptualization of Theory*. Lanham, MD: Rowman & Littlefield Publishers.

Messerschmidt, J. W. 2000. *Nine Lives: Adolescent Masculinities, the Body, and Violence*. Boulder, CO: Westview Press.

Meuser, Michael. 1998. *Geschlecht und Männlichkeit. Soziologische Theorie und kulturelle Deutungsmuster*. Opladen: Leske & Budrich.

Michaelis, Arno. 2015. "This is how you become a white supremacist." *The Washington Post*, June 25.

Miller-Idriss, Cynthia. 2009. *Blood and Culture: Youth, Right-Wing Extremism, and National Belonging in Contemporary Germany*. Durham, NC: Duke University Press.

Miller-Idriss, Cynthia. 2012. "The Extreme Goes Mainstream? Commercialized Right-Wing Extremism in Germany." *Perspectives on Europe* 42 (1): 15–21.

Miller-Idriss, Cynthia. Forthcoming. *The Extreme Gone Mainstream: Commercialization and Far Right Youth Subculture in Germany*. Princeton University Press.

Mosse, George L. 1985. *Nationalism and Sexuality: Respectability and Abnormal Sexuality in Modern Europe*. New York: Howard Fertig.

Nagel, Joane. 1998. "Masculinity and Nationalism: Gender and Sexuality in the Making of Nations." *Ethnic and Racial Studies* 21 (2): 242–269.

Nagel, Joane. 2005. "Nation." In *Handbook of Studies on Men and Masculinities*, edited by Michael S. Kimmel, Jeff Hearn, and R. W. Connell, 397–413. Thousand Oaks, CA: SAGE.

Nayak, A. 2005. "White Lives." In *Racialization: Studies in Theory and Practice*, edited by K. Murji and J. Solomos, 141–162. Oxford: Oxford University Press.

Patterson, Orlando. 2014. "Making Sense of Culture." *Annual Review of Sociology* 40: 1–30.

Pilkington, Hilary. 2010. "No Longer "On Parade': Style and the Performance of Skinhead in the Russian Far North." In *Russia's Skinheads: Exploring and Rethinking Subcultural Lives*, edited by Pilkington, Hilary, Elena Omel'chenko, and Al'bina Garifzianova, 143–165. London: Routledge.

Pyke, K. D. 1996. "Class-Based Masculinities: The Interdependence of Gender, Class and Interpersonal Power." *Gender & Society* 10: 527–549.

Richardson, Niall, and Adam Locks. 2014. *Body Studies: The Basics*. New York: Routledge.

Rios, Victor, and Rachel Sarabia. 2016. "Synthesized Masculinities: The Mechanics of Manhood among Delinquent Boys." In *Exploring Masculinities: Identity, Inequality, Continuity, and Changem*, edited by C. J. Pascoe and Tristan Bridges, 166–177. New York: Oxford University Press.

Rippl, Susanne, and Christian Seipel. 1999. "Gender Differences in Right-Wing Extremism: Intergroup Validity of a Second-Order Construct." *Social Psychology Quarterly* 62: 381–393.

Simi, Pete, Bryan Bubolz, and Ann Hardman. 2013. "Military Experience, Identity Discrepancies, and Far Right Terrorism: An Exploratory Analysis." *Studies in Conflict and Terrorism* 36: 654–671.

Surak, Kristin. 2013. *Making Tea, Making Japan. Cultural Nationalism in Practice*. Stanford, CA: Stanford University Press.

Todd, Anne Marie. 2004. "Environmental Consumer Ethics of Natural Personal Care Products." *Ethics & The Environment* 9 (2): 86–102.

Virchow, Fabian. 2008. "Die Bedeutung von Männlichkeitsstereotypen im Rechtsextremismus." Manuscript for *Brave Mädels und echte Kerle? Theorie und Wirklichkeit von Geschlechtsrollen im Rechtsextremismus*. Friedrich Ebert Stiftung Conference, Berlin, 23. January 2008.

Virchow, F. 2010. Tapfer, stolz, opferbereit—Überlegungen zum extrem rechten Verständnis, idealer Männlichkeit. In *Was ein rechter Mann ist...: Männlichkeit im Rechtsextremismus*, edited by E. L. Robert Claus and M. Yves, 39–52. Berlin: Karl Dietz Verlag.

Yuval-Davis, Nira, and Floya Anthias. 1989. *Women-Nation-State*. New York: St. Martin's Press.

# 'Sexually modern nativist voters': do they exist and do they vote for the populist radical right?

Niels Spierings, Marcel Lubbers and Andrej Zaslove

**ABSTRACT**

Populist radical right (PRR) parties have attracted anti-migration voters by claiming to serve the interests of nationally defined in-groups. Recently, several European PRR parties have shifted focus from protecting traditional values to protecting so-called modern Western values, including lesbian, gay, bisexual, and transgender rights. Here, we study whether PRR parties managed to attract voters who hold these modern values. In contrast with previous research, we do not position these voters with 'modern values' as necessary opponents of nativist voters. European Social Survey data linked to 29 elections demonstrate that the likelihood to vote for PRR parties is somewhat lower among lesbian and gay rights people, but not for those who have strong anti-migration attitudes. However, this effect differs across countries and in some cases, the 'sexually modern nativists' have the highest PRR voting likelihoods. This is not directly related to the parties' position on modern family values, but to the party system and alternative right-wing parties present.

## Introduction

The classic position of populist radical right (PRR) parties has been to defend the traditional family as the location where national identity was, and should be, reproduced. More recently, however, some of Europe's new PRR politicians have taken a different position; Pim Fortuyn[1] (Dudink 2016) and Geert Wilders (Akkerman 2015; De Lange and Mügge 2015), for example, project an image of tolerance towards gays and lesbians, arguing that such tolerance is part and parcel of the Western democratic tradition (Andersen 2013). From this point of view, these politicians argue, that it is imperative that tolerance towards LGBT people (lesbians, gays, bisexuals and the transgendered) should be protected from the perceived Islamic threat. This tension between Islam and 'secular modernity and tolerance' (Andersen 2013, 109) draws attention to discourses surrounding sexual identities and the framing of the PRR parties' anti-migration message. But the question is: does such a discourse resonate with voters? According to some unscientific Internet polls, Wilders' Party for Freedom (PVV) was the most popular among gay voters (see Spierings and Zaslove

2015a). Yet, at the same time, parties such as the Front National have been at the forefront of protests against legalizing same-sex marriage and less strict adoption laws (Akkerman 2015).

This apparent split in the PRR party family raises a series of important questions. For example: to what extent does the electorate mirror the parties' positions? And, do the parties' positions play a role in a voter's decision to vote for PRR parties? One study suggests that, in Northern European countries, the PRR parties might actually disproportionally attract 'pro-gay, but anti-immigrant' voters (Spierings and Zaslove 2015a). However, little to no systematic research exists on either the role of attitudes towards LGBT issues in PRR voting or whether PRR parties disproportionally manage to attract (or repel) voters supporting these attitudes, given the parties' claims of protecting or condemning unconventional or untraditional families and relationships. Combining programmatic voter and conflict theories with frame theory would suggest that the parties' positions affect the relation between attitudes and vote choice.

To date, most empirical studies have highlighted the strong impact of anti migration attitudes on voting PRR (Immerzeel 2015; Ivarsflaten 2008; Lubbers, Gijsberts, and Scheepers 2002; Norris 2005), emphasizing that cultural concerns are more important than economic concerns (Goodwin 2013; Ivarsflaten 2008; Lucassen and Lubbers 2012; Norris 2005; Rydgren 2008). The argument is that in Western Europe citizens perceive migrants as a threat since they are thought to possess different cultural practices and beliefs that would, in rather general terms, undermine national identity and cohesion. Sniderman and Hagendoorn (2007) argue that in most European countries, the largest source for conflict is over sexual norms, since there are few other issues on which migrants and natives in Europe vary so strongly. But, as already noted, European countries differ on the extent to which a progressive sexual norm is tied to the construction of national identity. This is often reflected in the programme of PRR parties, that is, regarding their focus and their framing of the countries national identity. Supply-side studies have shown that it is particularly the ethnicizing of other issues that is typical to PRR politics (Faist 1994; Yılmaz 2012); however, previous voter studies have not shown the relevance of sexual issues. In short, we question the extent to which those who support LGBT freedoms but hold anti-migration attitudes – sexually modern nativist voters – vote for PRR. In the process, we take both the demand and the supply sides into consideration. We focus on how anti-migration and pro-LGBT emancipation attitudes interact and/or reinforce or counteract each other.

This study uses data from over 30,000 respondents nested in 29 elections from 10 countries: Austria, Belgium, Denmark, Finland, France, Italy, the Netherlands, Norway, Sweden, and Switzerland. The voter data come from the six European Social Survey (ESS) rounds, which are coupled with Comparative Manifesto data from the electorally most successful PRR parties in Western Europe: the Austrian Freedom Party (FPÖ), the Flemish Interest (VB), the Danish People's Party (DF), True Finns (PS), the National Front (FN), the Northern League (LN), the List Pim Fortuyn/Party for Freedom (LPF/PVV), the Norwegian Progress Party (FrP), the Sweden Democrats (SD), and Swiss People's Party (SVP) respectively.[2] First, we assess, for the different countries and elections, how large the group of 'sexually modern nativists' is. We then analyse whether this particular group of voters (at the intersection of anti-immigrant and pro-LGBT attitudes) has a disproportionally high likelihood of voting PRR. And lastly, we test the supply-side dependency of the relationship by modelling if and how the position a party takes on the modern family is mirrored by support for PRR parties.

## Theoretical background

### *A demand–supply approach: party position and popular attitudes*

There is a growing consensus regarding the core ideological characteristics of the PRR. Mudde (2007) argues that the PRR combines populism with nativism and authoritarianism. As Mudde (2007) notes, populism is a thin-centred ideology which juxtaposes the 'pure people' with the 'corrupt elite' (Mudde 2007, 23). However, given that populism is a thin-centred ideology, it must attach itself with another ideology. The PRR combines populism with nativism and authoritarianism. Nativism is an ideology that seeks to define membership in the national community by way of belonging to 'the native group'; outsiders are, thus, seen as 'fundamentally threatening to the homogenous nation-state' (Mudde 2007, 19). Authoritarianism refers to the belief that there should be 'a strictly ordered society' and that transgressions of this order should be 'punished severely' (Mudde 2007, 23).

The extant literature on the PRR recognizes that explaining the rise, success, and also failure of PRR parties relies on a combination of both supply and demand (Mudde 2007; Rydgren 2007; Van Kessel 2015). Supply-side factors are often split into internal and external supply side: the former looking at party ideologies, organization, and framing, the latter focusing on the institutional context, such as party systems and/or electoral systems (Mudde 2007; Van Kessel 2015). Demand, on the other hand, focuses on those voter characteristics that may be structural and attitudinal, involving both individual positions and individual attitudes, as well as the larger socio-structural context that affects individual positions and attitudes (Mudde 2007). Thus, looking at both demand and supply, we can see that the success of PRRs is dependent not only on the choices made by voters driven by their personal (group) interests, attitudes, and issues they evaluate as important, but also on the way PRR parties frame political issues (Rydgren 2005). It may therefore be possible that the influence of attitudes towards LGBT issues on voting PRR actually stems from the interaction between supply and demand. To determine whether this is the case, our demand focus will be on the voters' attitudes and our supply focus will be on the parties' positions.

### *Cultural threat: anti-migration and attitudes towards homosexuality*

Regarding the popular demand for PRR parties, previous research has shown again and again that anti-immigration attitudes, often labelled as 'ethnic threat', are the strongest predictor in PRR voting, with political cynicism as a relevant runner-up (e.g. Ivarsflaten 2008; Norris 2005; Rydgren 2008; Van der Brug, Fennema, and Tillie 2000). This finding is commonly explained through realistic conflict theory, which suggests that migrants and natives are in competition over scarce resources (Coser 1956; Rydgren 2007), whereby natives are considered to be the out-group, threatening the material resources of the in-group and a threat to dominant cultural norms (McLaren 2003; Schneider 2008), often referred to as symbolic threat (Stephan and Stephan 2000). Threat ascription as such is, however, not restricted to migrants. Also, LGBT people have been seen as contesting existing sexual moral and norms of the nation. Research on prejudice and group-focused enmity, for instance, found that prejudice towards one group is associated with prejudice towards another (Zick, Pettigrew, and Wagner 2008) and more concretely also unfavourable attitudes towards LGBT people and immigrants have often been found to be (strongly) correlated (Inglehart 1997; Persell, Green, and Gurevich 2001; Whitley and Aegisdottir 2000). The overlap between attitudes towards migrants and LGBT people is even considered to be the central component in the non-economic dimension of the political landscape across politics in the West (Van der Brug and Van Spanje 2009). *Green–Alternative–Libertarian* (GAL) or postmaterialist values (including pro-migration and pro-LBGT attitudes) would be negatively associated with, and are often opposed to, *Traditional–Authoritarian–Nationalist* (TAN) values (Bakker et al. 2015; Inglehart 1997). From this perspective, one would expect that the more pro-LGBT emancipation, the less likely a person is to vote for PRR, and the more anti-migration, the more likely a person is to vote for PRR.

At the same time, focusing on competition over prevailing culture norms of a society and the rights that have been granted based on certain norms (Ivarsflaten 2005; Lucassen and Lubbers 2012), questions this juxtaposition. Regarding sexual norms, Sniderman and Hagendoorn (2007) found that, in the Netherlands, migrants are far more sexually conservative than natives. Perceiving migrants as possessing conflicting sexual norms could then actually be at the heart of anti-immigrant attitudes. Empirically, this is, for instance, reflected in the reinforcing impact of liberal sexual norms and anti-migration attitudes on voting for populist radical right in Norway and Sweden (Spierings and Zaslove 2015a).

This apparent contradiction in the literature might be resolved by realizing that while anti-migrant attitudes and anti-LGBT attitudes are associated, this association does not exclude possible pockets of voters (including LGBT people themselves) that combine pro-LGBT with anti-migration positions. Moreover, when the perceived cultural fault line between the migrant and the heartland cultures is perceived to revolve around the acceptance of homosexuality, then pro-LGBT citizens (and therefore also LGBT natives) can be expected to be led more by their anti-migration stance, because they weigh this more strongly against other issues. That would imply that this 'sexually modern nativist' group is the most likely to vote for PRR. A less strong interpretation would predict that pro-LGBT citizens might be less inclined to vote for PRR, but that this negative inclination is out weighted by perceiving a strong cultural threat among the group of voters who is in favour of LGBT emancipation but strongly anti-migration. In this case, the sexually modern nativists would be on par with other nativists, whereas among less anti-migration voters, pro-LGBT attitudes make more of a difference.

### Shifting party positions on sexuality

So far, we have assumed a rather homogenous understanding of the ethnicization of sexual politics on the political right. However, the perceived cultural conflict over sexual rights, between migrant groups and the so-called native population that Sniderman and Hagendoorn (2007) refer to, might be context dependent. For instance, the aforementioned authors positioned their work in the Netherlands, a country known to be one of the more sexually tolerant countries, but Western countries actually display quite a strong variation in the granting of rights to and political discourses around sexual minorities (Van den Akker, Van der Ploeg, and Scheepers 2013). In their study on voting PRR, Spierings and Zaslove (2015a) only found hints of this mechanism for some of the countries included.

Considering this diversity across Western Europe and as suggested by the demand–supply approach, the pattern described above is expected to be dependent on the political context and parties' positions. A disproportionally strong attraction of sexually modern nativist voters to PRR is most (or only) likely if the PRR party not only aims to diminish or halt migration, but if it has also incorporated pro-LGBT stances, at least in an ethnicized framework, claiming to provide particular protection against the cultural threat to LGBT freedoms.

PRR parties tend to defend the homogenous nation state, including the traditional family, and traditional moral values. However, not all PRR parties have always been explicit regarding their positions on women, as they tend to take the position that it is up to women and families to make their own decisions, implying that the parties support the dominant social order. At the same time, PRR parties clearly oppose affirmative action as put forward by the 'left-wing, feminist political elite' (Akkerman 2015; De Lange and Mügge 2015; Spierings and Zaslove 2015b). Also, when it comes to sexuality and the traditional family, PRR parties have supported traditional positions regarding, for example, same-sex marriage (Akkerman 2015; Spierings and Zaslove 2015b). In other words, support for homosexuality did not fit into the traditional picture of PRRs, but with the growing emphasis on Islam, an important turning point appears to have been reached.

In most cases, PRRs juxtaposed 'natives' with immigrants in rather general terms. But which groups the PRRs have specifically emphasized to be the main opponents of nationals' interests has changed over time (De Lange and Mügge 2015; Zúquete 2008). Whereas in the 1990s most of the PRRs focused on asylum seekers, people from former colonies, or non-Western immigrants in general, since 9/11, the parties have most explicitly focused on Muslims. Researchers have stressed that the cultural dissimilarities between European majorities and Muslims are emphasized more strongly, with Muslim asylum seekers particularly being singled out as outsiders (Lucassen and Lubbers 2012; Sniderman and Hagendoorn 2007). Following this change, more and more PRR parties have become defenders of liberal democracy, framing it as a European tradition of secularism and tolerance vis-à-vis what they view as a backward and perhaps even a medieval Islam (Andersen 2013; Betz and Meret 2009; Zúquete 2008).

While PRR have not often explicitly sought to protect gay and lesbian citizens, the growing emphasis on Islam has created a space for some populist radical right parties to implicitly, if not explicitly, defend the rights of (native) gay and lesbians. This has especially been the case in the Netherlands (Dudink 2016). Other PRR parties have also shifted position and became more ambiguous on LGBT issues. The Swedish Democrats, for example, were never very explicitly in favour of same-sex marriage, but stated that, as Islam forms a threat to sexual minorities, LGBT people should vote for them;[3] and even though the Danish People's Party voted against same-sex marriage, they did defend the rights of gays when a Gay Pride Parade was attacked by Muslims (Andersen 2013, 109).

The question is: considering this diversity in PRR parties' condition and national contexts, can attitudes towards LGBT people be a relevant predictor in voting for PRR parties across Western Europe? Bringing the demand and supply side together suggests that the effect for sexually modern nativists we described earlier should only be expected in countries where these parties have come to emphasize the contrast between 'us, the sexually-modern natives' and 'them, the traditional migrants'. Conversely, as long as these parties promote traditional family and sexual norms, it will be unlikely for voters with anti-migration but pro-LBGT attitudes to vote for the PRR.

## Hypotheses

Based on the existing literature, we can formulate the following two hypotheses.

*H1: The more a voter holds anti-migrant attitudes, the more likely it is they will vote for a PRR party.*

*H2: The more a voter holds pro-LGBT attitudes, the less likely it is they will vote for a PRR party.*

Considering the focus on Islam as a threat to Western liberal-democratic culture, including tolerance towards sexual minorities, we formulate the following new micro-level expectation.

*H3: The positive impact of holding strong anti-migrant attitudes on the likelihood of voting PRR is stronger among voters who hold pro-LGBT attitudes than among voters who hold traditional attitudes towards LGBT issues.*

Finally, in order to include the different positions on the modern family and LGBT emancipation among PRR parties, we add a demand–supply hypothesis.

*H4: The disproportionately positive likelihood of anti-migrant, pro-LGBT attitudes voters to vote for the PRR is stronger if the PRR party takes a less traditional position regarding family formation and LGBT rights.*

## Data and methods

### Survey data and dependent variable

We use all six rounds of the ESS data collection (ESS 2002–12b) and have selected the Western European countries and surveys in which the respondents could choose to vote for a PRR party. This refers to the respondents' self-reported choice of vote in the then most recent national election. We organized the data so that each respondent is nested in the most recent election in their country.[4] This allows us to combine voter- and party-level data, as the Manifesto Project includes party position per election (see below). Three elections were excluded because the number of PRR voters in those elections where too low to make reliable inferences (<25), resulting in the inclusion of 29 elections from 10 countries. For all countries, only the largest PRR party was included, either because there were no data on the second and smaller party in the Manifesto database or because the number of voters was too small. Party choice was recorded through two values: a vote for the PRR (1) or a vote for another party (0). Citizens who did not vote were not included.

   Table 1 provides an overview of all elections included by year and by country, also indicating the PRR party in that election. Almost all parties included are unequivocally part of the PRR party family (see Immerzeel 2015; Mudde 2007; Spierings et al. 2015; Van Kessel 2015). We also included the LPF for the 2002 and 2003 Dutch elections. As noted, there is debate over the status of the LPF; but we treat the LPF as functional equivalent to a PRR in the Dutch case (Rydgren and van Holsteyn 2005). Moreover, the parties' strong pro-LGBT rhetoric (De Lange and Mügge 2015; Dudink 2016) makes it a crucial case for our fourth hypothesis in the disaggregated analyses.

**Table 1.** The 29 elections and PRR parties included in the analyses.

| | Austria | Belgium (Flanders) | Denmark | Finland | France | Italy | Netherlands | Norway | Sweden | Switzerland |
|---|---|---|---|---|---|---|---|---|---|---|
| 1999 | | VB | | | | | | | | SVP |
| 2000 | | | | | | | | | | |
| 2001 | | | DF | | | LN | | FrP | | |
| 2002 | FPÖ | | | | FN | | LPF | | | |
| 2003 | | VB | | | | | LPF | | | SVP |
| 2004 | | | | | | | | | | |
| 2005 | | | DF | | | | | FrP | | |
| 2006 | FPÖ | | | | | | PVV | | | |
| 2007 | | VB | DF | PS | FN | | | | | SVP |
| 2008 | | | | | | | | | | |
| 2009 | | | | | | | | FrP | | |
| 2010 | | VB | | | | | PVV | | SD | |
| 2011 | | | DF | PS | | | | | | SVP |
| 2012 | | | | | FN | | PVV | | | |

Note: DF: Danish People's Party; FN: National Front; FPÖ: Austrian Freedom Party; FrP: Progress Party; LN: Northern League; LPF: List Pim Fortuyn; PS: True Finns; PVV: Party for Freedom; SD: Sweden Democrats; SVP: Swiss People's Party; VB: Flemish Bloc/Flemish Interest.

## Models

As the dependent variable is dichotomous and respondents are nested in different elections,[5] we have estimated multilevel logistic regression models, using the generalized linear mixed model function in SPSS. These multilevel models include a random intercept that captures the difference between voters in different elections and higher level explanatory variables can be included without deflating their $p$-values, which is crucial for election-level variables and explaining cross-election heterogeneity. As described elsewhere (Mood 2010), coefficients of logistic regression models cannot be compared across models and interaction terms should also be interpreted with care. For that reason, this study takes multiple approaches. Besides a pooled multilevel model, we also present disaggregate models per election, which provides insight into how effects differ by country by election and which contextual factors might be crucial, as well as help detect outliers (Spierings 2016). In addition, we will present the effects in terms of probabilities based on sample averages.

## Independent voter-level variables

The core micro-level explanatory variables in our hypotheses are anti-migration attitudes and attitudes towards LGBT rights. We measure anti-migration as a scale based on six items that ask people's views on allowing different immigrant groups into a country and the (negative) impact of the presence of immigrants,[6] which all tap into one underlying dimension.[7] These items are recoded to create six scales running from 0 to 1 and averaged. Second, attitudes towards LGBT rights, or more precisely LG rights, are measured by one item included in all ESS rounds: Gay men and lesbians should be free to live life as they wish. This variable is measured on a scale of five from completely disagree to completely agree.

We expect that the influence of strong anti-migration attitudes differs for the most pro-LGBT right people (or vice versa). This can be incorporated in two ways in the models. The first and seemingly most straightforward way is to include the two variables discussed above as well as their interaction term. This, however, cannot account for possible non-linear direct or interaction effects, whereas particularly the latter is the core of our theoretical expectation, as we focus on strong pro-LGBT and anti-migration citizens compared to all the rest. The second option is to create sets of dummies for both variables and add an additional dummy for our group interest similar to an interaction term (Brambor, Clark, and Golder 2006). This solves the issue above, but depends on defining certain cut-off points. For modelling the context-dependency of attitudes' effects on party positions, the second approach might also be slightly easier, as it avoids needing to include and interpret three-way interactions effects. In order to draw reliable conclusions, we have applied both methods and in the table with the pooled models we present both the dummy approach and the linear interaction models. For the other tables, the appendici provide the additional models. They show very similar results.

For attitudes towards lesbian and gay people, a dummy was created for each of the five scores. On anti-migration, five groups were made ranging from 0 to 0.2, 0.2 to 0.4, and so on. The last two groups are considered, respectively, to be respondents holding moderately strong and extremely strong anti-immigrant attitudes. As the descriptive analyses will show below, it is exactly these groups on which PRR electorates voters differ. The additional dummy for sexually modern nativists is therefore coded '1' for everyone who is strongly anti-migration, and most lesbian and gay rights. As will be shown below, roughly 6.5% of all respondents score 1 on this dummy.[8] If our contentions hold, we should find a positive coefficient for the sexually modern nativist group.

In addition to the core variables, a set of common control variables is included (see Immerzeel 2015; Ivarsflaten 2008; Lubbers, Gijsberts, and Scheepers 2002; Rydgren 2008; Spierings and Zaslove 2015a). We included a set of dummies as a detailed classification of people's occupational position, distinguishing between the self-employed, professionally employed, clerically employed, service-sector employed, blue-collar employed, agricultural occupations, military, unemployed, other non-employed, and employed but unknown. 'Authority or law & order' attitudes were measured by a scale (from 0 to 1) based on three items. Populist or anti-politics attitudes could be included as an index on political trust (from 0 to 1) based on the two items measuring the trust people have in parties and politicians (cf. Akkerman, Mudde, and Zaslove 2014; Schumacher and Rooduijn 2013; Spierings and Zaslove forthcoming). In addition to these core variables in the literature on voting PRR, we added an index that measured political engagement (from 0 to 1) and several demographic characteristics: education (years of schooling), age (years), sex (1 = female), religious attendance (7-point scale from 'never' to 'every day'), and religious commitment (11-point scale from not at all to very religious) (cf. Immerzeel, Jaspers, and Lubbers 2013).

### Election-level variables

To measure the positions of the PRR parties, we use the Manifesto data (Volkens et al. 2014). This is the only database covering all parties and countries.[9] The Manifesto data include items on family morality issues, which echoes issues regarding gay and lesbian rights, family issues, and the idea that individuals should be able to have the freedom to live their lives as they choose. Evidently, it would be better to have concrete data on all parties' LGBT emancipation positions, but these are not available in any comparative project. The traditional morality issue seems a reasonable proxy, including statements about the prohibition and suppression of immorality, divorce, and abortion, and the maintenance of the traditional family versus support for modern family composition.[10]

Based on the percentages of positive and negative sentences regarding morality issues, we have categorized the 29 PRR party platforms in 5 groups, the lowest scores indicating more traditional views on family life. The parties with only negative sentences form the lowest two groups: the 5 party platforms which devote most relative attention to the issue were coded '0'; the 12 others '1'. The platforms that included both positive and negative positions but had an overall negative score were given a '2'. The five platforms which did not pay explicit attention to the issue were coded '3', as they have not made the traditional family part of their manifesto, indicating that it is not an important issue for the party. The last and only party with more positive than negative sentences was given the highest score of '4'. Not surprisingly, this was the Dutch LPF in 2003; the party was named after its openly gay leader: Pim Fortuyn (see Dudink 2016).


## Analyses

### *The prevalence of 'sexually modern nativism'*

Before turning to the explanatory analyses, let us first establish the extent to which strong support for lesbians and gays living their lives freely is combined with strong anti-migration attitudes, 'sexually modern nativism'. Figures 1 and 2 illustrate that among PRR voters, people with (moderately and extremely) strong anti-migration attitudes are far more prevalent (Figure 1). Not surprisingly, those who possess particularly strong positive attitudes towards LGBTs are less common (Figure 2). These differences are in line with the generally accepted dimensionality of politics in which these two points of view are considered part of opposite poles, GAL (Green–Alternative–Libertarian) versus TAN (Traditional–Authoritarian–Nationalist). Voters close to the latter are expected to be PRR voters (see also Table 2 below). It is worth mentioning though that people with explicit anti-immigration attitudes are also in the minority among PRR voters, and so are the PRR voters expressing anti-LGBT attitudes.

Shifting our attention to the voters who deviate from the overall pattern and focusing more on the diversity among the population instead of the overall averages, we find that sexually modern nativists, who combine positions on both ends of the GAL–TAN scale, are no extreme rarity: in total, 6.4% of our sample takes a strong anti-migration position while also very strongly supporting freedom for lesbians and gays. Table 2 shows that the overall number of sexually modern nativists varies from 2% in Sweden and Switzerland to well over 10% in France, with Flanders and the Netherlands also touching the 10% mark. While the percentages of sexually modern nativists vary somewhat by year, none of the countries shows a clear increasing or decreasing trend. The differences mainly stress differences between countries. More generally, it is up for debate whether one considers the average of 6.4% a substantially significant group. In terms of number, we are talking about thousands of voters. For instance, even in Sweden, the 2.1% represents about one hundred thirty thousand voters; and in the Netherlands, the 8.4% in 2002 translates

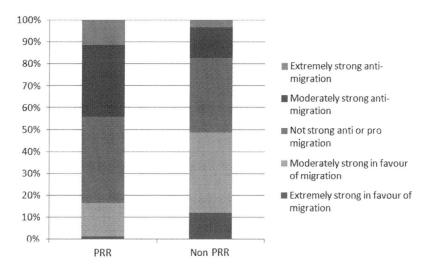

**Figure 1.** Voting for PRR parties and anti-migration attitudes.

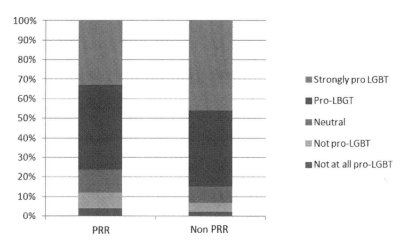

**Figure 2.** Voting for PRR parties and pro-LGBT attitudes.

to about eight hundred thousand voters. In other words, the percentages are relatively small, but in terms of potential votes, this group is sizable in multiparty systems. Based on our models, we will provide some more calculation of what these figures mean in terms of votes and seats.

A comparison of the prevalence of sexually modern nativist voters and the party manifesto classifications does not show a substantially or statistically significant relationship. For instance, among the voters in France, we find the largest share of sexually modern nativists. This is the case even though the French National Front on average scores a 1 on modern morality, putting it in the bottom three, together with the Northern League (IT) and Flemish Interest (BE). In general, it should, however, be remembered that the Manifesto Project's indicators for family morality issues measure a broader spectrum of issues than the parties' position on LGBT people.

**Table 2.** Percentage of voters with 'sexually modern nativist' attitudes per election.

|  | Austria | Belgium (Flanders) | Denmark | Finland | France | Italy | Netherlands | Norway | Sweden | Switzerland |
|---|---|---|---|---|---|---|---|---|---|---|
| 1999 |  | 6% |  |  |  |  |  |  |  | 2% |
| 2001 |  |  | 8% |  |  | 4% |  | 3% |  |  |
| 2002 | 7% |  |  |  | 11% |  | 8% |  |  |  |
| 2003 |  | 9% |  |  |  |  | 10% |  |  | 2% |
| 2005 |  |  | 6% |  |  |  |  | 3% |  |  |
| 2006 | 7% |  |  |  |  |  | 9% |  |  |  |
| 2007 |  | 6% | 6% | 3% | 13% |  |  |  |  | 3% |
| 2009 |  |  |  |  |  |  |  | 3% |  |  |
| 2010 |  | 10% |  |  |  |  | 10% |  | 2% |  |
| 2011 |  |  | 8% | 3% |  |  |  |  |  | 2% |
| 2012 |  |  |  |  | 11% |  | 8% |  |  |  |

Note: Weighted using the by the ESS provided design and stratification weight.

### The impact of sexually modern nativism on voting PRR

Table 3 presents the pooled models in which voting for PRR is explained. Model 1 includes anti-migrant attitudes and support for lesbians and gays living their lives freely, as well as the control variables, which behave as expected, validating the overall models. Our core variables show that the first and strongest indicators for voting PRR are the anti-migration attitudes. The influence of anti-migration attitudes is ordinal as the likelihood to vote for the PRR rises with the strength of the anti-migration attitudes, but the effect is not linear and, in terms of logged odds, with smaller differences between the strongly anti-migration voters. For the attitudes towards gay and lesbian people, a negative ordinal (but not linear) effect is found as well. The coefficient for the most anti-LGBT voters does not completely fit this, but this might indicate that the most anti-LGBT voters are a small group of highly traditional voters consistently voting (orthodox) Christian. Overall, the models in Table 3 as well as the additional analyses (see Appendix 1) support the first two hypotheses.

Part of the explanation of this effect being rather weak might also be that some voters with strong pro-gay rights attitudes strongly oppose the PRR, whereas others support PRR parties disproportionally as we hypothesized. Model 3 sheds more light on this. The dummy indicating those who combine strong anti-migration attitudes with pro-LGBT attitudes shows a positive coefficient and is statistically significant. Moreover, after including this dummy, the impact of pro-LGBT attitudes becomes somewhat weaker. These results are in line with Hypothesis 3, but the size of the effect is more difficult to assess given that these are logged odds coefficients. In Figure 3, the predicted probabilities of voting PRR are given, based on the coefficients in Model 2 and sample averages, for the most and least pro-LGBT voters per position on migration. This figure helps us to further interpret the results as it shows that the likelihood of voting PRR is indeed lower among those who are pro-LGBT emancipation. Actually, in terms of probabilities, the gap between those who are pro- and anti-LGBT emancipation widens when the anti-migration attitudes become stronger. However, and that is crucial for this study, this gap decreases again among the strong anti-migration voters (scores 4 and 5). For instance, among people without a strong or a neutral opinion on migration, the gap in likelihood to vote for PRR between pro- and anti-LGBT emancipation voters is 2.6 percentage points, while among the moderately strong anti-migration voters, it is only 1.0 percentage point. Or phrased differently, being rather neutral versus being a moderately strong anti-migration

**Table 3.** Multilevel models explaining voting for a populist radical right party in 29 elections across 10 European countries.

| | Model A1 Interval variables base model | | Model A2 Interval variables interaction model | | Model B1 Dummy variables base model | | Model B2 Dummy variables interaction model | |
|---|---|---|---|---|---|---|---|---|
| | Logged odds | SE | Logged odds | SE | Logged odds | SE | Logged odds | SE |
| *Core micro-level variables* | | | | | | | | |
| Anti-migration attitudes | 4.53*** | 0.12 | 3.06*** | 0.31 | | | | |
| 1: not against migration (ref) | | | | | ref | | ref | |
| 2 | | | | | 1.37*** | 0.15 | 1.35*** | 0.15 |
| 3 | | | | | 2.39*** | 0.15 | 2.36*** | 0.15 |
| 4 | | | | | 3.09*** | 0.15 | 3.00*** | 0.16 |
| 5: extremely anti-migration | | | | | 3.55*** | 0.16 | 3.45*** | 0.17 |
| Pro-LGBT rights | −0.08*** | 0.02 | −0.37*** | 0.06 | | | | |
| 1: strongly against | | | | | −0.01 | 0.12 | 0.01 | 0.95 |
| 2 | | | | | 0.22* | 0.09 | 0.22** | 0.09 |
| 3 (ref) | | | | | ref | | ref | |
| 4 | | | | | −0.08 | 0.06 | −0.09 | 0.06 |
| 5: strongly in favour | | | | | −0.19** | 0.07 | −0.28** | 0.07 |
| Interaction: anti-migration × pro-LGBT att. | | | 0.48*** | 0.09 | | | | |
| Dummy: Sexually modern nativist; ref = no | | | | | | | 0.21** | 0.08 |
| *Micro-level controls* | | | | | | | | |
| Occupation; ref = employed: blue-collar | | | | | | | | |
| Self-employed | −0.32*** | 0.08 | −0.32*** | 0.08 | −0.31*** | 0.08 | −0.31*** | 0.08 |
| Employed: professional | −0.75*** | 0.07 | −0.74*** | 0.07 | −0.75*** | 0.07 | −0.75*** | 0.07 |
| Employed: clerical | −0.39*** | 0.10 | −0.39*** | 0.10 | −0.41*** | 0.10 | −0.41*** | 0.10 |
| Employed: service-sector | −0.19* | 0.09 | −0.18* | 0.09 | −0.20* | 0.09 | −0.19* | 0.09 |
| Agricultural occupation | −0.23 | 0.30 | −0.23 | 0.30 | −0.17 | 0.30 | −0.17 | 0.30 |
| Military occupation | 0.05 | 0.40 | 0.39 | 0.41 | 0.06 | 0.40 | 0.05 | 0.40 |
| Unemployed | −0.05 | 0.11 | −0.05 | 0.11 | −0.03 | 0.11 | −0.03 | 0.11 |
| Non-employed | −0.36*** | 0.06 | −0.36*** | 0.06 | −0.36*** | 0.06 | −0.36*** | 0.06 |
| Unknown | −0.30 | 0.17 | −0.29 | 0.17 | −0.25 | 0.17 | −0.25 | 0.17 |
| Law & Order scale (0–1) | 0.51*** | 0.11 | 0.50*** | 0.11 | 0.55*** | 0.11 | 0.55*** | 0.11 |
| Political trust scale (0–1) | −0.13*** | 0.01 | −0.13*** | 0.01 | −0.14*** | 0.01 | −0.14*** | 0.01 |
| Political engagement scale (0–1) | −0.04 | 0.02 | −0.04 | 0.02 | −0.03 | 0.03 | −0.03 | 0.03 |
| Education: years of schooling | −0.05*** | 0.01 | −0.05*** | 0.01 | −0.05*** | 0.01 | −0.05*** | 0.01 |
| Age in years | −0.01*** | 0.00 | −0.01*** | 0.00 | −0.01*** | 0.00 | −0.01*** | 0.00 |
| Sex: female (ref = male) | −0.32*** | 0.04 | −0.32*** | 0.04 | −0.30*** | 0.04 | −0.30*** | 0.04 |
| Religious attendance (0–6) | −0.15*** | 0.02 | −0.16*** | 0.02 | −0.16*** | 0.02 | −0.16*** | 0.02 |
| Religious commitment (0–10) | −0.01 | 0.01 | −0.01 | 0.01 | −0.01 | 0.01 | −0.01 | 0.01 |
| Intercept | −1.92*** | 0.27 | −1.00*** | 0.32 | −1.95*** | 0.29 | −1.89*** | 0.31 |
| *Model statistics* | | | | | | | | |
| BIC | 232,608.528 | | 233,931.478 | | 235,011.510 | | 235,252.115 | |
| N | $N_{election}$=29; $N_{individual}$=39,271 | | $N_{election}$=29; $N_{individual}$=39,271 | | $N_{election}$=29; $N_{individual}$=39,271 | | $N_{election}$=29; $N_{individual}$=39,271 | |

Note: All models are two-level models with random intercepts at the election level.
Source: ESS round 1 to 6.
*$p < .05$.
**$p < .01$.
***$p < .001$.

increases one's likelihood of voting PRR by 8.3 percentage points among the most anti-LGBT voters, but 9.8 percentages points among the most pro-LGBT voters. At the same time, the figure shows that we cannot conclude that sexually liberal nativist are the most prone to vote for PRR. However, among the strong anti-migration voters, attitudes towards LGBT people are a weaker predictor of voting PRR. The additional analyses (see

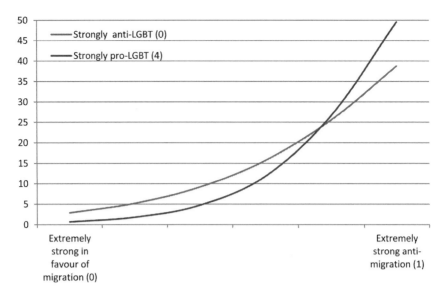

**Figure 3.** Predicted probabilities of voting for PRR parties. Note: estimations based on Model A2 in Table 3 and sample averages.

Appendix 1) confirm our third hypothesis, but it should be noted that the effect is small in terms of voting probabilities. Part of the story might be that there is a strong effect in some elections or countries, but no effect in others, which is the next step in our analysis.

### The context dependency of sexually modern nativism's impact

The analysis presented in Model 2 of Table 3 has been rerun per election (country-year) to see to what extent the effect varies. Since some of the more extreme subgroups with anti-migration and anti-LGBT attitudes become rather small after splitting the sample in 29 election-specific samples, we combined scores 1 to 3 for each variable into one group and took that as a reference in the dummy-based models. The 'sexually modern nativist' variables can be interpreted in the same way as above: a positive and statistically significant relationship indicates a disproportional tendency to vote for the PRR among sexually modern nativists compared to non-nativist progressive voters or nativist traditional voters. Table 4 shows the direction and significance of the interaction coefficients for each and every one of these 29 elections. Evidently, for precise interpretation, the main coefficients are crucial and we will include those below when focusing on the contexts in which an impact of sexually liberal nativism was found. For now, it suffices to say that in each election, there was a general positive main effect of anti-migration attitudes, whereas the effect of attitudes towards lesbian and gay people was less robust across elections.

Above all, Table 4 shows that the effects found above are not universal, but that the voting behaviour of sexually modern nativists is context dependent. In 9 of 29 elections, we find a positive statistically significant or marginally significant effect and all are positive and more substantive than the average effect found in Table 3.[11] No statistically significant relationships pointing in the other direction were found. Moreover, in four countries, for all or multiple elections, an effect was found: Austria, Norway, Sweden, and Switzerland.

**Table 4.** The additional logged odds on voting PRR for sexually modern nativists in the 29 elections.

| | Austria | Belgium (Flanders) | Denmark | Finland | France | Italy | Netherlands | Norway | Sweden | Switzerland |
|---|---|---|---|---|---|---|---|---|---|---|
| 1999 | | ++ | | | | | | | | ±± |
| 2000 | | | | | | | | | | |
| 2001 | | | − | | + | | | ±± | | |
| 2002 | ±± | | | | − | | − | | | |
| 2003 | | + | | | | | − | | | ± |
| 2004 | | | | | | | | | | |
| 2005 | | | + | | | | | − | | |
| 2006 | ++ | | | | | | − | | | |
| 2007 | | + | − | + | + | | | | | ±± |
| 2008 | | | | | | | | | | |
| 2009 | | | | | | | | ± | | |
| 2010 | − | | | | | | + | | ±± | |
| 2011 | | | ± | − | | | | | | − |
| 2012 | | | | | + | | − | | | |

Note: Only coefficient for interaction dummy; models are similar to pooled ones; not multilevel though. Underlined coefficients are statistically significant ($p < .10$) in the interval-based models; coefficients **in bold** are statistically significant in the dummy-based models;± indicates the direction of the interaction, whereby a + is the expected direction; ++ and − indicate the coefficient being larger than (−) 1.

To assess these effects further, we have plotted the predicted probabilities for the four countries in which a clear effect of sexually modern nativist was found (see Appendix 2 for the underlying models). For each of the countries, it holds that under the condition that voters are in favour of migration, the probability to vote for the PRR is larger among voters with strong anti-LGBT attitude than among voters with strong pro-LGBT attitudes. However, the figures show that this alters when voters have stronger anti-migration attitudes. Under the condition that voters have strong anti-migration attitudes, in Norway, Sweden, and Switzerland, people with *pro-LGBT* attitudes have a *higher* probability of voting PRR than people with anti-LGBT attitudes, whereas in Austria, the probabilities have then become the same. To give an indication of the effect sizes, we calculated the impact in terms of votes for the Swedish 2010 Riksdag elections. If we take out 'bonus' of the sexually modern nativist group, this translates roughly to the loss of a full seat in parliament for SD (Figure 4).

These results raise the question *why* this effect is found in some countries and not in others. This study is based on the assumption that both the demand and supply sides of PRR politics should be brought together in order to systematically assess and explain the dynamics at play. Based on both the voter (demand) and party (supply) literatures, we formulated the expectation that sexually modern nativist voters are likely to vote disproportionally PRR if the – by definition anti-migration – PRR party took a relatively more modern position on LGBT rights and freedoms – which is likely to be framed as part of the parties' anti-Islam agenda. To test this claim, we added to the multilevel models (Table 3; Models 2) the election-level variable that measures the family morality position of the parties and the interaction between this variable and the dummies for sexually modern nativist attitudes. This did not provide a substantially or a statistically significant interaction. Moreover, following Mood's (2010) discussion in interpreting interactions in logistic regression models, we also calculated whether there is a difference between the Manifesto platform scores for the cases for which we did not find a relationship in comparison with the ones for which we did (i.e. a statistically significant coefficient as reported in Table 4). There is no statistically significant difference between these groups either.[12] Our basic

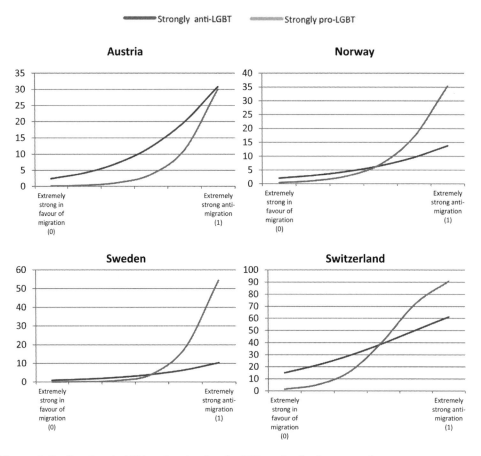

**Figure 4.** Predicted probabilities of voting for the PRR parties for four countries.

expectation formulated in Hypothesis 4 is refuted.[13] In the conclusion, we will reflect on this in greater detail.

## Conclusion

In a number of Western and Northern European countries, PRR parties have begun to emphasize the protection of LGBT people, rights, and freedoms against traditional Muslims, allegedly aiming to Islamize the West. In their view, Europe's progressive, modern culture would be endangered by such traditional views regarding the emancipation of women and LGBT people. This raises the question as to what extent voters with anti-immigrant but pro-LGBT attitudes (what we called 'sexually modern nativists') vote for PRR parties. To account for both demand- and supply-side explanations of voting behaviour, we alluded to both the voters' attitudes and the parties' position on LGBT issues. We found that sexually modern nativists are more likely to vote for PRRs than sexually traditional nativists, supporting our key hypothesis. The group of sexually modern nativists turned out to be a very clear minority in all countries under study, but their numbers can translate into multiple seats in parliament when it comes to elections. Moreover, this finding is of interest by itself: Why do some of the sexually modern voters hold nativist attitudes and others not? This is an interesting question for further research.

We found quite some variance between the countries under study on the extent to which sexually modern nativists were found to be more likely to vote for PRRs. In particular, in Norway, Sweden, and Switzerland, an effect was found that sexually modern nativist were more likely to vote for the PRR, and in Austria, the sexually modern nativist voters catch up with the rest. The variance between countries could not be explained by the differences between PRRs in their position on traditional family values, refuting one of our key hypotheses. Arguably, the strongest case of anti-Islam, pro-gay rights rhetoric was found in the Netherlands, with both Fortuyn (2002) and Wilders (2006, 2010, and 2012) (Akkerman 2015; De Lange and Mügge 2015; Dudink 2016),[14] but no effect has been found that suggested that sexually modern nativists were more likely to vote for these parties in the Netherlands (see also Spierings and Zaslove 2015a).[15]

A more fitting explanation for the country difference comes from broadening our supply-side scope by placing the PRR party in the larger party system, and particularly placing it within the context of the message of mainstream parties (i.e. non-PRR parties that are sceptical towards immigration). It has been argued that the presence of PRR parties in the party system has led mainstream right-wing parties to adopt stronger anti-migration positions (e.g. De Lange 2012). In some countries, these other parties are liberal-conservative parties, whereas in others, they are conservative or Christian-democratic parties. If the main anti-migration alternatives were traditional, we would expect a sexually modern nativist to vote for PRR parties, because this alternative does not match the voter's views on LGBT rights. If, on the other hand, the second-most anti-migration party is a liberal party that supports LGBT rights, sexually modern nativist voters might decide to vote for that party instead of the PRR party.

At first sight, this idea does explain that no relationship is found in Denmark, Belgium, and the Netherlands, where Venstre (DK), Open VLD (BE), and VVD (NL) are credible alternatives as conservative-liberal parties who are generally supportive of LGBT rights and a liberal family morality. Also, but in a somewhat less straightforward way, an alternative is available in Finland, France, and Italy: the major right-wing parties that are at least more liberal on LGBT issues than the PRR or include clear liberal factions.[16] In the six countries in which no clear effect was found, sexually modern nativists have a viable alternative when they are in the voting booth. This focus on the alternative anti-migration parties also seems to fit the cases in which a disproportional likelihood to vote for the PRR was found. Most straightforwardly, in Austria and Switzerland, the main alternative right-wing anti-migration parties are the (traditional) Christian-democratic ÖVP (AU) and CVP (SW).[17] In Sweden, the main right-wing alternative, the Moderate Party, is relatively pro-LGBT rights, but not strongly anti-migration in the period we studied. As the Moderate Party did make a right turn on this issue recently, it is an interesting test case for our suggested explanation here.[18] Similarly, the Norwegian case deserves more in-depth attention as the second-most anti-migration party – the Norwegian Conservative Party – is rather traditional, for instance, voting against same-sex marriage, but a few MPs deviated from the party line.[19]

The dynamics we proposed here should be studied in greater detail before strong claims can be made. The Islamizing or ethnicizing of progressive values has only relatively recently become a populist radical right party strategy to attract voters and it seems that the traditional parties that claimed to serve the interests of sexual minority groups have no clear answer to this shift among the PRR. Interviews with sexually modern nativist in the different countries could possibly provide more insight into the motivations to vote for or not to do so for the PRRs. Only for the Netherlands, the Manifesto data have explicitly revealed pro-gay, but nativist stances. Many of the other parties have been politically ambiguous, for example, voting against same-sex marriage, but referring to protecting gays when discussing the perceived threat of the Islamization of Europe. Therefore, further comparative research will require better indicators on PRR parties as well as their main contenders regarding positions on LGBT emancipation.

## Notes

1. We include the Lijst Pim Fortuyn as a PRR party, although it is a borderline case. Mudde (2007, 59) considers it to be a neo-liberal populist party, while others consider it to be a PRR party (De Lange and Art 2011). Following Rydgren and van Holsteyn (2005), we consider the LPF to be a functional equivalent of the PRR for the core question in this study.
2. We focus on PRR parties in Western Europe for two reasons. First, classifying parties in Central and Eastern Europe is tricky, as the boundary between the PRR and other types of populism is not always clear. Second, there are significant contextual differences between Western Europe and Central and Eastern Europe, both regarding supply and demand.
3. See T. Brandel "SD siktar in sig på hbt-röster". *Svenska Dageblat.* 28 July 2010.
4. If two survey rounds were held between elections respondents in both surveys are grouped in one higher level unit (e.g. the 2002 Austrian elections). If data were collected overlapping an election, we split the sample by the day of interview and linked respondents to different elections (e.g. ESS1 in Belgium).
5. Technically speaking, these elections are also embedded in countries. Approximately 15% of the variation is found at the country level (24% at the election level, and the rest at the individual level). However, our random intercepts capture these differences and including an additional level does not influence the results. We therefore present the simplest models in the text. In Appendix 1, the results from a three-level model and a country-fixed-effects model are given.
6. To what extent do you think [country respondent] should allow people from the poorer countries outside Europe to come and live here? (Allow many to come and live here; Allow some; Allow a few; Allow none.); How about people of a different race or ethnic group from most [country] people?; How about people from the poorer countries outside Europe?; Could you say it is generally bad or good for [country]'s economy that people come to live here from other countries? (Bad 0 through Good 10); Would you say that [country]'s cultural life is generally undermined or enriched by people coming to live here from other countries? (Undermined 0 through Enriched 10); Is [country] made a worse or a better place to live by people coming to live here from other countries? (Worse 0 through Better 10) (ESS 2002–12a).
7. Exploratory Factor Analysis: Eigen value 3.777; Bartlett's test $p<.001$; KMO 0.843; lowest loading 0.689; Cronbach's alpha 0.881.
8. Models were rerun with two 'interaction dummies' separating the moderately and extremely strong anti-migration respondents. Both showed highly similar interaction coefficients, but the latter group was only 1.5% and therefore did not reach statistical significance at conventional levels.
9. The Chapel Hill expert data are not coded per election and do not include Norway and Switzerland.
10. Other codes also include items relating to sexuality but tend to conflate it with other minorities, which is problematic for this study. For example, the manifesto items on equality measure positive attitudes towards equality policies, conflating sexual equality, class equality, and the position of underprivileged groups. Similarly, the item on 'underprivileged minority groups' can include statements supporting gay and lesbian people as well as ethnic minorities.

11. Given the small group size, we include marginally significant coefficients for now. Mostly, these were found for countries that showed a conventionally statistical significant relationship for another election as well.
12. A Mann–Whitney U test, for instance, shows a *p* value of .381; the two averages being 1.55 and 1.00, on the scale from 0 to 4.
13. Results can be obtained from the authors.
14. In the case of Wilders, it is actually more than claims making: the party supported the abolishment of the 'defiant clerks' (clerks who did not want to marry same-sex couples despite the law) in the parliamentary vote, even though this could have estranged the orthodox Christian party which government often needed to reach a majority (the PVV supported the minority government) in the Senate.
15. In terms of votes and political impact, this means that if the PVV would manage to increase the voting probability among the sexually liberal nativists of about 7% with only 10 percentage points, it gets an additional seat (they currently hold 12).
16. The Finnish National Coalition Party is a viable liberal and anti-migration party. For instance, it supports same-sex marriage (Bucken-Knapp et al. 2014; E. Tessieri, "National Coalition Party and Perussuomalaiset lead anti-immigration drive in Finland" *Migrant Tales,* 12 September 2014). In France and Italy, the major right-wing parties (Les Républicains [former UMP] and Forza Italia) are broad coalitions that include liberals and liberal-conservatives. For instance, Berlusconi has been said to be steering the party back towards its liberal roots (See "Pd-azzurri: asse sui diritti (senza Ncd)" *Corriere della Sera,* 4 January 2014; G. Dinmore "Berlusconi seeks return to liberal roots" *Financial Times,* 22 July 2012).
17. The liberal FDP is far less anti-migrant; the CVP is the foremost alternative to the SVP.
18. See M. Crow, "Sweden's Moderate Party Flipflop On Immigration" *The European Guardian – The Home of Europe's New Right*, 8 May 2015. The smaller strongest anti-migration party in Sweden, the Christian-democrats, is more traditional and thus not a real alternative either.
19. See S. Picheta "Norway new gay marriage law also grants new parental right" *Pinknews,* 12 June 2008.

## Disclosure Statement

No potential conflict of interest was reported by the authors.

## References

Akkerman, T. 2015. "Gender and the Radical Right in Western Europe: A Comparative Analysis of Policy Agendas." *Patterns of Prejudice* 49 (1–2): 37–60.
Akkerman, A., C. Mudde, and A. Zaslove. 2014. "How Populist are the People? Measuring Populist Attitudes in Voters." *Comparative Political Studies* 47 (9): 1324–1353.
Andersen, J. G. 2013. "Nationalism. New Right, and New Cleavages in Danish Politics: Foreign and Security Policy of the Danish People's Party." In *Europe for the Europeans: The Foreign and Security Policy of the Populist Radical Right*, edited by C.S. Liang, 103–123. Aldershot: Ashgate Publishing, Ltd.
Bakker, R., C. De Vries, E. Edwards, L. Hooghe, S. Jolly, G. Marks, J. Polk, J. Rovny, M. Steenbergen, and M. A. Vachudova. 2015. "Measuring Party Positions in Europe The Chapel Hill Expert Survey Trend File, 1999–2010." *Party Politics* 21 (1): 143–152.
Betz, H. G., and S. Meret. 2009. "Revisiting Lepanto: The Political Mobilization Against Islam in Contemporary Western Europe." *Patterns of Prejudice* 43 (3–4): 313–334.
Brambor, T., W. R. Clark, and M. Golder. 2006. "Understanding Interaction Models: Improving Empirical Analyses." *Political Analysis* 14 (1): 63–82.
Bucken-Knapp, G., J. Hinnfors, A. Spehar, and P. Levin. 2014. "No Nordic Model: Understanding Differences in the Labour Migration Policy Preferences of Mainstream Finnish and Swedish Political Parties." *Comparative European Politics* 12 (6): 584–602.
Coser, L. 1956. *The Functions of Social Conflict*. Glencoe: The Free Press.
De Lange, S. L. 2012. "New Alliances: Why Mainstream Parties Govern with Radical Right-Wing Populist Parties." *Political Studies* 60 (4): 899–918.
De Lange, S. L., and D. Art. 2011. "Fortuyn Versus Wilders: An Agency-Based Approach to Radical Right Party Building." *West European Politics* 34 (6): 1229–1249.
De Lange, S. L., and L. M. Mügge. 2015. "Gender and Right-Wing Populism in the Low Countries: Ideological Variations Across Parties and Time." *Patterns of Prejudice* 49 (1-2): 61–80.
Dudink, S. 2016. A Queer Nodal Point. Homosexuality in Dutch Debates on Islam and Multiculturalism. *Sexualities*, online first.
ESS Rounds 1-6: European Social Survey. 2002–12a. Documentation Report. Bergen, European Social Survey Data Archive, NSD – Norwegian Centre for Research Data for ESS ERIC.
ESS Rounds 1-6: European Social Survey Data. 2002–12b. Norwegian Social Science Data Services, Norway – Data Archive and distributor of ESS data.
Faist, T. 1994. "Immigration, Integration and the Ethnicization of Politics." *European Journal of Political Research* 25 (4): 439–459.
Goodwin, M. 2013. *The Roots of Extremism: The English Defence League and the Counter-Jihad Challenge*. London, UK: Chatham House.
Immerzeel, T. 2015. *Voting for a Change: The Democratic Lure of Populist Radical Right Parties in Voting Behavior*. ICS dissertation series, 223. http://dspace.library.uu.nl/handle/1874/308501.
Immerzeel, T., E. Jaspers, and M. Lubbers. 2013. "Religion as Catalyst or Restraint of Radical Right Voting?" *West European Politics* 36 (5): 946–968.
Inglehart, R. 1997. *Modernization and Postmodernization: Cultural, Economic, and Political Change in 43 Societies* (Vol. 19). Princeton, NJ: Princeton University Press.
Ivarsflaten, E. 2005. "Threatened by Diversity: why Restrictive Asylum and Immigration Policies Appeal to Western Europeans." *Journal of Elections, Public Opinion & Parties* 15 (1): 21–45.
Ivarsflaten, E. 2008. "What Unites Populist Radical Rights in Western Europe? Re-Examining Grievance Mobilization Models in Seven Successful Cases." *Comparative Political Studies* 41 (1): 3–23.
Lubbers, M., M. Gijsberts, and P. Scheepers. 2002. "Extreme Right-Wing Voting in Western Europe." *European Journal of Political Research* 41 (3): 345–378.
Lucassen, G., and M. Lubbers. 2012. "Who Fears What? Explaining Far-Right-Wing Preference in Europe by Distinguishing Perceived Cultural and Economic Ethnic Threats." *Comparative Political Studies* 45 (5): 547–574.
McLaren, L. M. 2003. "Anti-immigrant Prejudice in Europe: Contact, Threat Perception, and Preferences for the Exclusion of Migrants." *Social Forces* 81 (3): 909–936.

Mood, C. 2010. "Logistic Regression: Why We Cannot Do What We Think We Can Do, and What We Can Do About It." *European Sociological Review* 26 (1): 67–82.

Mudde, C. 2007. *Populist Radical Right Parties in Europe.* (Vol. 22, No. 8). Cambridge: Cambridge University Press.

Norris, P. 2005. *Radical Right: Voters and Parties in the Electoral Market.* Cambridge, UK: Cambridge University Press.

Persell, C. H., A. Green, and L. Gurevich. 2001, June. "Civil Society, Economic Distress, and Social Tolerance." *Sociological Forum* 16 (2): 203–230.

Rydgren, J. 2005. "Is Extreme Right-Wing Populism Contagious? Explaining the Emergence of a New Party Family." *European Journal of Political Research* 44 (3): 413–437.

Rydgren, J. 2007. "The Sociology of the Radical Right." *Annual Review of Sociology* 33: 241–262.

Rydgren, J. 2008. "Immigration Sceptics, Xenophobes or Racists? Radical Right-Wing Voting in Six West European Countries." *European Journal of Political Research,* 47 (6): 737–765.

Rydgren, J., and J. van Holsteyn. 2005. "Holland and Pim Fortuyn: A Deviant Case or the Beginning of Something New?" In *Movements of Exclusion: Radical Right-Wing Populism in the Western World,* edited by J. Rydgren, 41–63. Hauppauge, NY: Nova Science Publishers.

Schneider, S. L. 2008. "Anti-Immigrant Attitudes in Europe: Outgroup Size and Perceived Ethnic Threat." *European Sociological Review* 24 (1): 53–67.

Schumacher, G., and M. Rooduijn. 2013. "Sympathy for the 'Devil'? Voting for Populists in the 2006 and 2010 Dutch General Elections." *Electoral Studies* 32 (1): 124–133.

Sniderman, P. M., and A. Hagendoorn. 2007. *When Ways of Life Collide: Multiculturalism and its Discontents in the Netherlands.* Princeton: Princeton University Press.

Spierings, N. 2016. "Multilevel Analysis as Tool to Understand the Spatio-Temporality of Gender." *Politics & Gender* 12 (3), online publication, doi:10.1017/S1743923X16000398.

Spierings, N., and A. Zaslove. 2015a. "Gendering the Vote for Populist Radical-Right Parties." *Patterns of Prejudice,* 49 (1-2): 135–162.

Spierings, N., and A. Zaslove. 2015b. "Conclusion: Dividing the Populist Radical Right Between 'Liberal Nativism' and Traditional Conceptions of Gender." *Patterns of Prejudice,* 49 (1-2): 163–173.

Spierings, N., and A. Zaslove. Forthcoming. "Gender, Populist Attitudes, and Voting. Explaining the sex gap in Voting for Populist Radical Right and Populist Radical Left Parties." *West European Politics.*

Spierings, N., A. Zaslove, L. M. Mügge, and S. L. de Lange. 2015. "Gender and Populist Radical-Right Politics: an Introduction." *Patterns of Prejudice* 49 (1–2): 3–15.

Stephan, W. G., and C. W. Stephan. 2000. "An Integrated Threat Theory of Prejudice." In *Reducing prejudice and discrimination,* edited by S. Oskamp, 23–45. Hove, UK: Psychology Press.

Van den Akker, H., R. Van der Ploeg, and P. Scheepers. 2013. "Disapproval of Homosexuality: Comparative Research on Individual and National Determinants of Disapproval of Homosexuality in 20 European Countries." *International Journal of Public Opinion Research* 25 (1): 64–86.

Van der Brug, W., M. Fennema, and J. Tillie. 2000. "Anti-Immigrant Parties in Europe: Ideological or Protest Vote?" *European Journal of Political Research* 37 (1): 77–102.

Van der Brug, W., and J. Van Spanje. 2009. "Immigration, Europe and the 'new' Cultural Dimension." *European Journal of Political Research* 48 (3): 309–334.

Van Kessel, S. 2015. *Populist Parties in Europe: Agents of Discontent?* Houndmills, UK: Palgrave Macmillan.

Volkens, A., P. Lehmann, N. Merz, S. Regel, A. Werner, and H. Schultze. 2014. The Manifesto Data Collection. Manifesto Project (MRG/CMP/MARPOR). Version 2014b. Berlin: Wissenschaftszentrum Berlin für Sozialforschung (WZB).

Whitley, B.E., Jr., and S. Aegisdottir. 2000. "The Gender Belief System, Authoritarianism, Social Dominance Orientation, and Heterosexuals' Attitudes Toward Lesbians and Gay Men." *Sex Roles* 42 (11–12): 947–967.

Yılmaz, F. 2012. "Right-wing Hegemony and Immigration: How the Populist Far-Right Achieved Hegemony Through the Immigration Debate in Europe." *Current sociology* 60 (3): 368–381.

Zick, A., T. F. Pettigrew, and U. Wagner. 2008. "Ethnic Prejudice and Discrimination in Europe." *Journal of Social Issues* 64 (2): 233–251.

Zúquete, J. P. 2008. "The European Extreme-Right and Islam: New Directions?" *Journal of Political Ideologies* 13 (3): 321–344.

## Appendix 1. Alternative models testing sensitivity of results to estimation technique and operationalization.

| | Interval with country as additional level | | Interval with fixed effect for country effects | | Dummies with country as additional level | | Dummies with fixed effect for country effects | |
|---|---|---|---|---|---|---|---|---|
| | Logged odds | SE | Logged odds | SE | Logged odds | SE | Logged odds | SE |
| Anti-migration; ref = 1: not against migration | | | | | | | | |
| 2 | | | | | 1.35*** | 0.15 | 1.35*** | 0.15 |
| 3 | | | | | 2.36*** | 0.15 | 2.36*** | 0.15 |
| 4 | | | | | 3.00*** | 0.15 | 3.00*** | 0.16 |
| 5: extremely anti-migration | | | | | 3.46*** | 0.16 | 3.46*** | 0.17 |
| Anti-migration attitudes – continuous (0–1) | 3.07*** | 0.31 | 3.08*** | 0.31 | | | | |
| Pro-LGBT rights | | | | | | | | |
| 1: strongly against | | | | | 0.01 | 0.12 | 0.01 | 0.12 |
| 2 | | | | | 0.22** | 0.09 | 0.22** | 0.09 |
| 3 (ref) | | | | | | | | |
| 4 | | | | | −0.09 | 0.06 | −0.09 | 0.06 |
| 5: strongly in favour | | | | | −0.28** | 0.07 | −0.28** | 0.07 |
| Pro-LGBT rights – interval (1–5) | −0.37*** | 0.06 | −0.36*** | 0.06 | | | | |
| Sexually modern nativist (ref = no) | | | | | 0.21** | 0.08 | 0.21** | 0.08 |
| Interaction anti-migration × pro-LGBT rights | 0.48*** | 0.09 | 0.47*** | 0.09 | | | | |
| Micro-level controls included | | | | | | | | |

Note: All models are two-level models with random intercepts at the election level, unless mentioned otherwise.
Source: ESS round 1–6.
*$p < .05$.
**$p < .01$.
***$p < .001$.

## Appendix 2. Interaction models per country for which initial interaction effects were found.

| | Austria | | Norway | | Sweden | | Switzerland | |
|---|---|---|---|---|---|---|---|---|
| | Dummy | Interval | Dummy | Interval | Dummy | Interval | Dummy | Interval |
| Anti-migration; ref = 1: not against migration | | | | | | | | |
| 2 | 0.57 | | 1.09*** | | 2.04# | | 1.53*** | |
| 3 | 1.57* | | 1.94*** | | 3.79*** | | 2.52*** | |
| 4 | 2.08** | | 2.48*** | | 4.27*** | | 2.98*** | |
| 5: extremely anti-migration | 3.09*** | | 2.76*** | | 4.99*** | | 4.07*** | |
| Anti-migration attitudes – continuous (0–1) | | 2.91** | | 2.04** | | 2.49 | | 2.19** |
| Pro-LGBT rights; ref = 1: strongly against | | | | | | | | |
| 2 | 0.02 | | 0.28 | | −1.81 | | 0.49# | |
| 3 | −0.39 | | | | | | | |
| | | −0.22 | | −2.23# | | 0.47 | | |
| 4 | −0.80* | | −0.11 | | −1.83# | | 0.47# | |
| 5: strongly in favour | −1.75*** | | −0.07 | | −2.28# | | −0.15 | |
| Pro-LGBT rights – interval (1–5) | | −0.79** | | −0.41** | | −0.86 | | −0.62*** |
| Sexually modern nativist (ref = no) | **1.32** | | **0.29** | | **1.19#** | | **0.61*** | |
| Interaction anti-migration × pro-LGBT rights | | **0.78*** | | **0.71** | | **1.44#** | | **1.08*** |

Note: Only coefficients for interaction dummy are given; control variables are included in the models though (see Table 3).
Source: ESS round 1–6.
\*\*\*$p < .001$.
\*\*$p < .01$.
\*$p < .05$.
\#$p < .10$.

# 'EDL angels stand beside their men … not behind them': the politics of gender and sexuality in an anti-Islam(ist) movement

Hilary Pilkington

**ABSTRACT**
This article revisits the view that women are absent or insignificant across the extreme right spectrum. It draws on ethnographic research with grassroots activists in the English Defence League to explore whether a new generation of populist radical right movements offers a gender politics and practice capable of appealing to women and LGBT constituencies. It critically interrogates claims that the movement has made real shifts in the openness to, and roles played by, women and LGBT activists and asks whether the adoption of gender equality and gay rights rhetoric reflects such change or is an essentially instrumental move. Finally it considers how gender and sexual politics are played out in everyday practice in the movement. It concludes that while openness to women and LGBT supporters and activists is more than the top-down imposition of a strategically useful ideology, attitudes and behaviours among activists remain highly diverse, ambivalent and often conflicted.

## Introduction

Women are significantly underrepresented across the extreme right spectrum, from relatively moderate radical right political parties to the most extreme, violent neo-Nazi groups (Mudde 2014, 10). This article suggests there are compelling reasons to revisit this conclusion and to do so from a 'close-up' perspective. The first is that the rise across Europe of populist radical right (PRR)[1] parties and movements, whose ideologies are not 'a "normal pathology" unconnected to the mainstream' but a 'radicalized version of mainstream ideas' (Mudde 2007, 297), will extend the constituency of support at this end of the political spectrum beyond the characteristic 'twenty five-year-old unemployed man' (Bakić 2009, 201). Indeed, in some countries where the PRR has established itself in party systems, the gender gap may be disappearing (Spierings and Zaslove 2015a, 139–140). Secondly, PRR parties and movements offer a different 'supply' than the classic extreme right. Many have moved away from neo-Nazi roots, symbolism and unashamedly racist positions, which women have largely rejected (Blee and Linden 2012, 105), and some have incorporated gender equality and gay rights platforms into an anti-Islam or anti-multiculturalist ideology that extends their potential appeal to women and LGBT communities

(Akkerman and Hagelund 2007, 199). Thirdly, as such parties become 'mainstreamed', so stigmatisation – a documented barrier to women's participation (Blee and Linden 2012, 105) – decreases and women become increasingly visible including in leadership positions. Moreover, as a new generation of movements embraces digital media, women can engage in online activism that is more anonymous and more compatible with childcare and other home-based responsibilities. Fourthly, as these shifts render movements less closed in nature, so 'close-up' social research becomes more feasible, offering a potentially more nuanced picture than one of women in extreme right movements simply 'standing behind their men'.

This article draws on an ethnographic study of the anti-Islam(ist)[2] English Defence League (EDL) to ask whether the movement embodies a gender politics and practice different, and more appealing to women and LGBT constituencies, than the traditional extreme right. First, it critically interrogates whether there are real shifts in the openness to, and roles played by, women, gay, lesbian, bisexual and transgender people. Secondly, it assesses whether the movement's appeal to a human rights and equality based agenda to underpin its anti-Islam(ist) ideology is purely instrumental by analysing organisational ideologies and individual activists' views on gender roles and LGBT rights. Finally, it considers how gender and sexual politics are played out in practice among grassroots activists and asks whether, despite ideological shifts, the affective[3] dimension of the movement remains heterosexist and masculinist.

## Mapping the field

The field of study on gender and the extreme right is sparsely populated. This reflects the assumption that extreme right ideology – rooted in a broader rejection of human equality and an emphasis on traditional values – renders its parties and movements an inhospitable environment for women and sexual minorities.

The evidence for this is that women have been significantly less likely to support, or become active in, extreme right parties and movements (Kitschelt 2007, 1199). Indeed, this tendency is broadly confirmed for the new family of PRR parties in Europe too. Findings from the European Social Survey in 2010 show 11.6% of men compared to 8.2% of women had voted for PRR parties (Spierings and Zaslove 2015a, 136) while an online study (Facebook survey, $n = 10,667$) of support for PRR parties in 12 European countries found 75% of supporters to be male (Bartlett, Birdwell, and Littler 2011, 18). The literature on women's activism in the extreme right echoes that of voter preference studies in suggesting women's absence or insignificance. What is observed is 'a men's movement' where women, if present at all, are 'the girlfriends or wives of members' performing 'traditional supportive roles' (Ezekiel 2002, 54) or act 'primarily as helpmates' to male activists (Blee and Linden 2012, 107). Where women do take on prominent positions, moreover, this is because they are 'personally related to a prominent male in the same organisation' (Mudde 2014, 10). Recent scholarship, however, warns that right-wing women may not be so much absent as 'overlooked' (Blee and Deutsch 2012, 1) and a number of close up studies provide examples of women participating even in the violent dimensions of activism (Blee and Linden 2012, 110; Pilkington 2014).

The apparent absence of women is explained in the literature to date as a result of the ideological lack of appeal of such movements to women. Extreme right ideologies understand inequalities as 'natural' (de Lange and Mügge 2015, 63), emphasise a return to traditional values (Goodwin 2011, 13) and express profound homophobia (Ezekiel 2002, 55). Detailed analyses of voter preference suggest women are consistently less likely than men to vote for extreme right and PRR parties either for economic reasons or because their nativist[4] and authoritarian ideologies (see footnote 1) repel them. The greater appeal of nativist ideology to men may be determined by the higher frequency of negative outgroup attitudes among men (Dekker and van der Noll 2012, 114) while there is also evidence that negative attitudes towards Islam and Muslims are disproportionately concentrated among men (Field 2012, 159).

The role of ideology and policy on gender and sexuality in encouraging or deterring women and LGBT support for extreme right or PRR parties has become a matter of increasing interest following a shift, since the mid-1990s, towards the inclusion of women's and LGBT rights in party programmes where they are presented as 'core civilisational values of the West' under threat from migrant, especially Muslim, communities (de Lange and Mügge 2015, 62). The premise here is that, while a highly conservative understanding of gender roles and concern with the reproduction of the 'native' population, typical of classic extreme right parties, might alienate women, the framing of anti-Islam ideology as the protection of western traditions of gender equality and LGBT rights might extend the appeal of the European PRR to women and LGBT communities (Spierings and Zaslove 2015a, 142–143).[5] Amidst a wider public and political backlash to 'multiculturalism' across Europe, multicultural policies have been criticised for protecting cultural or religious groups perceived to suppress the rights of women and children (Akkerman and Hagelund 2007, 199). The Norwegian Progress Party and the List Pim Fortuyn (LPF) have used media debate on cultural practices such as honour killings, arranged marriages and genital mutilation to shift discourse on cultural diversity, immigration and citizenship away from multiculturalism and towards social cohesion (Akkerman and Hagelund 2007). These cultural practices are presented within a broader human rights and gender equality framework to portray 'Islamic values' as at odds with core liberal democratic values of democracy, individual autonomy, gender equality and freedom of expression (de Lange and Mügge 2015, 63). However, while such an instrumental adoption of 'pseudo-emancipatory gender policies' (Wodak and KhosraviNik 2013, 12, 28) is a cause for concern, its reach remains limited; the combination of anti-Islamic and pro-LGBT rhetoric is confined to date to PRR parties in northern Europe (Spierings and Zaslove 2015b, 168).

Finally, the existing literature has suggested that the low propensity of women to become active in extreme right movements is determined not only by the lack of appeal of its ideological message, but also by the inhospitable nature of its environment at the affective level. Evidence from a number of qualitative studies suggests extreme right movements forge 'an only-masculine world' (Ezekiel 2002, 57) governed by a complex ethics and aesthetics of homosocial friendship, loyalty, mutual support and intimacy (Pilkington, Omel'chenko, and Garifzianova 2010, 158) as part of an 'implied or explicit restoration of masculinity' (Kimmel 2007, 207). On the basis of their respective studies of extreme right activism in the USA and the Netherlands, Blee and Linden (2012, 103–105) argue that most women never experience the sense of belonging and comradeship that men gain from activism and are frustrated by how they are treated by men in their organisations.

Drawing on an empirical study of the EDL,[6] this article explores the evidence for the three main contentions set out in this brief overview of the current literature, namely:

that women are largely absent or insignificant in support for, or activism in, extreme right movements; that such absence is a result of the ideological lack of appeal of such movements to women; and that the mobilisation of gender equality and LGBT rights as part of a wider anti-Islam agenda might extend their appeal to women and LGBT communities.

## Introducing the English defence league

The EDL is a 'feet on the street' movement founded in 2009 to protest against 'militant Islam' and in support of the British military. It has no formal membership but there are 25–30,000 active supporters (Bartlett and Littler 2011) of whom between 200 and 3000 might attend a particular demonstration. Its mission statements distance the movement from classic far right organisations but its strong anti-Islam(ist) agenda has led it to be characterised as a social movement with a 'new far right' ideology (Jackson 2011a, 7), an 'Islamophobic new social movement' (Copsey 2010, 11) or an 'anti-Muslim protest movement' (Busher 2016, 20). In the media it is widely represented as part of the extreme right and 74% of those surveyed in a national poll by Extremis/YouGov (2012) considered it to be a 'racist organisation'.[7]

The published literature to date on the EDL is limited and attention to gender issues is rare. Copsey's (2010) study, based on secondary sources, captures the movement's origins and early activity (2009–2010). Bartlett and Littler's Facebook survey measures and characterises support for the movement but its sample is compromised by an over-representation of those sections of the population using digital media and by the inability to determine whether respondents were genuine supporters or 'trolls' (Bartlett and Littler 2011, 35). Jackson's (2011a, 2011b) analyses of the EDL focus on the role of social media in resource mobilisation rather than what motivates and sustains the movement and how this is gendered. Garland and Treadwell (2011) do consider the role of masculinity in the movement but draw on a limited empirical base (three interviews and covert observation at EDL demonstrations). The most comprehensive study to date is Busher's (2016) exploration of grassroots activism in the EDL in the London and Essex regions; 4 of his 18 interviewees were women although the gendered experience of activism is not addressed specifically.

Research to date on gender and the EDL suggests it is a classic movement of the extreme right in which women are insignificant. Both quantitative (Bartlett and Littler 2011, 5) and qualitative (Busher 2016, 17) studies suggest that no more than 20% of supporters and activists are women. Its affective environment, moreover, is steeped in male working-class solidarity (Blake 2011, 1) not least because of its close links with the football casual subculture (Copsey 2010, 9). EDL activism has been described thus as a form of 'protest masculinity' in which marginalised white working-class men articulate resentment and anger through the expression of hostility towards an Islamic 'other' (Garland and Treadwell 2011, 626).

## Methodological reflections

This article draws on an ethnographic study conducted over three years (April 2012 to July 2015) with activists in the EDL.[8] The primary site of observation was more than 20 EDL demonstrations including travel to and from them, usually by hired coach. This afforded the opportunity to observe (gendered) social interactions and cultural practices (around alcohol, drugs, food and money) and compare these observations with the narratives of interviewees. Other sites of observation included EDL divisional meetings, 'Meet and Greets', police liaison meetings, the Crown Court trial of two respondents and social occasions and informal gatherings. Online spaces were incorporated into the study as another site of everyday practice, communication, self-presentation and bonding of respondents (Hallet and Barber 2014, 309) but used primarily for communication and observation purposes.

Individuals were approached for interview either after meeting them at demonstrations or through a key informant. Thirty-five interviews were conducted, eight of which were with women. However, interactions and conversations with many more women are recorded through field notes and two women – Dee and Suzy – are cited here although no formal interview took place. Three respondents (two men and one woman) were open about being gay or lesbian. All respondents are referred to by assigned pseudonyms, citations are verbatim (and thus retain regional speech patterns or grammatical mistakes) and explicit agreement has been given to reproduce the photos[9] included in this article. Data were analysed using Nvivo 9.2 software.

How research relationships were formed and developed over time is discussed in detail elsewhere (see Pilkington 2016, 13–36). Being a woman did not prohibit access to the movement but shaped research relations. For example, I found myself subject to the same kind of rumour and assumptions about relationships with men in the movement endured by female EDL members (see below) and was drawn into some of the 'emotion work' (Duncombe and Jessop 2002, 107) performed by women in the group (such as 'talking down' men from potentially violent exchanges). While in some ways constraining, being positioned in this way also allowed insight into the gendered experience of EDL activism.

Of the multiple subject positions I took into the field, the most threatening to the management of relations with respondents was political standpoint. While other researchers have chosen not to disclose their own views (Crowley 2007, 619), I encouraged respondents to ask questions and answered as honestly as possible. I opened a Facebook account with a genuine profile and, when inviting people to be interviewed, suggested they talk to their divisional organisers or common Facebook friends before consenting. While openness about my own political position and interest in the movement made me subject to some unnerving exchanges and challenges, as relationships with respondents developed, I found that disclosure of difference could provide space for discussing issues and feelings that respondents might not share with those on the 'inside' (Bucerius 2013, 715). In practice, most respondents had a straightforward understanding of my position; I was there to 'report' what I saw. If I did that honestly, fairly and without prior prejudice, the fact that I had different views was not an issue.

## Men's parties or 'open to all'?

The EDL considers itself to have made a distinct break from traditional 'far right' parties not least through its policy of being 'open to all' regardless of ethnicity, faith, gender or sexuality. Nonetheless, men still significantly outnumber women among EDL activists and less than a quarter (eight) of respondents in this study were female. To interpret this as evidence of the movement's failure to live up to its claims, would be too simple, however. To understand what is a complex picture, we need to account for respondents' own narratives, which express their experiences of feeling comfortable, accepted and equal, *and* the constraints on this equality in practice observed during field research.

### 'Angels': standing beside their men?

Organisationally, openness to women is institutionalised through the women's division known as EDL Angels. The region in which this ethnography was conducted formed its own Angels group and Facebook page in 2014; its public page has over 17,000 'likes' (January 2016) and the closed group has 80 members. The regional group was initiated by Suzy and urges women to 'Stand up and be heard. It's not all about the fellas'. The page carries news and information similar to that shared in other EDL groups with a focus on violence towards children and women. However, there are no women's only events or actions and, thus, the Angels division has more symbolic than organisational significance; it is identified as a place for women to 'stand beside their men not behind them' (see Figure 1[10]).

As this image conveys, the iconography that accompanies the 'Angels' is not one of 'angelic' virtues of purity and innocence. As a rule EDL Angels are represented as active rather than passive and sexually assertive. Where this iconography is appropriated by women themselves (see Figure 2) it is not in the form of an 'angelic' figure but through attaching angel wings (a popular tattoo image symbolising aspiration, speed and elevation) to the EDL logo. In the symbolic space of the EDL therefore 'Angel' does not connote conservative femininity.

The significance of the Angels division should not be overestimated, however. While some activists went by Facebook names such as 'Angel Rachel', many women were unaware of, or ambivalent towards, the women's division. Rachel, a 48 year old with three grandchildren, supported the regional Angels group but viewed it rather cynically as part of Suzy's 'empire building' strategy (Field diary, 4 October 2014). Michelle, who was 29 and single at the time (although later formed a relationship, and had a child with, a male EDL member), sought to distance herself from any reputation of the Angels as sexually promiscuous: 'I wouldn't class myself as an EDL Angel in any way shape or form. I think they should rename themselves the Sticky Knicker Brigade to be fair [laughs].'

Although standing 'beside not behind their men' is intended as a statement of the equality and comradeship of women, the very placing of women in relationship to 'their men' ostensibly confirms studies of the extreme right that suggest women's activism is predicated on their ties to others in the movement (Blee and Linden 2012, 101). Such trajectories are termed 'compliant' (Linden and Klandermans 2007, 185) and in Linden and Klandermans' study of the Dutch extreme right, four of the five female activists interviewed are categorised as such (Blee and Linden 2012, 101). However, only two women activists in this study might be said to be'compliants' who drift into movements. One was 29-year-old Casey who saw her role primarily as to 'support' and 'help' her partner, who was a local EDL organiser. Most female respondents made conscious choices to become active, for example, after they recognised a need to vent their growing anger and frustration. In Michelle's case, this realisation was followed by a period of extensive social media communication with other members (via Facebook) before becoming

**Figure 1.** EDL Angels stand beside their men … Not behind them.

active herself. For Lisa, a 39 year old with mixed race heritage, in contrast, active member-ship began after she was approached by Rachel – who had noticed her 'British jobs for British people' sweatshirt – whilst out shopping in town. For Rachel herself, activism had been kick-started by an invitation by a (male) friend to attend a demonstration after which she took over running the local division as 'there was nobody else to do it'. Moreover, far from the stereotype of 'following a man into racism' (Blee 2002, 10), a number of female respondents in this study had not only entered the movement on their own initiative but had brought new recruits to it.

### Women's roles: high viz?

Blee and Linden (2012, 107) conclude from their respective studies that 'the needs and ambitions of women activists never fit into right-wing extremist parties and organizations dominated by men'. Such frustration of aspiration was not articulated in this study of EDL activism. Women were visible both online and physically in various 'admin' and organis-ational roles and as speakers at demonstrations (see Figure 3). Some expressed a desire to 'work my way up and, you know, put my ideas forward' (Lisa) and take on leadership

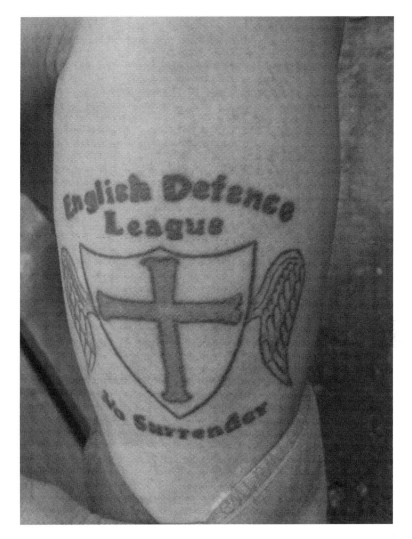

**Figure 2.** Rachel's EDL tattoo.

of the movement since they could 'do a better job' (Michelle). The example of Suzy's establishment of the regional Angels' group is indicative of the avenues open to those who sought formal roles (see also Busher 2016, 17).

The higher visibility of women in the EDL – in comparison to Ezekiel's (2002, 54–55) study for example – may be a product of the relatively flat organisational structure of the movement (Pilkington 2016, 42). At the time of research, women were included among the inner circle of Regional Organisers (Gail Speight) and the management team (Helen Gower)[11] and at least one woman was always among speakers at demonstrations.

This is not to suggest that women are not sometimes assigned, or assign themselves, a 'relegated status' (Kimmel 2007, 207). Women are often described as 'girlfriends' of male members (Rachel) or, like Casey, describe themselves as 'on the side line' despite frequently attending demonstrations and social events and often being central to their organisation.

**Figure 3.** Rachel and Lisa sporting their high viz stewards' vests.

> I help him [her partner who is a local EDL organiser] out, send all his letters off to the police and everything else, he's shit at things like, he just says it how it is and I'm like 'well you can't put that, you can't put this'. So, yeah [...] I do, running round the streets at half ten of a night getting things printed off [...] (Casey)

There is also some frustration with the laddish culture of the movement. Kylie, a 23-year-old mother of two whose dad and partner were EDL activists, described the EDL as 'coked up bald headed blokes running round the streets' while Michelle complained a Regional Organiser 'couldn't fucking organise a piss-up in a brewery'. Lisa became increasingly frustrated with the poor organisation of divisional meetings, which were called without agendas and often appeared to be an after-thought to the main event of 'getting pissed', and she subsequently left the movement. However, others left, or became less active, for family and relationship reasons-either because their partners disapproved of their participation or because they had small children.

### 'Tret with open arms': LGBT members

The creation of an active LGBT division within the EDL structure marks a definitive line in the sand from classic far right movements (Allen 2011, 288). Established in 2010, it declares itself to be 'a division of the English Defence League especially for Lesbian, Gay, Bisexual and Transgender people who support and identify with the aims and ideals of the EDL'.[12] The division is more than a smokescreen; its Facebook page – which has 3500 'likes' (January 2016) – carries news and information specifically related to LGBT issues and its rainbow flag was visible at demonstrations (see Figure 4). The flag was usually carried by Declan, the 19-year-old leader of the EDL LGBT division. At the EDL national demonstration in Newcastle in May 2013, Declan gave a speech, to much applause, challenging representations of the movement as comprising 'homophobic fascists' and criticising what he called the 'far left' for failing to consistently oppose homophobia (Field diary, 25 May 2013). Declan rejects suggestions of tokenism in EDL policy on LGBT rights and narrativises his own trajectory into the EDL (from the British National Party, which he had joined at the age of 13) as a conscious search for a movement that was 'open to all':

> I was starting to realise that I was gay and I came to realise that I couldn't be gay and in the BNP and just before I left I thought to myself 'is there any organisations out there with the same views as me that accept people of all backgrounds?' And that's when I found English Defence League. (Declan)

**Figure 4.** Declan holding a rainbow flag.

A lesbian respondent felt equally comfortable in the movement and chose to be open that, as she put it, she 'bats for the other side' (Field diary, 2 March 2013). A transsexual speaker at the Bristol demonstration was treated with respect and applauded for a speech in which she talked about being proud to be a transsexual EDL member and of the support she had received from the movement (Field diary, 14 July 2012). Indeed, the Bristol Gay Pride march was staged simultaneously with the EDL march in the city that day and a number of individuals chose to wave their rainbow flags alongside EDL demonstrators. On the basis of his own experience, Declan stated, 'I'm gay. I was tret [treated] with open arms since I first joined. It does not matter who you are or where you come from.' Thus, at first glance, the EDL seems to have fashioned itself into a relatively hospitable place for LGBT members.

## Gender and sexuality: organisational ideologies and personal views

The EDL might be seen as a classic example of the trend among PRR movements noted above towards the instrumental inclusion of women's and LGBT rights in party programmes; gender oppression and homophobia is referenced only in relation to the critique of 'Islamic cultures'. Among grassroots activists, gender equality was assumed and rarely discussed, except by three young men – Andrew (a 23-year-old graduate and Breivik sympathiser), Ollie (an 18-year-old college student) and Nick (a 16 year old recently excluded from school) – who attended EDL demonstrations but identified as national socialists and were primarily affiliated with a regional organisation of the Infidels. Mirroring the critique of multiculturalism, these young men understood feminism as a negative (and imposed) force that had distorted 'real' gender equality and infringed the rights of men. They called for the return to a world where:

> women respected men as men, as leaders, as people to be looked up to […] And men respected women as like a precious creation which God has made who they will show respect to, that they'll always love and care for. (Andrew)

Men and women are understood as having different but equal roles in society (Ollie) and transgression of this – women choosing a career over children – was considered 'wrong' (Nick). For this small group of fringe activists, gender – like ethnic and 'racial' – differences are biologically rooted; 'not everyone *is* equal' (Ollie). This distinction between the Infidels and mainstream EDL supporters appears to reflect the existence of distinct modern-traditional and neo-traditional gender positions among PRR parties identified by de Lange and Mügge (2015).

### 'Women […] have to walk behind their husband': gender, sexuality and anti-Islam(ism)

In contrast to the deafening silence on gender and sexuality, gender *in*equality and the abuse of women (and children) is a consistent feature of official and grassroots activists' characterisations of Islam. In its Mission Statement,[13] the EDL presents the movement as raising awareness of the perceived threat of Islam to British culture and society. It sets out the EDL's mission as promoting human rights against 'religiously-inspired intolerance and barbarity that are thriving amongst certain sections of the Muslim population in Britain'. Included, *inter alia*, in the list of acts of intolerance are 'the denigration and oppression of women, the molestation of young children, the committing of so-called honour killings, homophobia'. The movement aligns itself to the cause of protecting the rights of Muslim women stating that 'Muslims themselves are frequently the main victims of some Islamic traditions and practices' and argues that the government should ensure the protection of individual human rights 'including equal rights for Muslim women' (see footnote 13).

Gender and sexuality feature strongly in grassroots activists' associations of Islam with oppression and intolerance. In a telling contrast to the representation of EDL women standing 'beside their men not behind them' (see Figure 1), 47-year-old Jack suggests that in Islam 'Women are second-class citizens; they have to walk behind their husband'. The burqa is widely deployed as a symbol of gender oppression imposed by fathers or husbands as a means of control over women or to conceal violence towards women. Seventeen-year-old Kane, who as a child had suffered sustained abuse from his mother, reflected that 'It makes me think as well, why does Muslims wear burqas? Do they get beat up underneath there and they are hiding bruises?'.

Respondents perceive Islam to be the root cause of systemic violence towards women implemented through Sharia law and signifying the 'backwardness' or 'barbarity' of Islam. For 15-year-old Connor, it is associated with the brutal punishment of women for adultery or disobedience to their husbands while for his 18-year-old friend Chris, women are seen to lack equal rights before the law: 'If they dress provocatively, in their law, they can rape them. It's their own fault for dressing like it' (Chris). Linking the tropes of women's inequal- ity and *hudud* (fixed in the Quran) punishments, Declan argues that rape victims rather than perpetrators are punished:

> I seen in the You Tube video she is buried chest high 'cause she is raped by another Muslim man. When she got taken to a Sharia court, her case is half of a man's so they buried her up to her chest and they stoned her to death which I think is barbaric. (Declan)

The single most frequent association with Islam by respondents in this study, however, was 'paedophilia' and 'grooming gangs'. The centrality of this issue in respondent narra- tives reflects the fact that it was a key campaigning issue for the EDL due to a number of high profile court cases in the UK concerning the organised sexual exploitation of girls. This culminated in an independent inquiry into child sexual exploitation in the town of Rotherham (1997–2013) which concluded that at least 1,400 children had been sexually exploited – raped by multiple perpetrators, abducted, beaten and trafficked to other towns and cities – over that period (Jay 2014, 1). The majority of known perpetrators in Rotherham, including five men convicted in 2010, were of Pakistani heritage (ibid., 92). A key issue for the EDL was the claim that the police and other social welfare agencies failed to act in the interests of the children for fear of highlighting 'the ethnic issue'. The EDL set up a 'protest camp' outside the town's police headquarters over the summer of 2014 (see Figure 5) and in a speech at the national demonstration in the town (September 2014), Ian Crossland[14] attacked both the police and the social services for being 'too scared to offend Muslims' (Field diary, 13 September 2014).

A number of respondents emphasised that paedophiles are found among people of all ethnicities and religions but a direct link between Islam and the current phenomenon of grooming was also frequently asserted. It was argued that the veneration of the prophet Mohammed in the knowledge of his marriage to Aisha effectively sanctifies sexual activity with under-age girls and the logic of this argument is extended to the claim that white girls are the primary target of such grooming activity because attitudes within Islam to non-Muslims make them an object to be treated without respect (Field diary, 13 September 2014).

### Homosexuality and homophobia

EDL activists in this study described Islam as intolerant of sexual minorities. Connor associates Islam with 'the executing of gays' while Declan states Islam preaches that gays should be 'thrown off the top of a mountain'. One placard carried at the Bristol demonstration bore the hand written slogan 'Protect gays, children, females from Sharia law'.[15] In his speech at the national demonstration in Newcastle (May 2013), Declan denounced 'violent homophobia' among Muslims in Britain as a direct threat to gays and lesbians and claimed that among 'honour crimes' committed in the UK were cases of Muslim parents 'killing their gay children'. Earlier, in interview, Declan recounted that he had been 'attacked by Muslims for being gay' and that the police had failed to follow up his complaint for 'lack of evidence' despite his evident injuries.

Assessing the degree to which the pro-LGBT rights stance of the EDL is instrumental is difficult. Certainly the LGBT community is viewed as a potential ally against Islam(ism) and Connor concedes that homophobes are tolerated as long as they do not disrupt 'the cause' by making their views known. The pro-LGBT rights stance is used strategically to criticise 'the left' for failing to speak out against homophobia within the Muslim community and to equate 'Islamism' with Nazism. Moreover, according to Helen Gower, an influential

**Figure 5.** EDL posters and flags at the Rotherham protest camp.

member of EDL management team until 2014, the committee of Regional Organisers who led the EDL from October 2013 (following the resignation of co-leaders Robinson and Carroll), took a collective decision not to support LGBT rights.[16] On the other hand there is also a genuine sense of community with the marginalised; when asked what they thought about the Pride March taking place simultaneously with the EDL demonstration in Bristol, Connor said, he was '100 per cent with them' while his brother Ray expressed 'respect' for the marchers who were, like the EDL, on the streets to get their voices heard.

## Gender and sexual politics in practice: the affective dimension of EDL activism

If organisationally and ideologically the EDL is 'open to all', why does the movement continue to attract relatively few women and LGBT activists? A possible explanation is that they remain excluded from the affective dimension of activism – the 'affective solidarity' (Juris 2008, 66) forged through the 'reciprocal emotions' (Goodwin, Jasper, and Polletta 2001, 20) passing between participants in the course of activism. Indeed, studies of extreme right movements in the USA and the Netherlands suggest women participants tend not to develop strong ties with their organisation and become socially isolated (Blee and Linden 2012, 103–105). In contrast, in the EDL, the emotional dimension of activism appears as important as ideology. Affective bonds – friendship, loyalty, togetherness, belonging – are the most frequently cited meanings of activism in this study (Pilkington 2016) and 'affective practices' (Wetherell 2012, 4), such as demonstrating, are central to their formation. Women are not excluded from these practices; on the contrary, an online study found that female EDL supporters were more likely to participate in demonstrations while supporters who demonstrate are significantly more likely to consider themselves 'members' of the movement (Bartlett and Littler 2011, 28). However, this close up analysis reveals that the solidarities forged remain circumscribed by non-reflexive masculinist and heteronormative preconceptions and practices.

Women activists were observed participating in demonstrations and other events and experiencing the excitement that enhanced the pleasure of activism and the 'togetherness' that bound the movement. Michelle enjoyed the build up to demonstrations: 'you kind of psyche yourself up over the week before and then it comes to demo eve and that's it, nobody can sleep, so yeah it's proper exciting'. Tina, a 31-year-old mother of four who had recently begun studying Politics at university, enjoyed the 'banter' on the coach. Women participate in the drinking, smoking and other substance use as demonstrators 'get in the mood' and they experience the physical rush or 'buzz' of feeling part of a mass of bodies stretching 'as far as the eye can see' (Rachel). What distinguishes women's narratives from those of their male counterparts is the lack of reference to (or rejection of) the 'buzz' of violence; in demonstrating women sought 'a good day out' rather than a 'kick off'. In informal conversation, it also emerged that participation was sometimes a struggle; individual respondents said responsibility for children meant they had 'no time' to go on demonstrations or that they were 'not allowed to go' by male partners (Field diary, 29 September 2012).

The 'togetherness' experienced on 'a good day out' generates affective bonds of, on the one hand, friendship and loyalty and, on the other, belonging and family. Bonds of friendship and loyalty are articulated more frequently in male respondents' narratives stressing the importance of 'having each others' backs' especially at demonstrations. Through physically standing by one another, male respondents develop meaningful relationships in the movement:

> These are my real mates. I class these as family now. The EDL are my family. [...] My mates what I knew before the EDL they ran off and left me. But the EDL they stay by each other's side. (Kane)

Enduring friendships and bonds were forged and sustained by women also but past negative experiences meant they were articulated more cautiously. Rachel's trust and friendship had been betrayed by a member of her division who disappeared owing her money after she had supported him through the break-up of his marriage and an escalating drug habit (Field diary, 2 March 2013 and 20 July 2013). Suzy had been beaten up after she recognised from CCTV footage that a young EDL member – whom she had taken in as a lodger and acted 'like a second mother' to – had been responsible for a burglary at her place of work. While the wrong done to Suzy was 'sorted' by a group of EDL men (Field diary, 4 October 2014), such incidents demonstrate that, in practice, affective bonds are characterised by frustration, anger and hurt as well as solidarity, loyalty and security.

The sense of belonging and family is underpinned by a more diffuse affective solidarity rooted in feelings of care and concern. Lisa notes 'one of the best things about EDL is that I've felt welcome and I've felt part of like family' (Lisa). However, while male respondents' narratives suggest they find a profound ontological security – often missing from their childhood or adolescence – through feeling part of the EDL 'family', female respondents' narratives are less lyrical. This is partially because, the EDL 'family', like other families, is a site of material and emotional labour that is disproportionately borne by women (Reay 2004, 59). It is also because while the affection and emotion rooted in interpersonal relationships can fuel activism, they can also undermine it (Brown and Pickerill 2009, 32–33). In this study, bitter arguments often started with accusations of 'shagging around' and led to individuals being removed from Facebook pages, stripped of admin positions and made to feel as if they were no longer welcome at demonstrations (Field diary, 4 October 2014). Rachel, who found herself falsely accused of having a relationship with a local organiser, expressed frustration at 'the way everybody is interested in who's sleeping with whom rather than the cause' (Field diary, 29–30 April 2013). The emotional labour involved is not exclusively performed by women; one male division leader complained that he spent a lot of time resolving problems caused by relationships between activists. However, in the context of generally unreconstructed masculinities within the movement, these experiences are not gender-neutral. Female respondents were particularly vulnerable to the rumour mill and were more likely to be condemned for engaging in relationships. Notwithstanding the active roles women take in the movement, therefore, the integrity of their participation is undermined by assumptions that it is motivated by the desire to find a partner and the continued existence of sexual double standards for men and women (Crawford and Popp 2003). As Connor put it, 'Most of the EDL lasses are in it for cock. [...] I do think some of them are slags'. At the same time, women could be criticised for *not* engaging in such relationships; a regional organiser did not trust one female activist, he said, because she flirts with blokes with 'no intention of giving them anything' (Field diary, 2 March 2013). Thus affective solidarity is prescribed as masculine even when it includes women; travelling back late at night from a particularly gruelling demonstration, Jack expressed the bonding effect of the experience by giving me a hug and announcing 'you're one of the *boys* [my emphasis] now' (Field diary, 1 September 2012).

While traditional notions of femininity are challenged or transgressed to some degree by women in the movement, traditional masculinity goes unquestioned. Female respondents mocked EDL merchandise being produced in pink for women, playfully associated themselves with being 'a tomboy' and found creative ways to combine identities such as establishing an 'EDL baby division'. Such acts, however, take place amidst a barrage of masculinist sexual 'banter' – language, jokes, comments on women's physical attributes and bottom pinching – which was routine to the point of being invisible to women activists. EDL images and iconography also perpetuate the sexual objectification of women; the same regional Angels division Facebook page that carried the image recreated in Figure 1 also displayed a photo of Daily and Sunday Sport glamour model, Kelly Bell, barely clad in a St George's cross bikini. Of course men are also targets of such 'banter'. Male respondents subjected each other to insults about their appearance, sexual prowess or their wives and mothers (Field diary, 2 March 2013) while a metrosexual man passing on the street provoked a football style chant of 'What the fucking hell is that?' to be struck up by the men on the coach (Field diary, 7 September 2013).

The battle against homophobia within the EDL is also far from won. Declan had left his original EDL division because individuals in it had 'called me an embarrassment' and 'said that the EDL should not allow gays'. He had also been 'punched in the face' by an 'anti-gay' EDL supporter at a demonstration in 2011. At the fringe of the movement, Nick was strongly against the gay marriage bill because 'it says in the bible that homosexuality is wrong' while Andrew called for the recriminalisation of homosexuality because 'it spreads disease and it spreads immorality within communities, and it destroys families'. Individuals within the mainstream movement are often conflicted and uncertain about their views. With regard to the Bristol demonstration discussed above, one respondent commented that, on that day, he had held the 'gay flag' for some people marching with the EDL until they started kissing next to him: 'nothing against 'em', he said, 'but within limits' (Field diary, 7 October, 2013).

## Conclusion

This article argues that while support for, and activism in, the extreme right remains numerically dominated by men, it is no longer a closed or ideologically inhospitable environment for women or LGBT activists. The 'gender gap' among voters for PRR parties is smaller than often suggested, the masculinity of such parties overemphasised and their ideological direction of travel likely to attract more women in the future (Spierings and Zaslove 2015a, 159–160). In the EDL, while women remain a minority, the movement is not a 'men's party'. Women are visible within the inner circle of power and are active as 'admins', local organisers and stewards. There are significant obstacles to women's greater participation, including childcare and other family responsibilities, but women in this study experienced neither thwarted ambition nor isolation within the movement. For the most part they had joined on their own initiative and enjoyed, alongside male activists, the 'buzz' of demonstrations and the affective bonds generated.

The EDL is one of a new generation of PRR movements and parties to adopt gender equality and LGBT rights platforms to 'expose' what is envisaged as an oppressive and intolerant Islamist ideology. The instrumental nature of this position is evident in the fact that the EDL does not promote gender equality and LGBT rights in and of themselves; rather, they are 'defended' against a perceived threat from 'Islamic culture'. However, the movement falls short of capitalising on the potential for new tactical alliances around gender and LGBT rights; reflecting perhaps that ideology and policy on gender and sexuality remain relatively unimportant among reasons for the support of extreme and PRR movements and parties (Spierings and Zaslove 2015a, 150). Findings therefore reveal a contradictory picture. They expose the limits to progressive views on gender and sexuality within the movement whilst also providing observational evidence that declarations of greater openness to women and LGBT supporters constitute more than lip-service to the top-down imposition of a strategically beneficial ideology. In practice, attitudes and behaviours among activists are diverse, ambivalent and conflicted; as such they constitute a more radical variant of mainstream population attitudes rather than a highly ideologised, pathological fringe (Mudde 2007).

Blee and Linden (2012, 98) argue that the experience of participation by men and women in the extreme right is highly gendered. This article has sought to flesh out the substance of these gendered experiences particularly in relation to the affective dimensions of activism. Differences in experience, it is concluded, stem from the wider gendered environment of the movement which, while 'open to all' and accepting of 'transgression' in terms of femininities and the rights of LGBT people to fight for their rights, still leaves in place a largely unreconstructed masculinity that governs everyday interactions. In this context, women's integrity is undermined by men's claims they are 'in it for the cock' but also by women's protection of their own reputation through criticism of other women. This confirms the real constraints on female solidarity in male-dominated movements and subcultures (Leblanc 2006, 8; Pilkington, Omel'chenko, and Garifzianova 2010, 70–71). Thus, while the evidence from this 'close-up' research suggests that PRR movements may no longer be wholly inhospitable environments for women and LGBT people, their inclusion into the affective dimension of activism remains constrained; women may stand 'beside' rather than 'behind their men' in the EDL but as yet they do not stand beside each other.

## Notes

1. 'Populist radical right' characterises parties and movements which, unlike inherently antidemocratic movements of the 'extreme right', are nominally democratic whilst upholding a core ideology combining nativism, authoritarianism and populism (Mudde 2007, 25–31).
2. The characterisation of the EDL is contentious (see Pilkington 2016, 3–4). The term 'anti-Islam (ist)' is adopted here to indicate the claim to be against Islam*ist* ideology (as opposed to Islam as a religion) alongside routine slippage into anti-Islam or anti-Muslim prejudice.
3. 'Affective dimension' is used as shorthand for the roles played in social movements by feeling (as a personal sensation), emotion (as the social display of feelings) and affect (as the non-conscious movement from one experiential state to another) (Massumi 2004 , xvii; Shouse 2005).
4. Nativism is understood here as the resistance to groups and forces perceived as threatening nationhood, national identity or culture and calls to preserve the state exclusively, or primarily, for members of the native group.

5. The evidence to date, however, suggests that gender ideology plays a relatively small role in voter preference; the most important predictor of voting for such parties remains nativist and anti-immigrant attitudes (Spierings and Zaslove 2015a, 150).
6.  For a more detailed outline of the origins, development and current organisational structure of the movement, see Pilkington 2016, 37–59.
7. This proportion is of those who had heard of the EDL, see http://extremisproject.org/2012/10/the-english-defence-league-edl-what-do-people-think/.
8. The study was undertaken as part of the MYPLACE (Memory, Youth, Political Legacy and Civic Engagement) project funded under the European Union Seventh Framework Programme (FP7-266831), see https://myplaceresearch.wordpress.com/
9. All images in this article are photos taken by the author except Plate 1 which is reproduced with permission of the EDL.
10. This image is recreated from a similar one, with unknown authorship, in the gallery on the regional Angels' Facebook page.
11. Both have since left the movement acrimoniously.
12. See https://www.facebook.com/EDL.LGBT.Division/info/?tab=page_info
13. See http://englishdefenceleague.org/about-us/mission-statement/.
14. Crossland subsequently (December 2015) became leader of the EDL.
15. See http://www.thisisbristol.co.uk/pictures/Bristol-EDL-march-anti-EDL-protests/pictures-16536026-detail/pictures.html)
16.  In a post (24 May 2014), reproduced by Hope not Hate, Gower claims this was central to her departure from the movement, see http://www.hopenothate.org.uk/blog/insider/edl-on-the-brink-3840.

## Disclosure statement

No potential conflict of interest was reported by the author.

## Funding

This work was supported by the Seventh Framework Programme [FP7-266831].

## References

Akkerman, T., and A. Hagelund. 2007. "'Women and Children First!' Anti-Immigration Parties and Gender in Norway and the Netherlands." *Patterns of Prejudice* 41 (2): 197–214.
Allen, C. 2011. "Opposing Islamification or Promoting Islamophobia? Understanding the English Defence League." *Patterns of Prejudice.* 45 (4): 279–294.
Bakić, J. 2009. "Extreme-Right Ideology, Practice and Supporters: Case Study of the Serbian Radical Party." *Journal of Contemporary European Studies* 17 (2): 193–207.
Bartlett, J., J. Birdwell, and M. Littler. 2011. *The New Face of Digital Populism*. London: Demos.
Bartlett, J., and M. Littler. 2011. *Inside the EDL: Populist Politics in a Digital Age*. London: Demos.
Blake, B. 2011. *EDL: Coming Down the Road*. Birmingham: VHC.
Blee, K. 2002. *Inside Organized Racism: Women in the Hate Movement*. Berkeley: University of California Press.
Blee, K., and S. Deutsch. 2012. "Introduction." In *Women of the Right: Comparisons and Interplay Across Borders*, edited by K. Blee and S. McGee Deutsch, 1–17. University Park: Penn State University Press.
Blee, K., and A. Linden. 2012. "Women in Extreme Right Parties and Movements." In *Women of the Right: Comparisons and Interplay Across Borders*, edited by K. Blee and S. McGee Deutsch, 98–116. University Park: Penn State University Press.
Brown, G., and J. Pickerill. 2009. "Space for Emotion in the Spaces of Activism." *Emotion, Space and Society* 2: 24–35.

Bucerius, S. M. 2013. "Becoming a 'Trusted Outsider': Gender, Ethnicity, and Inequality in Ethnographic Research." *Journal of Contemporary Ethnography* 42 (6): 690–721.

Busher, J. 2016. *The Making of Anti-Muslim Protest: Grassroots Activism in the English Defence League.* London: Routledge.

Copsey, N. 2010. *The English Defence League: A Challenge to Our Country and Our Values of Social Inclusion, Fairness and Equality.* London: Faith Matters.

Crawford, M., and D. Popp. 2003. "Sexual Double Standards: A Review and Methodological Critique of Two Decades of Research." *The Journal of Sex Research* 40 (1): 13–26.

Crowley, J. 2007. "Friend or Foe? Self-Expansion, Stigmatized Groups, and the Researcher Participant Relationship." *Journal of Contemporary Ethnography* 36 (6): 603–630.

Dekker, H., and J. van der Noll. 2012. "Islamophobia and Its Explanation." In *Islamophobia in the West: Measuring and Explaining Individual Attitudes*, edited by M. Helbling, 112–123. London: Routledge.

Duncombe, J., and J. Jessop. 2002. "'Doing Rapport' and the Ethics of 'Faking Friendship'." In *Ethics in Qualitative Research*, edited by M. Mauthner, M. Birch, J. Jessop, and T. Miller, 108–123. London: SAGE.

Ezekiel, R. 2002. "An Ethnographer Looks at Neo-Nazi and Klan Groups: The Racist Mind Revisited." *American Behavioral Scientist* 46: 51–71.

Field, C. D. 2012. "Revisiting Islamophobia in Contemporary Britain, 2007–10." In *Islamophobia in the West: Measuring and Explaining Individual Attitudes*, edited by M. Helbling, 147–161. London: Routledge.

Garland, J., and J. Treadwell. 2011. "Masculinity, Marginalization and Violence: A Case Study of the English Defence League." *British Journal of Criminology* 51 (4): 621–634.

Goodwin, M. 2011. *Right Response: Understanding and Countering Populist Extremism in Europe.* A Chatham House Report. London: Royal Institute of International Affairs (Chatham House).

Goodwin, J., J. M. Jasper, and F. Polletta. 2001. "Why Emotions Matter." In *Passionate Politics: Emotions and Social Movements*, edited by J. Goodwin, J. M. Jasper, and F. Polletta, 1–24. Chicago: University of Chicago Press.

Hallet, R., and K. Barber. 2014. "Ethnographic Research in a Cyber Era." *Journal of Contemporary Ethnography* 43 (3): 306–330.

Jackson, P. 2011a. "The English Defence League: Anti-Muslim Politics Online." In *Far-Right.Com: Nationalist Extremism on the Internet*, edited by P. Jackson and G. Gable, 7–19. Northampton: Searchlight Magazine and The Radicalism and New Media Research Group.

Jackson, P. 2011b. *The EDL: Britain's 'New Far Right' Social Movement.* Northampton: RNM Publications, University of Northampton.

Jay, A. 2014. "Independent Inquiry into Child Sexual Exploitation in Rotherham 1997–2013." http://www.rotherham.gov.uk/downloads/file/1407/independent_inquiry_cse_in_rotherham.

Juris, J. 2008. "Performing Politics: Image, Embodiment, and Affective Solidarity During Anti-Corporate Globalization Protests." *Ethnography* 9 (1): 61–97.

Kimmel, M. 2007. "Racism as Adolescent Male Rite of Passage: Ex-Nazis in Scandinavia." *Journal of Contemporary Ethnography* 36 (2): 202–218.

Kitschelt, H. 2007. "Growth and Persistence of the Radical Right in Postindustrial Democracies: Advances and Challenges in Comparative Research." *West European Politics* 30 (5): 1176–1206.

de Lange, S., and L. M. Mügge. 2015. "Gender and Right-Wing Populism in the Low Countries: Ideological Variations Across Parties and Time." *Patterns of Prejudice* 49 (2): 61–80.

Leblanc, L. 2006. *Pretty in Punk: Girls' Gender Resistance in a Boys' Subculture.* New Brunswick: Rutgers University Press.

Linden, A., and B. Klandermans. 2007. "Revolutionaries, Wanderers, Converts, and Compliants: Life Histories of Extreme Right Activists." *Journal of Contemporary Ethnography* 36 (2): 184–201.

Massumi, B. 2004. "Translator's Foreword: Notes on the Translation and Acknowledgements." In *A Thousand Plateaus*, edited by G. Deleuze and F. Guattari, ix–xvi. London and New York: Continuum Books.

Mudde, C. 2007. *Populist Radical Right Parties in Europe.* Cambridge: Cambridge University Press.

Mudde, C. 2014. "Introduction: Youth and the Extreme Right: Explanations, Issues, and Solutions." In *Youth and the Extreme Right*, edited by C. Mudde, 1–18. New York, London and Amsterdam: IDebate Press.

Pilkington, H. 2014. "'My Whole Life is Here': Tracing Journeys Through 'Skinhead'." In *Rethinking Youth Cultures in the Age of Global Media*, edited by D. Buckingham, S. Bragg, and M-J. Kehily, 71–87. Basingstoke: Palgrave Macmillan.

Pilkington, H. 2016. *Loud and Proud: Passion and Politics in the English Defence League*. Manchester: Manchester University Press.

Pilkington, H., E. Omel'chenko, and A. Garifzianova. 2010. *Russia's Skinheads: Exploring and Rethinking Subcultural Lives*. London and New York: Routledge.

Reay, D. 2004. "Gendering Bourdieu's Concepts of Capitals? Emotional Capital, Women and Social Class." *Sociological Review* 52 (S2): 57–74.

Shouse, E. 2005. "Feeling, Emotion, Affect." *M/C Journal*, 8 (6). http://journal.media-culture.org.au/0512/03-shouse.php.

Spierings, N., and A. Zaslove. 2015a. "Gendering the Vote for Populist Radical-Right Parties." *Patterns of Prejudice* 49 (1–2): 135–162.

Spierings, N., and A. Zaslove. 2015b. "Conclusion: Dividing the Populist Radical Right Between 'Liberal Nativism' and Traditional Conceptions of Gender." *Patterns of Prejudice* 49 (1–2): 163–173.

Wetherell, M. 2012. *Affect and Emotion: A New Social Science Understanding*. London: Sage.

Wodak, R., and M. KhosraviNik. 2013. "Dynamics and Politics in Right-Wing Populism in Europe and Beyond: An Introduction." In *Right-Wing Populism in Europe: Politics and Discourse*, edited by R. Wodak, M. KhosraviNik, and B. Mral, xvii–xxviii. London: Bloomsbury.

# Women and Golden Dawn: reproducing the nationalist habitus

Alexandra Koronaiou and Alexandros Sakellariou

**ABSTRACT**

This article focuses on the place and role of women in the ideology of the Greek neo-Nazi political party Golden Dawn (GD). The article considers the place of women in GD's ideology as well as how GD envisages the role of women in society. It asks whether this vision of women's role is reflected in the participation of women in the party's activities. Based on a content analysis of material derived from the party's official websites, it is argued that women play a key role in GD's ideological edifice. This is evident in the party's concern with the construction of a *nationalist habitus* for women. This habitus is rooted in ideas of anti-feminism, motherhood and family and the primacy of nation and nationalist sentiment in determining women's lives.

## Introduction

The xenophobic, sometimes racist, discourses of extreme-right movements and parties are well-known and have been extensively studied (e.g. Davies 1999). However, less well-studied are the ideological viewpoints, opinions and social representations of contemporary extreme-right movements as they relate to the role of women in both private and public spheres and women's participation in such groups. The vast majority of fascist movements in Europe have fervently promoted the view that women's place is first and foremost in the domestic sphere and their main goal is raising children (Blee 1996; Mosse 1997). For the extreme-right gender is a biological fact, given by nature, rather than a social and cultural construction; it belongs to the sphere of the natural or the divine order of the world (Lesselier 1991). In the 'new order' extreme-right movements want to solidify the family as society's foundation and the primary location of women as mothers and wives. This excludes them from the public sphere and from higher office, despite the fact that over the last two decades a number of ultra-conservative and nationalist parties have had women leaders.[1]

This article considers the place of women in Golden Dawn (GD)'s ideology, how the party envisages the role of women in society and whether this vision of women's role is reflected in the participation of women in the party's activities. It begins by contextualising the case of GD in the wider literature on the relationship between fascism/the extreme-right and women. This is followed by an outline of the notion of 'habitus' and how it is employed in the subsequent analysis. The history and place of GD in Greek society are then presented briefly and an overview of the material gathered and analysed is provided. Finally, the findings of the analysis are outlined in thematically structured sections.

## Women, fascism and the extreme-right: past and present

It is only in the last three decades that the relationship between women and fascism has generated any significant interest in historical or sociological research fields. Research conducted to date has been concerned primarily with historical fascism leading to well-elaborated studies focusing on the place of women in Italian Fascism (De Grazia 1992; Gori 2004; Pickering-Iazzi 1995), during Weimar and Nazi Germany (Bridenthal, Grossman, and Kaplan 1984; Lower 2013; Moser-Verey 1991; Scheck 2004) or both (Durham 1998). These studies draw some common conclusions regarding how fascist regimes envisaged the role of women. They establish that motherhood was supported and promoted by fascist regimes in a way that mythologised but also nationalised women's bodies (De Grazia 1992) in as much as women's purpose was to act as vessels of the nation by raising 'new men' who would fight for the nation. Thus, as Durham (1998, 133) argues, fascism cannot be considered a purely masculine movement pursuing a misogynist agenda (although it often demonstrates such characteristics). In its effort to recruit female members and increase its popularity, fascism experienced serious internal tensions regarding women's rights and, on occasion, political expediency led to the expression of opposition to traditionalist patriarchy and the promotion of policies designed to appear to accept and promote women's equality (Durham 1998, 1). Thus, there is a certain ambiguity in Italian Fascist policy regarding women, which emphasised motherhood whilst also demanding women's participation in society (Gori 2004, 1). Recent research has also challenged existing knowledge about women as passive agents under the Nazi regime in Germany through its uncovering of the participation of women in brutal acts on the Eastern front (Lower 2013).

Research in the field of extreme-right studies also focused almost exclusively on men until around 30 years ago. Women in the extreme-right were overlooked or considered unimportant; certainly, they were not considered active agents in the construction of right-wing ideology or the mobilisation of right-wing movements or parties. The study of organised racism was deeply, but invisibly, gendered; the committed racist usually appeared as male while women racists existed in the shadows, lurking behind husbands and boyfriends (Blee 1996, 680). Over the last few years, a blossoming literature on right-wing women, using in-depth interviews and oral history, has demonstrated that rightist activism has almost never been the sole province of men (Bacchetta and Power 2002; Blee and Deutsch 2012, 1). Female participation in organised racism may well be bound by affect but is not irrational and certainly less capricious than suggested in earlier research (Blee 2002, 5–6, 1996, 698). However, these studies appear to confirm that the key tenets of ideology concerning the role of women in society identified in the study of historical fascism are found also among contemporary extreme-right groups and movements.

Bacchetta and Power (2002) identify common elements in the role of women in right-wing extremist groups. These include gender essentialism as well as a dualistic sense of public and private spheres according to which women are associated with private, less visible and often subordinated aspects of daily life and politics, while public, visible and dominant spaces are reserved for men. However, they also note (Bacchetta and Power 2002) that traditional structures of women's subordination and men's authority may be advanced even though women sometimes pursue political goals in public, assertive, and aggressive ways that are antithetical to notions of women's 'proper place'. Indeed Blee and Deutsch (2012, 3) also demonstrate through a series of case studies that the boundary between public and private, while an important dimension of women's right-wing politics, is far from constant; right-wing women can transgress, even erase, the borders between these spheres as well as uphold them.

Existing studies on women and right-wing extremism demonstrate that such parties do not attract massive numbers of women as members and voters (Mudde 2007, 6). The British National Party, for example, has tried unsuccessfully to attract women through the formation of a family circle (Goodwin 2011, 87, 137, 180). However, in recent years women have become highly active and risen in the hierarchy of such political parties. Marine Le Pen in France is the most well-known, but far from the only, example. Krisztina Morvai of Jobbik in Hungary, formerly a militant feminist, is today an openly anti-Roma, Islamophobic and anti-Semitic Member of the European Parliament. Barbara Rosenkranz, known as the 'mother of the Reich', of the Freedom Party of Austria (FPÖ) is currently serving as the Minister of Building Law and Animal Protection of the State of Lower Austria (since 2008) and was the FPÖ candidate for the Austrian presidential elections in 2010. Indeed, such women often are extremely modern in their personal lives whilst retaining fascist, racist and anti-Semitic positions.[2]

Before turning to the specifics of GD's ideology, two points should be emphasised. The first is that connection between women and nation/nationalism is not new; it has been discussed and analysed by scholars from a range of perspectives (see, for example: Halkia 2007; Hogan 2009; McClintock 1995; Ranchod-Nilsson and Tetreault 2000; Yuval-Davis 1997; Yuval-Davis and Anthias 1989) and the findings of these existing analyses will be drawn on below. Second, the findings of this research raise the question of whether it is possible to talk about a specifically nationalist ideology regarding the place of women in society at all. In practise, most of the values and ideas supported by fascist, neo-fascist and extreme-right parties about women are not innovative but replicate conservative and patriarchal values from the past. While this holds true for the case of GD as well, it is also important to note that in its open denunciation of feminism and its claim that homosexuality is an obstacle to the reproduction of the nation, GD goes well beyond other political parties in Greece. Moreover, GD brings a new militaristic dimension to these traditional attitudes, by positioning women not only as the reproducers of the Greek nation but more specifically of Greek *soldiers*. In the analysis presented, therefore, we show how traditional conservative and patriarchal ideas are appropriated by GD but reworked and reproduced in distinctive ways.

### *The nationalist habitus*

In light of the suggestion above that conservative and patriarchal attitudes are both embedded in societies but also reworked by social agents, we propose the notion of 'habitus' to be a useful theoretical tool for our analysis. Originating in Aristotelian ethics, habitus has been developed for sociological analysis, especially in the work of Max Weber and Pierre Bourdieu. According to Bourdieu (1984, 170), habitus is neither created through free will nor determined by social structures, but is the outcome of the interplay between the two over time. Habitus is created via social rather than individual processes; it is not fixed and changes under different conditions (Navarro 2006, 16). For Bourdieu habitus is a filter that individuals use to structure their own perceptions, experiences and practices and which shapes one's mental and physical being. Habitus helps mould one's natural propensity and sense of one's place, but it is also an internalisation of external forces and conventions. Habitus supplies at once a principle of sociation and individuation; sociation because the categories of judgment and action emerging from the social world are shared by those who are subjected to similar social conditions and conditioning, and individuation because each person has a unique trajectory and location in the world (Wacquant 2006, 319).

Applying this notion of habitus to the contemporary Greek political context, we suggest that GD might be considered to be seeking to reproduce a nationalist habitus for women, which includes specific values, ideas and lifestyle rooted in existing paradigms derived both from international and Greek history. This habitus consists of fundamental elements such as anti-feminism, anti-homosexuality/pro-heterosexuality and, most importantly, motherhood enacted through family formation and child-raising. For GD, this nationalist habitus should be accepted and followed in their everyday activities by every 'real' Greek woman. The fact that the vast majority of the texts uploaded on GD's Women's Front (WF) website are written by women suggests that some women indeed have started to internalise and reproduce this habitus.

## The rise of Golden Dawn in Greek society

The economic and social crisis that Greece has been experiencing since 2010 has deeply affected political and social life. One of the most salient developments is the remarkable electoral success and entry into the Greek parliament of a formerly marginal political formation, GD. The crisis has enabled the party to foster an extreme anti-leftist, xenophobic, racist and authoritarian discourse focused on anti-immigrant and anti-Islamic (Sakellariou 2015a, 54–57, 2017 Forthcoming) scapegoating, which rejects what is now Greece's third democratic political system (established in 1974). GD's impressive electoral leap in 2012, as well as its growing influence particularly among young people (Koronaiou et al. 2015, 231–249; Koronaiou, Lagos and Sakellariou 2015, 193–123) and penchant for extremist discourse and violent activism (Georgiadou 2013, 75–101), has attracted the attention and concern of the media, the public and academia (Christopoulos 2014; Ellinas and Lamprianou 2016; Paraskeva-Veloudogianni 2015; Tsiakalos 2015; Vasilopoulou and Halikiopoulou 2015). Although GD's power and electoral success erupted at the peak of the economic crisis in 2012, the first signs were evident in the 2010 local elections when the party gained 5.29% of the votes (and elected a city councillor) in Athens and polled as high as 8.38% in some districts.[3] Thus any attempt to connect the rise of GD and the financial crisis in a linear and deterministic way is superficial; the crisis was not the sole cause, but rather a pretext, behind which we need to seek the deeper reasons for the party's appeal especially to young people (Sakellariou 2015b, 12–14). The party has continued to register significant electoral support. In the 2012 June elections, GD captured 6.92% of the vote and gained 18 seats in the Greek Parliament (in the first elections, in May, it had won 6.97% of the vote which translated into 21 seats). Through 2015, GD's support held up; in January it won 6.28% of votes and 17 seats, and in September it won 6.99% of the vote and 18 seats. In the European elections of 2014, GD won its highest proportion of the vote, 9.39%, and secured three seats in the European Parliament.[4]

## Methodology

Our analysis is based on documentary online material collected from the official websites of GD.[5] The material is drawn primarily from the website of the women's organisation of the party, WF (http://whitewomenfront.blogspot.gr/), but also from GD's official webpage (http://www.xryshaygh.com/) and the website of the party's youth division (Antepithesi/ Counterattack) (http://www.antepithesi.gr/). All these sites carry articles regarding women's place in GD's ideology, their role in contemporary society and in a future ideal national-socialist society and their participation in the party's activities. Online material was selected as a primary source for our analysis because GD's exclusion from mainstream media, especially following the arrest and prosecution of the party's leadership for mem-bership of a criminal organisation,[6] means the majority of its work to promote its ideology and reach wider audiences has been conducted via the Internet. Indicative of the impor-tance GD assigns to the Internet and social media is the fact that one of the first slogans GD used on the former youth division's webpage was 'turn off your TV, you will find us on the Internet'.

Discourse contributes to the composition of the rules and regulations of social life as well as of relations, identities and institutions (Fairclough 1992, 65). The analysis of dis-course has become, therefore, a very important tool for social scientists in their efforts to study and understand society and social relationships. Discourse analysis treats a wide range of linguistic or non-linguistic material – speeches, reports, manifestos, histori-cal events and interviews – as 'texts' and 'writings' that enable subjects to experience the world of objects, words and practices (Howarth 2000, 10). The particular mode of analysis applied to the material gathered for this article is qualitative, thematic content analysis (Grawitz 2004, 133–231; Kyriazi 2001, 283–301). The categories of analysis are grouped around the following four themes: women in society; motherhood and family; female examples from history; and participation. The categories were arrived at after studying the collected material – totalling more than 2,500 downloaded pages – from all three web-sites between December 2007 and July 2016.

## The Women's Front

The website of the WF, which was the main source of our data collection, started in 2007 and was last updated on 9 March 2013. The website is dedicated to women and includes the following main sections: GD; Local Organisations; Green Department (ecology); Nation-alist Ecology; ELAM (division in Cyprus); Products; and Videos. There is a link also to an 'Ideological Library' which includes ideological texts, but this is accessible only to invited members. Other links include: a 'Kitchen' with recipes for traditional Greek food but also with advice on how to produce home-made cosmetics; a link to the WF of the Cyprus brother-organisation website; a link to 'Meander' a periodical publication of GD;

and a link to 'Art Selection', which includes texts and images on women and/in the arts from ancient and modern times. There are two further interesting links: one to a website dedicated to Ioannis Metaxas, a Greek dictator during the interwar period (1936–1940), which carries digitised versions of the contemporary periodical entitled 'Youth';[7] and a second to the website of 'Homefront', described as 'a publication for the racially conscious home', published by the Women for Aryan Unity.[8]

Among the major topics presented and discussed on the website are: the current social, political and financial crisis especially after 2010; religion; nationalist ideology – historical or related to contemporary nationalist movements across Europe and beyond; anti-leftist and anti-communist ideas and attitudes;[9] immigration, multiculturalism and the rise of Islam.[10] These, however, are general themes that form the nucleus of GD's ideology and can be found on the other party websites as well (Koronaiou et al. 2015; Koronaiou, Lagos and Sakellariou 2015). Material from the two other official websites of GD noted above was also used in the analysis, since the party's official website and the youth division's official website regularly propagate texts about the role of women in contemporary societies in general and in Greek society in particular.

## Women as mothers: commitment to the nation and the white 'race'

The dominant theme found on GD's websites concerns the role of women as mothers. One of the first texts uploaded on the website (WF, 'Our fatherland gets old', 17 October 2007) highlights the low birth rate in Greek society as a key problem. In this text the modern woman who prioritises her career over her role as mother is criticised, but the party's main complaint concerns the lack of financial and infrastructural support for mothers raising children. The author of the text praises, on the one hand, the Mussolini regime for its additional taxation of the childless and, on the other, the Third Reich, for establishing the organisation 'Mother and Child'[11] and creating a comprehensive system of protection (including health, security and financial support) for mothers and their children. Finally, the issue of abortion[12] is discussed as directly related to the question of motherhood and the need for more children (WF, 'The social consequences of abortions', 12 September 2010; WF, 'Europe commits suicide', 13 April 2010). The text ends with some advice for both men and women:

> Although some people fear precisely this, our race [the white 'race'] must realise that it has the capacity to achieve and perpetuate its numerical predominance. By forming a family and meeting the challenge of educating and providing for their children, men will feel there is a meaning to their existence in this world. [On the other hand] women [through the formation of a family] will accept their nature - the only true liberation is to give birth and raise children.

The protection of the white 'race' through the birth of children is one of the main themes for GD. Through its discourse on the role of women as mothers, motherhood becomes not only a private issue and a role played out in the private sphere, but also a matter for the public sphere since it is tied up with the protection and reproduction of the white 'race' in general and the Greek nation in particular (see Figure 1). In the image accompanying the above mentioned text, for example, a white, blonde girl is pictured looking ahead, probably to the future, with a caption that reads 'Europe: Protect her … '. Images like this one are taken from foreign extreme-right websites or blogs and the message is clear. Europe, and the white 'race', is personified as a young woman in need of protection from immigrants and this can only come about through the birth of more white children. Not surprisingly, therefore, another key dimension of WF discourse is praising those who have more than three children (WF, 'The mother with many children today', 18 August 2010) while linking low fertility rates with the rise in immigration not only into Greece but into Europe in general (WF, 'Low fertility and immigrants', 7 June 2010).

As a consequence, family becomes the end goal for people, especially women (WF, 'The crisis is moral, not financial', 10 December 2011), and the values and role of the family are discussed and praised frequently (WF, 'Family, today, yesterday, tomorrow', 15 December 2011). As stated in one of the analysed texts:

> The end goal of every person is the formation of a healthy and happy family. This should be the goal of every man and every woman, because everything else is sick and serves the interests of the 'new world order'. (WF, 'The crisis is moral, not financial', 10 December 2011)

According to a male member of GD, in a text uploaded to the WF website, family – the most important institution for the transmission of values, ideals and traditions – has been heavily affected by current austerity measures and is in deep crisis. Family is described as 'home', 'refuge', the 'flame' and the 'light' and is considered the first and most fundamental link in any society in which the ideals of Blood and Honour dominate.

> In our world people are connected with each other through the bonds of Blood and Honour and family is the first teacher of the race and should have a primary and non-negotiable role. The values and the ideals of the family are indissolubly connected with Tradition and Nation. (WF, 'Family, today, yesterday, tomorrow', 15 December 2011)

For GD this means that women are to be revered as reproductive vessels through which the 'race' is realised (WF, 'Women of today and of yesterday', 3 December 2008). This position has been supported by GD Members of Parliament (MPs) on occasions such as international women's day in March 2016, when the wife of the party's leader and GD MP argued that under nationalism women are respected and recognised and that motherhood is a holy obligation, a duty and an honour.[13] Halkia (2007, 383) suggests that, in being called upon to give birth to children (and reject abortion) women's uteruses are used to fill the empty showcases of the nation.

**Figure 1.** 'The racial issue' (WF, 28 November 2010).

As in other extreme-right parties and organisations (Lesselier 1991; Litt 2004; Perry 2004), the most important role ascribed to women is motherhood, since through motherhood women reproduce the Greek nation and the white 'race'. This is a paradigm rooted in historical fascism, but which reframes motherhood within the public sphere through the 'nationalisation of women' (De Grazia 1992, 1–16). The formation of family and the birth of children are no longer purely private issues but play a crucial role for the nation. In this way, women are subjects of the nation destined for a supposed higher purpose. At the same time, the ideological platform 'Race-Family-Party-State' serves as an operative of a historically inherited fascism and a strong mechanism of normativity fuelled by the persistent denial of different forms of sexuality (Macciocchi 1976).

This idea was articulated clearly in the following text:

> We, women, must be proud of our gender and of the gift nature gave us, to create life. […] The greatest energy that a woman can offer to a national society and its people is her children. […] We have to be worthy first as wives and then as mothers. For worthy husbands, better children and a healthy nation. (Antepithesi, 'Woman as energy', 1 July 2016)

Using Bourdieu's notion of habitus, we might suggest that, through this kind of ideological rhetoric about that nature and the role of women in society, GD is attempting to produce a nationalist habitus regulating women's sense of their place in society. GD reproduces specific patterns and representations for women to follow, which serve to structure their own perceptions, experiences and practices. In this way GD steers women towards the internalisation of a set of ideas and practices by which they become 'real' women.

## The place of women in society: criticism of the present and ideals for the future

GD criticises the modern view of women in the West as independent in society. For example, one can find criticism of feminism, consumption, advertising and homosexuality in the online narratives.

> Unfortunately, mainly because of the western pattern, future mothers decide not to get fat and lose their figure, instead of reproducing their species. Couples are not willing on any account to reduce their uncontrollable consumer activity, nor are they willing to deprive themselves or put themselves out for the sake of a child. The financial situation has made things worse. (Antepithesi, 'The immigration problem', 29 March 2013)

Feminism is considered a major factor in the creation of the current demographic problem not only in Greece, but, as GD sees it, throughout the white 'race'. This explains their complete antipathy towards feminist ideas and groups (Antepithesi, 'Looking forward', 8 April 2014). Here lies a difference between GD and other European parties of the extreme-right. While, in some extreme-right parties, women have begun taking leading roles, presenting themselves as modern, ordinary women, who can combine caring for their families and raising their children with leadership roles,[14] GD completely rejects this model. GD is an explicitly anti-feminist party and argues that women are mothers and wives first. They should work or participate in society only after fulfilling that role and, even then, not in male fields but in those areas dictated by their 'nature'. As a consequence, while in some political parties of the extreme-right we could argue that a kind of feminist revival is taking place this is certainly not the case for GD.

Consumption and its influence on women's way of life is another point of discussion and criticism. According to views expressed on GD websites, women have become a material product, interested only in their appearance.

> Women nowadays have become consumable objects, first of all because they don't respect themselves. Being a woman doesn't mean pretending to be a stupid chicken. [...] Feminism isn't about being equal with men. This is against our nature and incompatible with natural laws. We should take our lives in our hands with pride and without any manly crutches. (WF, 'Woman-human being or woman-consumable object?', 15 September 2008)

Consumerist consciousness is according to the party, primarily cultivated through advertising. This makes it an object of considerable criticism (WF, 'Adverts', 2 January 2013) alongside pornography and the exploitation of women in the porn industry (WF, 'Eros: The gift of the Gods', 10 November 2007).

Homosexuality is another issue that is discussed in direct relation to women and gender issues in general. Gender, it is stated, is not socially constructed but 'purely genetically and biologically predetermined, in the same way as race' (Antepithesi, 'Gender: Genetically predetermined', 29 April 2013) (Figure 2).

This is referred to as 'the gender ideology' and contributors to the websites take positions against homosexuality and the rights of homosexuals contemporary Greek society, arguing that 'the neutralisation of gender, political correctness and human rights [regarding homosexuals] are against the values of this country' (Antepithesi, 'The

**Figure 2.** 'Give your daughter your singularity. Choose a father for her from your own race!' (WF, 'Preserve variety in humanity', 3 February 2009).

gender ideology', 24 March 2014). This is a direct criticism of, and clear attack on, homosexuality, which 'dominates the public sphere with all these faggots who are boring because they are only talking about their passion'. As one contributor to the website argues:

> I am heterosexual and I am proud of it. I am proud to live normally [...]. I am heterosexual and I am proud that normal people, and people I respect and appreciate, don't point a finger at me. I am heterosexual and I am proud that I can, and I want to, have a family. I am heterosexual and I am proud that I don't suffer from psycho-somatic problems. I am heterosexual and I am proud that I don't abuse my nature. [...] And I am not going to account or apologise for this to anyone. I am a woman and I am proud of the fact that I like men; normal men - rough ones. [...] Not half-gay men. [...]. (WF, 11 December 2007)

As a consequence, independent heterosexual women are considered extremely important for the nation:

> We are neither stupid chicks, nor prostitutes. We are women ready to take the helm of our own lives, not live in the shadow of our men. We are not anyone's puppet. We are, and we will always be, the other half of the sky. Our country needs us! (WF, 'Women of today and yesterday', 3 December 2008)

GD's women are presented as capable of managing their own lives, but they are also men's supporters, partners and companions (WF, 'The partner', 13 December 2008). This leads us to argue that GD supplies women simultaneously with mechanisms for sociation and individuation. Sociation because the categories of judgment and action emanating from GD are shared by those subjected to similar social conditions and conditionings, and individuation because each person nonetheless internalises a unique combination of these structuring patterns and thus occupies a singular location in the world (Wacquant 2006, 319). GD argues that each woman is special, but at the same time needs to conform to the nationalist habitus in order to belong to the greater family of the nation. The imagined community of the nation is one of flesh and blood, imagined through the categories of 'race' and gender (Hogan 2009, 13).

## Women of GD in the national-socialist society

All these problems that, according to WF, women face in contemporary modern, consumerist societies will be eliminated in the future national-socialist society, because 'the nationalist woman, together with the nationalist man are the only healthy cells of a dying people' (Antepithesi, 'GD's youth pioneer in the fight for intellectual liberation (part 2)', 23 July 2015).

> Following in the footsteps of our ancestors, GD's women do not lower themselves to sex objects or fake beautiful dolls [...]. Against the current that wants women to be pointless and greedy consumerist beings, GD's women give an example of following a way of life based on simple, natural values. Motherhood is the highest duty for GD's women in order to protect the race. [...] A man and a woman fulfill each other since they are two different substances, with different roles. As a consequence, there is no issue of equality. In nationalism the nation comes first, and this means that everyone cooperates for the National State. (Antepithesi, 'Women in people's community', 7 April 2013)

The women of GD are presented as educated, emancipated and capable of defending themselves without forgetting their role as future mothers. They must also participate in the everyday fight against those who are against the Greek nation and be proud of that (WF, 'The woman of GD', 24 October 2012).

In a national-socialist society women will have responsibilities and obligations due to their importance to the success of the nation. They are viewed as dynamic and capable of performing in public life. In the ideal society of national-socialism the virtues of women will be developed for the benefit of the society and women will take the place they deserve. However, motherhood is not separated from action and other activities (WF, 'Woman and Politics', 19 October 2007). A national-socialist woman who rejects the current model of a woman who is only interested in fashion and entertainment becomes, by definition, a heroine (WF, 'Jeanne D' Arc', 15 October 2007). Furthermore, it is argued, the role of a woman is that of a mother, a host, a partner and also of a special member of society, having the capacity and the duty to defend in her own way her ideals, values, institutions and traditions that are disappearing. 'This is the kind of women Greece used to produce, and not fake dolls without any content' (WF, 'Women-objects or guards of the institutions?', 11 October 2012). This discourse demonstrates that fascist conceptions of female gender and body (health, motherhood, beauty) remain strong in the dominant ideas about women (Mosse 1997).

## Heroic figures from the past

This raises the question as to whether there are role models and historical figures that could become exemplary paradigms for contemporary women. As might be expected, national-socialist Germany is the main historical example discussed on the WF website. Nationalism-socialism is characterised as a revolutionary ideology and is presented as a model, alongside ancient Sparta, regarding the place of women (WF, 'Women in national-socialism', 28 August 2010). It is argued that current economic circumstances will lead to the rise of national-social-ism and implied that women will once again take up their place as mothers of the nation against dominant feminist ideologies. Even on Valentine's Day, WF employs a photo from Nazi Germany in order to create a sense of nostalgia (see Figure 3). In this picture we see a

**Figure 3.** 'A picture of another time' (WF, 14 February 2009).

couple lying down, embracing, in a place that looks like a beach and with small swastika flags above them. Although it is not clear from where this picture comes, or if it is real, its purpose is to present an image of an ideal past during the Nazi regime that women should internalise for the construction of a contemporary nationalist habitus.

Apart from the German paradigm, particular reference is made to the Metaxas dictatorship (1936–1940), a nationalist regime, through a special text dedicated to the place of women in it, and through the use of archival material (photos) from that time period (WF, 'Women under the 4th of August regime', 4 August 2007).

Ancient Sparta is also used as a historical model for the role of women in society (WF, 7 June 2010) and even described as the first national-socialist society (WF, 28 August 2010). Physical activity, motherhood, sexual life and independence are presented as the main examples that every society should follow regarding the place of women. Women in ancient Sparta are presented as: exercising rigorously in order to become healthy mothers; tough, especially with their boys, in order to prepare them for battle; and selective about their partner because of the importance of motherhood for the reproduction of the 'race' in terms of eugenics. Finally, women in Sparta are portrayed as independent beings, able to maintain and manage their own property, including land, without being controlled by men.

While these are examples of societies that might be emulated in terms of the role of women, the website also carries items about individual heroic figures. These are either women who participated in the revolutionary struggle against Ottoman Rule during the nineteenth century and died for the national cause (WF, 16 February 2009; WF, 5, 7, & 9 February 2008) or ancient figures such as Hypatia who was an astronomer and mathematician murdered by the Christian mob in Alexandria, Egypt (WF, 16 July 2007). Through these figures it is implied that women are not only mothers, restricted to the private sphere of home, but could also be fighters and scientists; independent characters especially when they are committed to a higher cause. The use of historical or even religious figures from the past is not an innovation of GD. The Front National in France, for example, has used such figures as the Virgin Mary and Joan of Arc as paragons of virtue for women to follow. This practice represents a further element of the construction of a nationalist habitus since it requires women to internalise not only the ideology of GD regarding the natural role of women in society but also to study, follow and internalise female role models from the past in order to emulate them in the 'new' nationalist society under construction.

## Participation in Golden Dawn's activities

Women participate in many activities of GD presented on the party's websites. This participation, and its public presentation, increased after the first electoral breakthrough of GD in the local elections of 2010 and still more after the party's entry into parliament in 2012. Women participate in commemoration rallies of the battle of Thermopylae (WF, 27 July 2010; WF, 18 July 2011), of the fall of Constantinople to the Ottomans in 1453 (WF, 29 May 2010) and others. Many texts presented on the WF website are accompanied by photos as a demonstration of the dynamic participation of women in the party's rallies.

In addition, women participate in acts of solidarity such as the distribution of food to the poor and homeless or visiting families and giving them food, clothes (see Figure 4) or toys for children (WF, 6 December 2011; WF, 25 October 2011; WF, 26 September

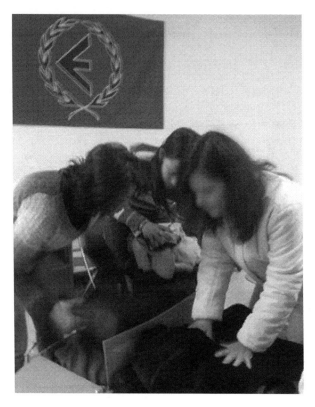

**Figure 4.** 'Collecting clothes' (WF, 6 December 2011).

2011; WF, 28 December 2012). The beneficiaries of these GD actions are exclusively ethnic Greeks.

Women also participate in the propagation of GD's ideology through the distribution of leaflets and the party's official newspaper and in demonstrations against immigrants (WF, 25 November 2010). GD and the WF organise meetings in some of the party's local offices in order to strengthen the ties between women through organisational discussions (WF, 24 December 2012), ideological speeches, for example on 'The place of women in people's community' (WF, 16 October 2010) and meetings 'about the Greek nationalist woman and her importance in national struggles' (GD, 12 May 2016).[15] The party also supports the right of women to serve in the army and undertake military service,[16] if not obligatory service when they turn 18, then at least voluntarily. This position is justified by the party on the grounds that the current situation, in which women are not allowed to enter the armed forces as soldiers, reproduces inequalities between men and women. Through these kinds of activities GD attempts to rebut the criticism that it is a male organisation whose ideology confines the role of women to that of stay-at-home mothers. However, from the analysis of GD's texts and the images that accompany them, the division of labour based on gender roles is evident. Women are essentially participating in charitable activities for poor and socially excluded Greek people and families and, in this way, they reproduce the stereotype that women are more sensitive and suited to work on issues related to disabled people, children, older people etc.

A crucial question in terms of participation and support for GD is what the impact of all the above is on women. Confirming Lesselier's (1991) findings on support for the Front National in France, electoral data on support for GD show women tend to be less attracted to such ideologies than men. According to the exit polls[17] for the January 2015 elections, 8.5% of men but only 3.8% of women voted for GD. Other polls have also shown[18] that men are more likely to vote for GD compared to women (10% and 4%, respectively). These data were confirmed by the survey of young people undertaken as part of the Memory, Youth, Political Legacy and Civic Engagement (MYPLACE) project.[19] There again, 8.8% of young men and 3.2% of young women voted for GD during the elections of June 2012.

We might also consider women's participation in GD through evidence on their visibility in the party's organisational structure and in parliament. Of GD's current 18 MPs only two are women, of which one is the GD leader's wife. In the elections of May 2012, only one of 21 MPs was a woman (the leader's wife); in the elections of June 2012 only one of 17 was a woman (again the leader's wife); and in the elections of January 2015 two of 17 were women, including the leader's wife. Finally, all three European Parliament members elected in 2014 are men. These findings suggest that while GD wants women to be active, this activism should be within specific gender and sex constraints. These constraints, they believe, are determined by nature and women's social and political activity should never interfere in the performance of their principal role as mothers and child-bearers.

## Conclusions

The analysis of GD's websites suggests that a central political focus and target for the party is women. Although this interest in women has been traced back to the mid-1990s (Psara 2014), it took the form of a more open call to women after the formation of the WF and, in particular, after the first electoral success of GD in the municipal elections of 2010.

This analysis of GD's discourse and representations of gender has found that they bear significant similarities to those of historical fascism. Nation, 'race' and family, all seen as rooted in natural differences, are emblematic of the 'discourse of order' that many contemporary extreme-right and neo-Nazi movements adopt. GD's ideological discourse about women is deeply embedded in assumptions about the natural, biological differences between men and women. It is a discourse that reproduces racism, sexism, social inequalities and the domination of men. Women are welcomed to participate in politics through electoral participation, participation in the party's local organisations and in various forms of activism. While such activism involves mainly 'female' activities like cooking and the distribution of food, toys and clothes to poor families, it also includes participation in rallies, writing slogans on walls, etc. Thus, while the division of labour based on natural characteristics is evident in GD's ideology this does not mean women are expected to remain exclusively within the domestic sphere of the home. The crucial distinction emphasised by GD is that women's participation in such activities should not undermine motherhood and domesticity and the reproduction of the national soldier as part of a nationalist agenda.

Our analysis suggests GD's ideology envisages women's participation in all five of the ethnic and national processes – biological reproduction, the reproduction of boundaries, the production of ideology and culture, the signification of difference; and national and military struggles – identified by Yuval-Davis and Anthias (1989, 7) as the five major, but not exclusive, ways in which women have tended to participate in ethnic and national processes and in relation to state practices. We suggest that, specifically, GD seeks to reproduce a nationalist habitus for women based on existing historical examples derived either from Greek antiquity or from fascist regimes. In addition to the fundamental role of motherhood, this habitus is characterised by anti-feminism, heterosexuality and the rejection of a consumerist society that has turned women into sexual objects. Of course, habitus implies the physical embodiment of cultural values and this is what is striven for by GD through its ideology. Women, they suggest, should occupy a separate habitus in which they accept and submit to existing social conditions; they should not seek equality with men since this contradicts their nature, which is viewed as essentially different to that of men. GD constructs its ideology on this habitus – it is a core component of its nationalist ideological corpus – because it addresses directly the very existence, and protection, of the nation, which is GD's main priority. In light of multicultural policies and demands for gender equality, GD tries to cultivate a nationalist habitus for women based on particular ways of behaving within the nationalist community. This habitus, as the party implies, needs to be not only followed by every woman for the good of the nation, but also internalised and naturalised in everyday life. While many of these ideas about women are not new and have been supported by right-wing, patriarchal and conservative groups and political parties in Greece before, GD appropriates and reproduces them in distinctive ways and presents itself as the contemporary protector of the nationalist habitus.

## Notes

1. Marine Le Pen of the Front National is the most obvious example but other women leaders include Pia Kjaersgaard of Denmark's People's Party, Siv Jensen of Norway's Progress Party and Sarah Palin, a leading figure of the conservative Tea-Party in the United States.
2. http://www.marieclaire.fr/,extreme-droite,20240,451373.asp (last accessed 27 September 2016).
3. GD is not a new phenomenon. Its history goes back to 1980s (Psaras 2012, 11–96).
4. In 1994, GD participated for the first time in the elections to the European Parliament gaining only 0.11% of the votes.
5. A first analysis of some of this material took place within the framework of the FP7 EU research project Memory, Youth, Political Legacy and Civic Engagement (MYPLACE 2011–2015). For more details, see Koronaiou and Deliveris (2014).
6. In 18 September 2013 an antifascist musician was murdered by a GD supporter, who was arrested and confessed his crime. Thereafter, the government compiled 32 criminal cases and sent them to the public prosecutor, so that the involvement of GD members and supporters and MPs in criminal activity could be examined. All of them were accused of being members of a criminal organisation, based on the Greek penal code. Currently all the party's MPs and other group members are on trial.
7. http://ioannismetaxas.gr/Periodiko_Neolaia.html (last accessed 27 September 2016).
8. http://wau14.com/homefront/our-magazine/ and http://www.wau14.com/ (last accessed 27 September 2016).
9. http://whitewomenfront.blogspot.gr/2010/10/blog-post_20.html 'I don't talk to communists' (WF, 20 October 2010) (last accessed 27 September 2016).
10. Almost all the texts uploaded in the Women's Front website use pseudonyms.
11. It is not clear to which association the author of the text refers. Only one women's association persisted under the regime (the association of Gertrud Bäumer, Die Frau or Woman), until 1944, but was placed under the guardianship of the Reich Minister of People's Education and of Propaganda, Joseph Goebbels (Moser-Verrey 1991, 32). Rudolf Hess established the

Deutsches Frauenwerk which with the women's branch of the Nazi party, the NS-Frauenschaft, aimed to become a mass organisation (Vincent 2011, 42).

12. This is an issue that is returned to on the website in subsequent years as well.
13. http://www.xryshaygh.com/enimerosi/view/elenh-zaroulia (last accessed 27 September 2016).
14. http://www.marieclaire.fr/,extreme-droite,20240,451373.asp (last accessed 27 September 2016).
15. See for example http://www.xryshaygh.com/enimerosi/view/gia-thn-ellhnida-ethnikistria-ekdhlwsh-sta-grafeia-ths-t.o.-boreiwn-proasti (last accessed 27 September 2016).
16. This is suggested by the party in its Political Theses, clarifying, though, that women will serve in offices and they will be exempted if they are mothers. See http://www.xryshaygh.com/kinima/thesis (last accessed 27 September 2016).
17. For more information see http://www.metronanalysis.gr/exit-poll-CEB2CEBFCF85CEBBC EB5CF85CF84CEB9CEBACF8ECEBD-CEB5CEBACEBBCEBFCEB3CF8ECEBD-CEB9CEB1CEBD-2015/ (last accessed 27 September 2016).
18. For more information see http://www.publicissue.gr/wp-content/uploads/2012/06/koinwniko_profil_b6_2012.pdf (last accessed 27 September 2016).
19. MYPLACE (Memory, Youth, Political Legacy and Civic Engagement) was an FP7 research project (2011–2015). For more information on the project, its structure, goals and outcomes, see www.fp7-myplace.eu.

## Disclosure statement

No potential conflict of interest was reported by the authors.

## References

Bacchetta, Paola, and Margaret Power, eds. 2002. *Right-Wing Women: From Conservatives to Extremists around the World*. New York, NY: Routledge.

Blee, M. Kathleen. 1996. "Becoming a Racist: Women in Contemporary Ku Klux Klan and Neo-Nazi Groups." *Gender and Society* 10 (6): 680–702.

Blee, M. Kathleen. 2002. *Inside Organized Racism: Women in the Hate Movement*. Berkley and Los Angeles, CA: University of California Press.

Blee, M. Kathleen, and Mc Gee Deutsch, eds. 2012. *Women of the Right: Comparisons and Interplay across Borders*. Pennsylvania, PA: The Pennsylvania State University Press.

Bourdieu, Pierre. 1984. *Distinction. A Social Critique of the Judgment of Taste*. Cambridge, MA: Harvard University Press.

Bridenthal, Renate, Anita Grossman, and Marion Kaplan. 1984. *When Biology Became Destiny: Women in Weimar and Nazi Germany*. New York, NY: Monthly Review Press.

Christopoulos, Dimitris, ed. 2014. *Το Βαθύ Κράτος και η Ακροδεξιά [The Deep State and the Extreme-Right]*. Athens: Nissos.

Davies, Peter. 1999. *The National Front in France. Ideology, Discourse and Power*. London: Routledge.

De Grazia, Victoria. 1992. *How Fascism Ruled Women. Italy, 1922–1945*. Berkley and Los Angeles, CA: University of California Press.

Durham, Martin. 1998. *Women and Fascism*. London: Routledge.

Ellinas, Antonis, and Iasonas Lamprianou. 2016. "How Far Right Local Party Organizations Develop: The Organizational Buildup of the Greek Golden Dawn." *Party Politics*. Advance online publication. doi:10.1177/1354068816641337.

Fairclough, Norman. 1992. *Discourse and Social Change*. Cambridge: Polity Press.

Georgiadou, Vassiliki. 2013. "Right-Wing Populism and Extremism: The Rapid Rise of Golden Dawn in Crisis-Ridden Greece." In *Right-Wing Extremism in Europe*, edited by Ralf Melzer, and Sebastian Serafin, 75–101. Berlin: Friedrich Ebert Stiftung.

Goodwin, Mathew. 2011. *New British Fascism. Rise of the British National Party*. Oxon: Routledge.

Gori, Gigliola. 2004. *Italian Fascism and the Female Body: Sport, Submissive Women and Strong Mothers*. London: Routledge.

Grawitz, Madeleine. 2004. *Μέθοδοι των Κοινωνικών Επιστημών [Social Sciences Methods]*. Athens: Odysseas.

Halkia, Alexandra. 2007. *Το Άδειο Λίκνο της Δημοκρατίας. Σεξ, Έκτρωση και Εθνικισμός στη Σύγχρονη Ελλάδα [The Empty Cradle of Democracy. Sex, Abortion and Nationalism in Contemporary Greece]*. Athens: Alexandria.

Hogan, Jackie. 2009. *Gender, Race and National Identity. Nations of Flesh and Blood*. New York, NY: Routledge.

Howarth, David. 2000. *Discourse*. London: Open University Press.

Koronaiou, Alexandra, and Aristotelis Deliveris. 2014. "Golden Dawn and Greek Youth." MYPLACE Research Report. http://www.fp7-myplace.eu/documents/D7_1/Cluster%201%20Right%20Wing%20and%20Patriotic%20movements/MYPLACE_WP7.1REPORT_PUA_Golden%20Dawn%20(Greece).pdf.

Koronaiou, Alexandra, Evangelos Lagos, Alexandros Sakellariou, Stelios Kymionis, and Irini Chiotaki-Poulou. 2015. "Golden Dawn, Austerity and Young People. The Rise of Fascist Extremism among Young People in Contemporary Greek Society." In *Radical Futures? Youth, Politics and Activism in Contemporary Europe*, edited by Hilary Pilkington, and Gary Pollock, 231–249. Oxford: Willey-Blackwell.

Koronaiou, Alexandra, Evangelos Lagos, and Alexandros Sakellariou. 2015. "Singing for Race and Nation: Fascism and Racism in Greek Youth." In *Digital Media Strategies of the Far Right in Europe and the United States*, edited by Helga Druxes, and Patricia Simpson, 193–213. New York. NY: Lexington Books.

Kyriazi, Nota. 2001. *Η Κοινωνιολογική Έρευνα [Sociological Research]*. Athens: Ellinika Grammata.

Lesselier, Cluadie. 1991. "De la Vierge Marie à Jeanne d'Arc: Images de femmes à l'extrême droite." *L'Homme et la société, Femmes et sociétés* nos. 99-100: 99–113.

Litt, S. Jacouelyn. 2004. "Normalizing Racism: A Case-Study of Motherhood in White Supremacy." In *Home-Grown Hate: Gender and Organized Racism*, edited by Abby L. Ferber, 92–107. New York, NY: Routledge.

Lower, Wendy. 2013. *Hitler's Furies: German Women in the Nazi Killing Fields*. New York, NY: Houghton Mifflin Harcourt.

Macciocchi, Antonietta-Maria. 1976. "Les femmes et la traversée du fascism." In *Éléments pour une analyse du fascisme, tome I*, 128–278. Paris: Union générale d'édition.

McClintock, Anne. 1995. *Imperial Leather. Race, Gender and Sexuality in the Colonial Contest*. New York, NY: Routledge.

Moser-Verrey, Monique. 1991. "Les femmes du troisième Reich." *Recherches Feminists* 4 (2): 25–44.

Mosse, L. Georges. 1997. *L'image de l'homme. L'invention de la virilité moderne*. Paris Abbeville: Tempo.

Mudde, Cas. 2007. *Populist Radical Right Parties in Europe*. Cambridge: Cambridge University Press.

Navarro, Zander. 2006. "In Search of a Cultural Interpretation of Power: The Contribution of Pierre Bourdieu." *IDS Bulletin* 37 (6): 11–22.

Paraskeva-Veloudogianni, Despoina. 2015. *Ο Εχθρός, Το Αίμα, Ο Τιμωρός [The Enemy, The Blood, The Avenger]*. Athens: Nissos.

Perry, Barbara. 2004. "White Genocide: White Supremacists and the Politics of Reproduction." In *Home-Grown Hate: Gender and Organized Racism*, edited by Abby L. Ferber, 71–91. New York, NY: Routledge.

Pickering-Iazzi, Robin, ed. 1995. *Mothers of Invention: Women, Italian Fascism and Culture*. Minneapolis: University of Minnesota Press.

Psara, Aggeliki. 2014. "Έμφυλες πτυχές του ελληνικού νεοναζισμού [Gendered Aspects of the Greek Neo-Nazism]." *Archeiotaxio* 14: 129–156.

Psaras, Dimitris. 2012. *Η Μαύρη Βίβλος της Χρυσής Αυγής [The Black Bible of Golden Dawn]*. Athens: Polis.

Ranchod-Nilsson, S., and M.-A., Tetreault, eds. 2000. *Women, State and Nationalisms*. London: Routledge.

Sakellariou, Alexandros. 2015a. "Anti-Islamic Public Discourse in Contemporary Greece: The Reproduction of Religious Panic." In *The Revival of Islam in the Balkans: From Identity to Religiosity*, edited by Arolda Elbasani, and Olivier Roy, 42–61. Basingstoke: Palgrave Macmillan.

Sakellariou, Alexandros. 2015b. "Golden Dawn and its Appeal to the Greek Youth". Athens: Friedrich Ebert Foundation. http://library.fes.de/pdf-files/bueros/athen/11501.pdf.

Sakellariou, Alexandros. 2017 (Forthcoming). "Islam and Politics of Fear in Greece: Migration, Terrorism and 'Ghosts' from the Past." *Nationalities Papers*.

Scheck, Raffael. 2004. *Mothers of the Nation: Right-Wing Women in Weimar Germany*. Oxford: Berg.

Tsiakalos, Giorgos. 2015. *Για τη Ναζιστική Ακροδεξιά και την Πολιτική Καθημερινότητα στην Εποχή της Κρίσης [For the Nazi Extreme-Right and the Political Routine in Times of Crisis]*. Thessaloniki: Epikentro.

Vasilopoulou, Sofia, and Daphne Halikiopoulou. 2015. *The Golden Dawn's 'Nationalist Solution'. Explaining the Rise of the Far-Right in Greece*. New York, NY: Palgrave Macmillan.

Vincent, Marie-Bénédicte. 2011. *Histoire de la société allemande au XXe siècle. Tome I. Le premier XXe siècle. 1900–1949*. Paris: La Découverte.

Wacquant, Loic. 2006. "Habitus." In *International Encyclopedia of Economic Sociology*, edited by Jens Beckert, and Milan Zafirovski, 317–321. London: Routledge.

Yuval-Davis, Nira. 1997. *Gender and Nation*. London: Sage.

Yuval-Davis, Nira, and Floya Anthias, eds. 1989. *Woman-Nation-State*. New York, NY: Palgrave MacMillan.

# Afterword: next steps in the study of gender and education in the radical right

Kathleen Blee

Gender is key to the radical right today, and in the past. Traditional masculinity is etched into its practices and images, especially those of aggression, authority, brutality, and comradeship. Gender also shapes who participates in radical right politics and parties and on what basis. Despite their masculinist cast, radical right parties and movements have incorporated women in a variety of roles, from symbols of the nation or race that rightists vow to safeguard, to members, supporters, and even, on occasion, leaders. And gender issues are core to the ideological basis of the far-right. Since radical rightists favor social hierarchies, such as those that privilege native-born citizens over many immigrants, whites over nonwhites, and Christians over non-Christians, most also fervently support gender hierarchies that favor men over women. Yet some far-right movements and parties proclaim their support for women's rights in an effort to attract female followers or to substantiate their insistence that white Christian citizens provide women with greater rights and opportunities than do followers of Islam.

Education is also central to the agendas and strategies of the radical right. This may seem surprising as formal education is widely regarded as a way to promote tolerance and undermine the possible appeal of radical right ideas, especially to young people. However, as the articles in this issue demonstrate, schooling has a complex relationship to the radical right. Schools may inoculate students by teaching complex ideas that counter the simplistic claims of the far-right and exposing them to diverse people and ideas. On the other hand, some radical rightists target educational institutions as locations for recruiting new followers and distributing their ideas.

The radical right relies as well on informal educational processes. Loosely structured far-right movements seek to spread their ideologies into the broader population to create a base of followers. Institutionalized radical right parties similarly depend on disseminating propaganda to convince voters that their ideas and agendas are correct and possible to achieve through electoral power. Ideological campaigns may be structured to extend beliefs that are already widely held among their intended population, as, for example, by intensifying racism or xenophobia and convincing potential followers that the radical right can protect society against nonwhites or immigrants. Ideological campaigns can also be structured to promote ideologies and ways of thinking that are not already widely accepted, such as virulent Islamophobia or anti-Semitism. Both kinds of campaigns have specific goals of learning and re-learning that seek to commit people to radical rightist ideas that can be highly conspiratorial, illogical, and dangerous in their implications for action.

Scholars have paid attention to gender in the radical right and, to a lesser extent, to education in the radical right, but few have studied these factors simultaneously. Yet, as the articles collected in this issue illustrate, looking at the intersection of masculinity/femininity and learning makes it possible to identify the gendered processes whereby people learn to accept radical right ideas as well as the educational implications of the gendered nature of radical right politics and political recruiting. It brings into focus rarely studied aspects of the radical right and opens novel questions and lines of inquiry for future researchers.

An example of the creative possibilities found by examining education and gender through a single lens is Cynthia Miller-Idriss' analysis of how rightist ideologies are etched into the masculine body. By wearing clothing and products that display far-right ideologies, young German men both learn and reinforce the ideologies of the radical right through their bodies. Such radical right bodily presentations build on conventional gender expectations – such as that young men will display aggressive masculinity – at the same time that they assert the wearer's knowledge of and loyalty to the messages of the far-right. Miller-Idriss' work is an example of how scholarship at the intersection of gender, education, and politics can detect new ways in which politicized processes of learning can change bodies as well as minds. It also exposes the extent to which transmitting radical right ideologies through gender-coded bodily presentations can be as, or even more, effective in securing followers for far-right parties and movements than more traditional means such as broadcasting radical ideologies through websites, speeches, and printed propaganda.

Another example of the value of a gender/education analytic lens is Anita Stasulane's study of the Latvia National Front (LNF). She shows how women have become central players and guardians of the odd blend of radical rightism and esoterism that constitutes the LNF's secret wisdom. Such an emphasis on secret knowledge is an important factor in the appeal of many radical rightist politics across time and place which promise to provide followers with special insights or facts that are hidden from the general public such as the common trope that Jews engage in secret conspiracies to control the economy or manipulate the political world. Stasulane pushes this insight in a productive new direction by showing how a politicized secret knowledge can also be gendered. Her study should prompt scholars to explore whether women have an unexpected influence over ideological messages in other radical right politics, especially those infused with spirituality and other practices in which women are traditionally central players.

Attending to both gender and education reveals the complicated politics of sexuality in the radical right, as demonstrated in several articles in this issue. Hilary Pilkington's study of the English Defence League (EDL) describes its recognition of gay and lesbian contingents, in striking contrast to the decided homophobia of most radical right groups. The EDL's support for these sexual minority groups is not covert, as it allows rainbow flags to be flown at its rallies. Yet, as Pilkington cautions, such displays are not meant to encourage EDL supporters and others to accept sexual diversity or sexual minorities. Rather, the EDL's strategy is to enhance the visibility of non-immigrant gays and lesbians in Britain to legitimate its argument that such civil liberties are endangered by immigrants who adhere to the anti-gay beliefs of traditional Islam. The EDL thus wields gendered sexuality as a counter-educational narrative for its members and the wider public: its purported acceptance of gays and lesbians in Britain serves to highlight its claims of sexual oppression by Muslims. This case study raises broader questions about the multivalence of gendered symbols in radical right propaganda, suggesting that scholars should consider the complex layering of overt and covert messages that are broadcast by right wing extremists.

The politics of sexuality varies by national context, as shown in the analysis of data on voting in 10 European countries by Niels Spierings, Andrej Zaslove, and Marcel Lubbers. A number of radical right parties in Europe have shifted toward greater tolerance of LGBTQ persons in recent years, a transnational diffusion across highly nationalist parties that is clearly propelled by their opposition to Islamic immigration to the continent. Yet Spierings and his colleagues find that European voters respond to radical right messages of anti-immigration and sexual tolerance in very different ways across nation and time. Their article demonstrates the importance of understanding the contexts in which radical right parties create and broadcast message to voters, especially when these messages include unexpected ideas such as acceptance of sexual minorities. A very different stance toward sexual minorities is found in George Severs' study of the twentieth century British National Party (BNP) which targeted gay men as a social problem. Indeed, the BNP sought to broaden its appeal to the public by engaging in a campaign that Severs terms *homohysteria*, a description that underscores the uneven association between radical right and homophobic ideologies.

The juxtaposition of articles that demonstrate the very different ways in which European radical right parties handle issues of sexual diversity opens interesting questions for scholars working within gender and education. Under what conditions do radical right parties and movements incorporate sexual ideologies within their educative agendas? When do they advance seemingly progressive ideologies, such as sexual tolerance, for strategic purposes, and what complications follow from such a strategy?

A different slant on gender and education in the radical right is found in the study of the modern-day Greek far-right party Golden Dawn by Alexandros Sakellariou and Alexandra Koronaiou. They show how Golden Dawn harnesses internet technologies to quickly spread ideas of ultra-nationalism, anti-feminism, and white supremacism, a new and effective mode of ideological education for the radical right. A similar theme is taken up in the study by Jennifer Meyer which shows how an advocate of German national socialism in the last century sought to spread an ideology of radical right quasi-feminism by penetrating the nation's schools and professions and broadening women's opportunities in public life. These contrasting works suggest the need to pay attention to the precise modes of public education that are employed by radical rightists, as well as to the gender context in which ideological messages are distributed. Do radical rightists make use of modes of ideological transmission that require people to participate in highly visible politics, such as rallies, or that allow people to participate in the privacy of their homes, such as the Internet? Are private forms of messaging more effective in reaching a broad group of potential female supporters than are more public forms?

There are other questions of education and gender that might prove fruitful for scholars of the far-right. One is whether women and men recruits to radical right parties and movements are educated in a similar manner and toward the same ideological ends. Are there limits to the information provided by radical rightists to their women recruits compared to men? Are the beliefs that radical rightists broadcast to outsiders tailored differently to reach women and men?

A second area that needs further research is the process of un-learning radical right doctrines. In situations in which social groups have developed strongly negative beliefs about an antagonist group in the context of a civil war or violent conflict, repairing social bonds involves un-learning hatreds and stereotyped beliefs. The same is true of those who have learned the ideologies and intergroup hatreds that are promoted by the radical right. Although even highly committed radical rightists can change their political beliefs, little is known about whether the process of political un-learning is different for men and women.

Finally, the model of studying the intersection of gender, education, and radical right politics evident in this issue provides a new way to analyze the accelerating capacity of technology to spread radical right political messages and affect political outcomes worldwide. This issue goes to print just as Donald Trump has been elected to the U.S. presidency, an outcome that may have been aided by torrents of fake news items meant to undermine Trump's female opponent that were propelled across social media by sophisticated technologies. The election results were aided as well by the public exposure of politically sensitive emails stolen by internet hackers, who may have been tied to networks of extreme misogynist computer hackers and gamers, and by the circulation of memes, symbols, and ideas from the shadowy world of so-called *alt-right* white supremacists, xenophobes, and anti-feminists. The complexities of these political processes require careful attention to the many dimensions of gender and of educational messaging operating in the radical right today.

# Index

family as location of national identity 84–5
fascism 34–5, 126–9, 133, 139–40; women's roles 127–9
fascist-Futurist paradigm 34
'feet on the street' movement 109; see also British Defence League
female leaders on radical right 50–66; conclusion 63–4; emergence of LNF 52–3; esoteric background of LNF 53–5; esoteric interpretation of feminine 55–7; female-promoted discourse in LNF 60–63; introduction 50–51; prominent position of females in LNF 59–60; radical right in Latvia 51–2; women's mission in LNF 57; women's participation in LNF 57–8
female participation in LNF 57–8
female visibility on PRR stage 50–51
female-promoted discourse in LNF 60–63
feminist education for German girls 24–7
feminist revival 132–4
First World War 16
football casual subculture 109
Fortuyn, Pim 84, 92, 99
Fountaine, Andrew 39–40
Frau, Die 16
Frauenverein Reform 24
free speech 10
Freedom Party of Austria 128
French Revolution 22–3
Fröbel, Friedrich 20–22
Front National 85, 93, 137, 139
future of study of gender/education and radical right 10–11, 144–7

Garda, Aivars 53, 55, 57–62
Garda's girls 59–60
Garland, Carol 42, 109
gay British neo-Nazis 35
gay emancipation 35, 85, 87, 89, 92, 94, 98–100
'gay plague' 42; see also HIV/AIDS
GD see Golden Dawn
gender dimorphism 23
gender equality as primary educational goal 3, 23–4
gender esentialsim 127–8
'gender gap' 121–2
gender ideology 134–5
gender oppression 117
gender politics in EDL 106–125
'gender question' 20–22
gender and radical right 3
gender-equal education 22–7; call for 'new male ethics' 26–7; de-Jewified schools 23–4; feminist education for German girls 24–6; measuring intelligence 22–3
German 'de-Jewified' schools 23–4
German far right 67–83; conclusion 79–80; data, methods 68–72; dual articulations 79; embodying extremism 73–4; introduction

67–78; male comradeship/belonging 74–6; masculinity/embodiment of nationalism 72–3; resistance, power, machismo 76–9
Germania 17
Germanisation 24
Geschlecterfrage 20–22
Gestapo 21
Golden Dawn 126–43; conclusion 139–40; heroic historical figures 136–7; introduction 126–7; methodology 130; place of women in society 133–6; rise of in Greek society 129–30; women, fascism, extreme right 127–9; women as mothers 131–3; Women's Front 130–31; women's participation in GD activities 137–9
Goldschmidt, Henriette 20–21
Goodwin, Matthew J. 35–6
Gottlieb, Julie V. 34
Gottschewski, Lydia 21
Gower, Helen 118–19
graffiti 69
grassroots activism 37, 109, 116
Greek society and GD 129–30
Griffin, Nick 33, 35, 41–2
grooming 117–18
Günther, Hans F. K. 18–19

habitus 126–43
hacking 147
Hagendoorn, A. 85, 87
Halkia, Alexandra 132
Hardman, Anne 74, 78
hate groups 2
hegemonic masculinity 68, 72–4, 78–80
heroic historical figures 136–7; see also Golden Dawn
Hesse, Rudolf 74
heteronormative conformity 39
high viz roles for women 112–14
historical roles of women 127–9
Historikerinnenstreit 15–17
Hitler, Adolf 17, 21, 24–5, 37
Hitler Youth 68
HIV/AIDS 37, 41–4
Holocaust 17, 37–8
Homefront 131
homohysteria 33–49; see also British National Party, 1982–1999
homophobia 33–49, 107–9, 115, 117–21, 145; in BNP 33–49; in EDL 118–19
homosexuality 38, 62–3, 86–7, 118–19, 134–5; attitudes towards 86–7; and homophobia 118–19
homosocial spaces 3, 108–9
honour killing 117
Hunke, Sigrid 17
hypermasculinity 74
hypotheses on nativism 89

Made in the USA
Middletown, DE
02 April 2021